D1573066

CONTEMPORARY FURNITURE

An International Review of Modern Furniture, 1950 to the Present

Edited by Klaus-Jürgen Sembach

Architectural Book Publishing Company
New York 10016

Translation of the introductory texts into English by Mark Borill

First published in the U.S.A. 1982
by Architectural Book Publishing Co., Inc.

Library of Congress Cataloging in Publication Data

Contemporary furniture.

   Selection of photos. Originally published in: New
furniture=Neue Möbel. With new captions and introd.
   Includes index.
   1. Furniture–History–20th century. I. Sembach,
Klaus-Jürgen. II. New Furniture. III. Title: Neue
Möbel, 1950–1982.
NK2395.C67   749.2′049   81-19108
ISBN 0-8038-9526-7   AACR2

Printed in Germany

Contents · Inhalt

The series "New Furniture" has appeared eleven times at regular intervals. It began in 1951 and then it was customary for a volume to appear every two, or at the very latest every three years. The chain was broken in 1971, and this present edition contains, along with much that is new, above all a resumé of the contents of previous volumes.

A dispassionate conclusion might be that development in the past ten years has stagnated and that it is apparent that there have not been enough examples to warrant further reports. Does this mean that good furniture has become unfashionable, or has designers' imagination failed them?

The problem can probably not be regarded in such simple terms. The disruption we observe is more deep-seated. Our attitude towards the symbols of progress is not the same as it used to be; the social changes in the past ten to fifteen years have played their part in forming our attitude towards the materialisation of objects in our environment. Our awareness of the way architecture and ambience function has become more acute and more critical. There has been a general spreading of scepticism of the "latest development". Even attempts to create radical changes renounced a new outward appearance. The different attitudes of different generations is indeed striking: whereas progressive ways of thinking after the first world war went hand in hand with an endorsement of the avant garde in architecture and design, the situation fifty years later was exactly the opposite. The direction was towards forms from the past, not from the future.

The younger generation's indifference, and even contempt, for modern furniture, expressed by its preference for cheap, old things, showed at the same time, however, that it took modern products seriously. Their value was appreciated so little that people thought they could be accepted straight away and without much thought. They represented too much for that. They were the representatives of an age that was mistrusted. After all, furniture does more than just carry out a function; it reflects convictions as well. The affinity of convictions and outward form has been stressed over and over again—both positively and negatively. Show me how you live and I will tell you what you are like. In this respect furniture acquires a psychological, and even a political meaning.

If one pursues the attitude described above into the present—and it is by no means a thing of the past—then today's catch-phrase should be: no future = no modern design. It is easy to come back with a reply to that. One only has to turn round the equation: no modern design = no future. If one accepts this premise, it is a reminder that if new technical—and that also means commercial—developments do not occur, the roots of our existence are thereby endangered. To wish to deny this, or to alter it radically, would be like living in a topsy-turvy utopia. The most that can be achieved is a modification of the trend, directing it with more care and greater awareness. The furniture industry is perhaps a good example of this, cultivating as it does at the moment an increased sense of tradition instead of offering new trends at any price. This refers to the fact that it increasingly reissues "classics", that is to say furniture that was designed fifty or more years ago. The new trend in this is the production of old furniture that does not, however, seem so old as to be out of date. This policy does not ignore, as does the antiques trade, the production side; it merely uses it in another way.

But that is only one aspect of this ingenious process. What is so special about it is that traditional objects are produced which still have the aura of the avant garde. The past and the future are drawn together in a remarkable way. One is not operating somewhere in the distant past but in one's own, still tangible, short history, and one senses at the same time that these things will survive much that is younger than they are. It must come as a surprise to untrained observers to discover how old the ideas are that led to the creation of these objects. They will hesitate to decide in favour of them today and postpone the decision until they have got more used to them.

It could be argued that this represents the perfect solution, the happy mean in every respect. The demand for both the past and the present can be catered for simultaneously and with absolute conviction. And so we have reached a standstill; the demand for the future has been put off for the time being. One could cynically add the speculation that the young people who reject this furniture today are the best customers for these quasi-old things tomorrow, as this furniture enables them to take the unavoidable step forward without having to reject the conviction that progress is suspect. The necessary distance still remains.

If one refrains from regarding furniture principally as documenting certain attitudes, the fact that its further development has recently come to a standstill points to another phenomenon. Here it is less a matter of something generally encountered than of an individual problem. In connection with furniture, the purely functional aspects confront the emotional. We do not only live with furniture, we also live through it. In time it becomes part of ourselves and it continually express something of our expectations and wishes. It can break free of us easily through simple decay, for us to escape from it is less easy since we need it in more than one respect.

Our instinct for freedom has increased lately and it does not only include external conditions but also the objects that surround us. Any kind of harassment is troublesome, the material no less than the mental. Objects have the power to be a burden on one's existence merely by being there, not to mention their formal quality.

It is not necessary to go back to the nightmarish situation at the end of the 19th century to discover the reasons why individual people would like to avoid having too much furniture. More recent developments have, of course, taken this need increasingly into account, but they were only partially successful. It was a hard road to the desired emptiness. Art Nouveau brought about the first change, both formal and in the number of objects filling a room. But the aesthetic demands they made increased considerably; they required that one's whole life should be turned into an art form. Rooms were not arranged so much according to their owners as vice versa. Very few people were willing or able to make such a sacrifice.

The picture began to become clearer in the 1920s but the purist stance assumed was hardly able to serve as a generally valid model with which people could identify. They were able to understand and appreciate its purported severity, but its absolute demands had a confusing effect that was not very inviting. What was displayed was more a purifying form for the moment than one that could be endured for a longer period of time. The balance between the formal intention to make a statement on the one hand and the expectation of a free, relaxed way of life on the other, which came about around 1930, came too late to be able to have an effect in the highly charged political and economic climate at the time. Now, however, half a century later, what came out of that period—as has already been noted—have become the main ingredients of our formal view of the world. The exemplary designs from the years 1925 to 1933 now hold sway in Olympus. The new gods on the highest pedestal are the furniture from that period. Zeus is the Barcelona armchair (ill. 36) by Mies van der Rohe, Aphrodite the chaise longue (ill. 19) by Le Corbusier and Pallas Athene his small armchair (ill. 18). One could distribute the whole mythological cosmos in this way; there would be no lack of examples. So now that lucid severity which had been longed for for such a long time has become reality after all. The ideal has materialised. If the matter is thus regarded, many of us live in paradise. The furniture mentioned above had never completely disappeared from the market, but real acclamation for it has only come in the past few years, when it became apparent how well it fitted into the general mood of the age. At the same time, people set about greatly increasing the numbers of the club. Today it is possible to choose among numerous examples from the late 1920s and early 1930s. However, before this situation was reached several intermediate phases had to be overcome. This book deals mainly with them.

It is impossible to overlook the fact that the results of the post-war years have turned out somewhat more profane that the heroic products of the early years would have led one to expect. Much was obviously created to challenge the gods; still some has the appeal of its mongrel origins. The furniture of Charles Eames and Arne Jacobsen, all of it from about 1950, is without doubt entirely legitimate and well-behaved progeny. It demonstrates the virtues of a second generation. Its appearance is lighter, more unhampered and somewhat less concerned with posture than that of its forbears. The positioning of the chairlegs is characteristic of this: they are pushed nonchalantly forward at an angle and are not squared off so severely. The offspring behave confidently, just like someone does who knows he comes from a good family.

This new beginning was truly auspicious. Around 1950 it was possible to believe that development could be continued after a grey interval and not be disturbed a second time. If one leafs again through the first volume of "New Furniture" today, one is surprised how much of what one remembers as being good already existed then—in 1951. Apart from the above-mentioned objects, that is also true for the chairs by Max Bill, Egon Eiermann, and Hans J. Wegner.

The ability of these things to please while at the same time being demanding was new, and reduced their elitist character. They do not have the same effect as the high schools of interior design. But this agreable quality was obviously misunderstood to mean that it could be unhesitatingly imitated. The consequence of this slight relaxation in style was that the dam broke and a flood of inferior products was washed ashore. The standard of furniture from the 1950s was terrible; the most favoured form resembled molluscs—the kidney-shaped table, typical for that time, is still remembered today with foreboding. Characteristic of the 1950s is the steep plunge from the good model to the poor copy.

The second question posed at the beginning of this introduction has not yet been answered. Has designers' imagination failed them? This question is probably phrased wrongly as well. Here it not so much a matter of ability itself than of the necessity of having to prove this ability. This book is able to do just that, to show what has been tried out and produced in the past thirty years. Some designs were useful, others were not. This long process of elimination and evaluation naturally involved a certain amount of disillusionment. Everything that we really need is there already. This is something everyone has to accept these days. No future for modern design? At this very moment rather extreme objects are being produced whose affected style is able to suggest that kind of desperation.

The future probably lies in those half-designed objects now being developed so successfully in Sweden. Their form and price place them very cleverly between junk and solid bourgeois household effects, between somewhat gaudy casualness and rather solid order. Is this the adequate solution for reduced needs? Only volume 13 of the "New Furniture" series can answer that question.

Elfmal ist die Reihe »Neue Möbel« mit großer Regelmäßigkeit erschienen. Sie begann 1951, und es war dann Usus, alle zwei, spätestens aber nach drei Jahren den nächsten Band folgen zu lassen. 1971 riß die Kette ab, und heute liegt eine Ausgabe vor, die neben einigem Neuen vor allem ein Resümee dessen enthält, was in früheren Bänden gezeigt worden ist.
Ohne Sentimentalität kann daraus geschlossen werden, daß die Entwicklung in den letzten zehn Jahren gestockt hat und daß es offensichtlich nicht mehr genügend Beispiele gegeben hat, um weiter darüber berichten zu können. Heißt das nun, daß gute Möbel unmodern geworden sind oder fällt den Entwerfern nichts mehr ein?
Wahrscheinlich kann das Problem nicht so einfach gesehen werden, wie das eben geschehen ist. Die Störung, die wir beobachten müssen, reicht tiefer. Unser Verhältnis zu den Symbolen des Fortschritts ist nicht mehr das alte; gesellschaftliche Wandlungsprozesse der letzten zehn bis fünfzehn Jahre sind nicht ohne Einfluß geblieben auf unsere Einstellung zu den Materialisationen in unserer Umgebung. Das Bewußtsein für die Wirkungsweise von Architektur und Ambiente hat sich geschärft und ist kritischer geworden. Skepsis hat sich ganz allgemein gegenüber »Neuem« verbreitet. Selbst Versuche, die darauf zielten, radikale Veränderungen zu schaffen, verzichteten darauf, äußerlich ein neues Gewand zu tragen. Der Unterschied im Verhalten der Generationen war wirklich frappant: gingen nach dem Ersten Weltkrieg die fortschrittlichen Gesinnungen weitgehend Hand in Hand mit einem Bekenntnis zur Avantgarde in Architektur und Gestaltung, so war das fünfzig Jahre später genau umgekehrt. Man orientierte sich an vergangenen Formen, nicht an zukünftigen.
Die Gleichgültigkeit, wenn nicht Verachtung, die eine jüngere Generation zeitgemäßen Möbeln zukommen ließ, indem sie billige alte Dinge vorzog, bewies aber zugleich auch, daß sie die modernen Erzeugnisse wichtig nahm. Ihr Stellenwert wurde nicht so gering eingeschätzt, daß man sie schlichtweg und ohne großen Gedankenaufwand glaubte übernehmen zu können. Dafür erschienen sie zu belastet. Sie waren die Repräsentanten einer Gegenwart, der man mißtraute. Möbel sind schließlich mehr als nur Funktionsträger, sie spiegeln auch Überzeugungen wider. Die Affinität von Gesinnung und äußerem Arrangement ist immer wieder gern betont worden – im Guten wie im Schlechten. Zeige mir, wie Du wohnst, und ich sage Dir, wer Du bist. Insofern kommt Möbeln ein geistesgeschichtliche, wenn nicht gar politische Bedeutung zu.
Setzt man nun die eben geschilderte Einstellung bis in die Gegenwart fort – und sie ist noch keineswegs überwunden –, dann müßte die Parole des Tages heißen: no future = no modern design. Eine Antwort kann darauf leicht gegeben werden, man braucht nur die Gleichung umzustellen: no modern design = no future. Folgt man diesem Satz, dann wird mit ihm daran erinnert, daß, wenn neue technische – und das heißt auch kommerzielle – Entwicklungen ausfallen, damit weitgehend die Basis unserer Existenz gefährdet ist. Das leugnen oder radikal ändern zu wollen, würde bedeuten, im Sinne einer auf den Kopf gestellten Utopie zu handeln. Was bestenfalls erreicht werden kann, ist eine Modifizierung des Verlaufes, seine Steuerung mit mehr Vorsicht und größerer Bewußtheit. Die Möbelindustrie bietet dafür vielleicht ein besonders gutes Beispiel, wenn sie jetzt statt Novitäten um jeden Preis verstärkt Traditionspflege anbietet. Gemeint ist damit das Phänomen, in zunehmendem Maße »Klassiker« wiederaufzulegen, also Möbel, die vor fünfzig und mehr Jahren entworfen worden sind. Die Neuheit liegt hier somit im Herstellen von Altem, das aber wiederum nicht so alt ist, daß es wie von gestern wirkt. Bei diesem Verfahren werden im Gegensatz zum Handel mit Antiquitäten die Kapazitäten der Produktion nicht außer acht gelassen, sondern nur in anderer Weise genutzt.
Aber das ist nur die eine Seite des patenten Vorgehens. Das Besondere an dem Prozeß ist ja, daß man Traditionelles herstellt, das immer noch die Aura der Avantgarde hat. Vergangenheit und Zukunft berühren sich hier in merkwürdiger Weise. Man bewegt sich nicht irgendwo in der Historie, sondern in der eigenen, noch überschaubar kurzen Geschichte, und ahnt zugleich, daß diese Dinge vieles überleben werden, das jünger ist als sie. Ungeschulte Betrachter muß es überraschen, zu erfahren, wie alt die Ideen sind, die zur Geburt der Gegenstände geführt haben. Sie werden zögern, sich heute schon für sie zu entscheiden, sondern das für später aufschieben, wenn die Gewöhnung größer geworden ist.
Man könnte nun argumentieren, daß hier das Ei des Kolumbus gefunden worden sei, der in jeder Hinsicht goldene Mittelweg. Gleichzeitig und mit ungeteilter Überzeugung kann sowohl dem Bedürfnis nach Historie wie nach Gegenwärtigkeit gedient werden. Ein schöner Stillstand ist erreicht, die Frage nach der Zukunft ist vorübergehend suspendiert. Zynisch könnte man noch die Vermutung anfügen, daß die jungen Verweigerer von heute morgen die besten Kunden für die quasi-alten Dinge sein werden, denn ohne ihre Überzeugung aufgeben zu müssen, daß Fortschritt verdächtig ist, können sie mit diesen Möbeln das unumgängliche Avancement vollziehen. Die nötige Distanz bliebe immer noch.
Sieht man einmal davon ab, in Möbeln grundsätzliche Dokumente für bestimmte Gesinnungen zu erblicken, so verweist der Umstand, daß ihre Weiterentwicklung in jüngerer Zeit ins Stocken geraten war, auch noch auf ein anderes Phänomen. Es geht dabei weniger um eine übergeordnete und allgemeine Erfahrung als um ein individuelles Problem. Beim Umgang mit Möbeln stehen den rein funktionalen Aspekten die emotionalen gegenüber. Wir leben nicht nur mit Möbeln, sondern auch durch sie. Im Lauf der Zeit wachsen sie uns zu, und stets drücken sie etwas aus von unseren Erwartungen und Wünschen. Sie können uns zwar leicht entkommen durch einfachen Zerfall, wir ihnen aber weniger mühelos, da wir sie in mehr als einer Hinsicht brauchen.
Unser Gefühl für Freiheit hat sich in letzter Zeit gesteigert, und es bezieht dabei nicht nur die äußeren Bedingungen mit ein, sondern auch die Gegenstände, die uns umgeben. Bedrängungen sind in jeder Weise hinderlich, die dinglichen nicht weniger als die geistigen. Dinge vermögen das Dasein schon allein durch ihre bloße Existenz zu belasten, von ihrer formalen Qualität einmal ganz abgesehen.
Es ist nun gar nicht notwendig, bis zu den alptraumhaften Situationen zurückzugehen, die gegen Ende des 19. Jahrhunderts herrschten, um die Ursachen für den Wunsch zu entdecken, warum einzelne Menschen gern einem Zuviel an Möbeln entgehen möchten. Zwar hat die jüngere Entwicklung zunehmend auf dieses Bedürfnis Rücksicht genommen, aber sie konnte sich dabei immer nur teilweise durchsetzen. Der Weg zu der erhofften Leere war mühsam. Eine erste Änderung brachte der Jugendstil, formal wie auch in der Anzahl der Gegenstände, die ein Zimmer füllten. Aber dafür stieg deren ästhetischer Anspruch, sie verlangten gleichsam, das ganze Leben zu einer Kunstform zu machen. Räume richteten sich nicht so sehr nach ihren Besitzern, als vielmehr diese sich nach ihnen. Ein solches Opfer wollten und konnten nur wenige bringen.
In den zwanziger Jahren begann sich das Bild zu klären, doch die puristische Haltung, die dabei eingenommen wurde, war kaum dazu geeignet, als allgemein gültiges Identifikationsmodell zu

9

dienen. Die vorgegebene Strenge konnte zwar verstanden und gewürdigt werden, doch ihr Abso-
lutheitsanspruch wirkte verstörend und wenig einladend. Was man vorgeführt bekam, war mehr
eine für den Moment bedachte Läuterungsform denn eine solche, mit der man es längere Zeit
hätte aushalten können. Der Ausgleich zwischen dem formalen Bekenntniswillen einerseits und
der Erwartung nach einer freien, unangestrengten Lebensführung andererseits, der sich um
1930 vollzog, kam dann zu spät, um innerhalb des sowohl politischen wie wirtschaftlichen Span-
nungsfeldes von damals noch wirksam werden zu können. Jetzt jedoch, ein halbes Jahrhundert
danach, sind – wie schon gesagt – die Ergebnisse von einst aufgerückt zu den Top-Ingredienzien
unserer formalen Weltsicht. Was zwischen 1925 und 1933 an Vorbildlichem entstanden ist, be-
herrscht heute den Olymp. Als die neuen Götter stehen die Möbel von damals auf dem höchsten
Podest. Zeus ist der Barcelona-Sessel (Abb. 36) von Mies van der Rohe, Aphrodite die Liege
(Abb. 19) von Le Corbusier und Athene dessen kleiner Sessel (Abb. 18). Diese Art der Zuweisung
ließe sich fortsetzen für den ganzen mythologischen Kosmos, an Beispielen würde es nicht
mangeln.
Nun ist also jene lichte Strenge doch noch Wirklichkeit geworden, nach der man sich so lange
gesehnt hatte. Das Ideal hat sich materialisiert. Sieht man die Sache so an, dann leben einige
von uns im Paradies. Zwar waren die oben genannten Möbel nie ganz vom Markt verschwunden,
aber richtig gefeiert wurden sie erst in den letzten Jahren, als sich herausstellte, wie exzellent
ihre Existenz ins allgemeine Zeitgefühl paßte. Zugleich ging man daran, ihre Gesellschaft erheb-
lich zu erweitern. So kann man denn heute unter zahlreichen Beispielen aus den späten zwanziger
und frühen dreißiger Jahren wählen. Bis es jedoch zu diesem Zustand kam, mußten einige Zwi-
schenstationen überwunden werden. Hauptsächlich von ihnen handelt nun dieses Buch.
Nicht zu übersehen ist dabei, daß die Ergebnisse der Nachkriegsepoche etwas profaner ausgefal-
len sind, als es die heroischen Zeugnisse der Frühzeit hätten erwarten lassen. Vieles ist offenbar
gemacht worden, um die Götter herauszufordern, einiges hat immerhin den Reiz der bastardarti-
gen Herkunft. Durchaus legitime und sehr wohlgeratene Abkömmlinge sind zweifellos die Möbel
von Charles Eames und Arne Jacobsen, die alle um 1950 entstanden sind. Sie weisen die Vorzüge
einer zweiten Generation auf. Ihr Auftreten ist legerer, freizügiger und etwas weniger um Haltung
bemüht als das der Väter. Bezeichnend ist dafür die Stellung der Stuhlbeine: sie werden ungeniert
schräg nach vorn geschoben und bleiben nicht mehr streng angewinkelt. Die Sprößlinge geben
sich mithin so selbstbewußt, wie das nun eimal jemand tut, der weiß, daß er aus einer guten
Familie stammt.
Diese neuen Anfänge waren wirklich verheißungsvoll. Um 1950 konnte es so aussehen, als
ob es möglich wäre, nach einer grauen Zwischenzeit die Entwicklung so fortzuführen, daß sie
nicht ein zweites Mal gestört würde. Blättert man heute den ersten Band »Neue Möbel« wieder
durch, dann ist man überrascht, wie viel von dem, was an Gutem im Gedächtnis geblieben
ist, schon damals – 1951 – auf der Welt war. Das gilt neben den schon erwähnten Dingen
vor allem für die Stühle von Max Bill, Egon Eiermann und Hans J. Wegner.
Die Fähigkeit dieser Dinge, mit Anspruch zu gefallen, war neu und reduzierte ihren Elitecharakter.
Sie wirkten nicht mehr wie die ganz hohe Schule der Wohnerziehung. Aber diese freundliche
Eigenschaft wurde offensichtlich dahingehend mißverstanden, sie bedenkenlos imitieren zu kön-
nen. Die leichte Lockerung in der Haltung hatte zur Folge, daß die Dämme brachen und eine
Flut von Minderwertigem an Land gespült wurde. Die durchschnittliche Möbelproduktion der
fünfziger Jahre war miserabel, sie gebar mit Vorliebe molluskenhafte Gebilde – der dafür typische
Nierentisch ist bis heute in ominöser Erinnerung geblieben. Das schnelle Abgleiten vom guten
Vorbild zum schlechten Abklatsch ist dabei bezeichnend für den Befund der fünfziger
Jahre.
Noch nicht beantwortet ist die zweite Frage, die am Anfang stand: Fällt den Entwerfern nichts
mehr ein? Vermutlich ist sie falsch gestellt. Es geht hier nicht mehr primär um das Können
selbst als um die Notwendigkeit, dieses Können noch unter Beweis stellen zu müssen. Gerade
dieses Buch vermag zu belegen, was im Lauf der letzten dreißig Jahre alles schon ausprobiert
und in die Welt gesetzt worden ist. Lauter Ideen, die entweder sinnvoll waren oder auch nicht.
Dieser lange Auscheidungs- und Wertungsprozeß mußte ein bestimmtes Maß an Ernüchterung
mit sich bringen. Was wir wirklich brauchen, gibt es inzwischen alles schon. An dieser Erfahrung
kommt heute niemand mehr vorbei. No future for modern interior design? Gerade jetzt tauchen
reichlich exaltierte Dinge auf, die in ihrer manierierten Haltung auf eine derart gestimmte Verzweif-
lung hindeuten könnten.
Vermutlich liegt die Zukunft in jenen halbgestalteten Dingen, die heute mit großem Erfolg in
Schweden entwickelt werden. Mit ihrem Anspruch und Preis bewegen sie sich sehr geschickt
zwischen Sperrmüll und gutbürgerlichem Hausrat, zwischen etwas buntem Zufall und ziemlich
viel solider Ordnung. Die adäquate Lösung für ein vermindertes Bedürfnis? Jedoch das kann
erst der 13. Band der Reihe »Neue Möbel« beantworten.

The return of historical influences noticeable at the moment is a quite general phenomenon of our time. It is not a uniform orientation and displays at least two aspects. One is a move towards the historical as a result of a general love of the past, the other because it sees a better form for modern things in the past. The first attitude is ill-considered, opportunist and sentimental for the most part. It is usually described by the term "nostalgia", and it is basically against everything modern. The second is based on the conviction that using traditional ideas represents a more sensible kind of progress than creating new ones. It judges the historical according to its present value, and sees it relatively and not absolutely.

If one transfers this characterisation of present trends onto the level of practical examples, the recreated furniture of Charles Rennie Mackintosh is a representative of the first aspect. The two high-backed chairs (ills. 5, 6) can really only be noted because of their ludicrousness, and not because they are decisive for us in any way. They were once an ingenious challenge and remind us of the time when vehement attacks on logic and functionality were still allowed. It is indicative of the attitude that led to their renaissance that it is these designs that have been reproduced and not those that really make sense and are useful–for example, the runged chairs Mackintosh designed for the Willow Tearoom in Glasgow.

A similar situation is to be found with the chairs and armchairs of Josef Hoffmann (ills. 7–9), whose period can be clearly seen in the same way, but which are nevertheless a great deal more practicable than the Scot's. They were designed from the outset with functionality in mind– and not intentionally contrary to it. It could also be doubted whether it makes sense to reproduce the furniture of Gerrit Thomas Rietveld (ills. 11, 12). At the time the red and blue chair was created it was more of an artistic demonstration using a chair as an example than a chair with exemplary artistic form. But its bulky appearance is deceptive : it is comfortable to sit in. The zigzag chair by the same designer was the forerunner of a form that is more convincing now in plastic than in wood, which is unsuitable for such treatment. Rietveld's furniture gives the impression of being museum exhibits that have got into much too profane surroundings by mistake. Whereas one knows from the start that one cannot use Mackintosh's chairs, one feels with Rietveld's that one is not allowed to. One may admire them but not try them out.

The furniture that can be included in the second category we mentioned is the kind that was designed in the 1920s and the early 1930s and which "is still as modern today as it was then" (ills. 13–49). There is a completely different justification for continuing to produce it than there is for the return of examples of Art Nouveau. It does not represent quotes from the past whose selection is more or less accidental. It demonstrates that a continuity of proven designs makes sense and is possible. This observation is not only supported by the furniture of Ludwig Mies van der Rohe (ills. 31–34, 36–38), Marcel Breuer (ills. 23, 26–30) and Alvar Aalto (ills. 40–49) ; it becomes clearer when one looks at the examples from the Thonet production (ills. 2, 3), for the most part anonymous and whose "timelessness" is a continued source of admiration. Their presence provides a vital corrective for the present.

Die Wiederkehr von Historischem, die gerade beobachtet werden kann, ist ein Zeitphänomen ganz allgemeiner Art, das jedoch nicht einheitlich ausgerichtet ist, sondern zumindest zwei Aspekte aufweist. Der eine zielt auf Historisches aus einer generellen Vergangenheitsliebe heraus, der andere, weil er in historischen Dingen die bessere Form des Zeitgemäßen sieht. Die erste Einstellung ist weitgehend unreflektiert, opportunistisch und sentimental, sie wird gern mit der Bezeichnung »nostalgisch« umschrieben. Im Grunde richtet sie sich gegen alles Gegenwärtige. Die zweite basiert auf der Überzeugung, daß Tradieren zeitweise eine vernünftigere Art des Fortschritts darstellt als die Kreation von Neuem. Sie beurteilt Historisches im Hinblick auf seinen aktuellen Wert, sieht es also relativ und nicht absolut.

Überträgt man diese Charakterisierung momentaner Tendenzen auf die Ebene praktischer Beispiele, dann vertreten die wiederaufgelegten Möbel von Charles Rennie Mackintosh sicherlich die erste Auffassung. Besonders die beiden hochlehnigen Stühle (Abb. 5, 6) können eigentlich nur wegen ihrer Skurrilität Beachtung finden, nicht aber, weil sie in irgendeiner Weise für uns verbindlich sind. Sie waren einmal geistvolle Herausforderungen und erinnern nun an eine Zeit, der es noch gestattet war, in vehementer Form gegen Logik und Funktionalität anzugehen. Bezeichnend für die Haltung, die zu ihrer Renaissance geführt hat, ist, daß gerade diese Modelle wieder produziert werden und nicht solche, die wirklich sinnvoll und nutzbar sind – etwa den Sprossenstuhl, den Mackintosh für den Willow Tea Room in Glasgow entworfen hat.

Ähnlich verhält es sich mit den Stühlen und Sesseln von Josef Hoffmann, denen ihr Zeitstil gleichfalls deutlich anzusehen ist, die aber trotzdem wesentlich praktikabler sind als die des Schotten (Abb. 7–9). Ihre Manier war von vornherein auf Benützbarkeit angelegt – und nicht bewußt gegen sie. Bezweifelt werden könnte auch, ob es sinnvoll ist, die Möbel von Gerrit Thomas Rietveld erneut herzustellen (Abb. 11, 12). Der Rot-Blau-Stuhl war schon zu seiner Entstehungszeit eher eine künstlerische Demonstration am Beispiel eines Stuhles als ein Stuhl mit beispielhafter künstlerischer Ausformung. Aber seine sperrige Erscheinung täuscht: man sitzt gut in ihm. Der Zickzack-Stuhl des gleichen Entwerfers nahm eine Form voraus, die heute in Kunststoff überzeugender wirkt als in Holz, das für eine derartige Behandlung denkbar ungeeignet ist. Im Grunde gleichen Rietvelds Möbel jetzt Museumsstücken, die aus Versehen in viel zu profane Umgebungen geraten sind. Weiß man bei Mackintosh von vornherein, daß man seine Sitzmöbel nicht benutzen kann, so hat man bei Rietveld das Gefühl, es nicht zu dürfen. Bewunderung ja, Erprobung aber nein.

Der zweiten, anfangs genannten Tendenz zugerechnet werden können die Möbel, die in den zwanziger und beginnenden dreißiger Jahren entstanden sind (Abb. 13–49) und die »heute so modern sind wie damals«. Ihr Fortleben hat eine ganz andere Berechtigung als die Wiederkehr der Beispiele aus dem Jugendstil. Sie stellen keine historisierenden Zitate dar, deren Auswahl mehr oder minder zufällig erfolgte, sondern sie bekunden, daß eine Kontinuität des Bewährten sinnvoll und möglich ist. Diese Beobachtung muß sich jedoch nicht nur auf die Möbel von Ludwig Mies van der Rohe (Abb. 31–34, 36–38), Marcel Breuer (Abb. 23, 26–30) und Alvar Aalto (Abb. 40–49) stützen, noch deutlicher wird sie an den im Grunde anonymen Beispielen der Thonet-Produktion (Abb. 2, 3), deren »Zeitlosigkeit« immer wieder verblüffen kann. Ihre Anwesenheit bildet ein unverzichtbares Korrektiv für die Gegenwart.

1 **Werner M. Moser** 1929 Switzerland

Chair of wood with rattan seat
Stuhl aus Holz mit Sitz aus Rohrgeflecht
Horgen-Glarus

2 **Works Design** 1859 Austria

Chair "No. 14" of bentwood with rattan seat
Stuhl »Nr. 14« aus Bugholz mit Sitz aus Rohrgeflecht
Thonet

3 **Works Design** 1870 Austria

Armchair "No. 209" of bentwood with rattan seat
Armstuhl »Nr. 209« aus Bugholz mit Sitz aus Rohrgeflecht
Thonet

4 **Charles Rennie Mackintosh** 1918 Great Britain

Table "D.S.2" and armchair "D.S.4" of ebonized ashwood with sea grass seat
Tisch »D.S.2« und Armstuhl »D.S.4« in schwarz gebeizter Esche mit Sitz aus geflochtenem Seegras
Cassina

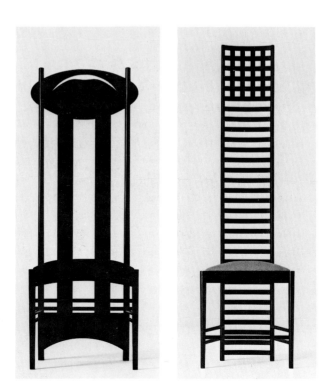

5 **Charles Rennie Mackintosh** 1897 Great Britain

Chair "Argyle" of ebonized ashwood with upholstered seat
Stuhl »Argyle« in schwarz gebeizter Esche mit Polstersitz
Cassina

6 **Charles Rennie Mackintosh** 1902 Great Britain

"Hill House 1" chair of ebonized ashwood with ladder back and upholstered seat
Stuhl »Hill House 1« in schwarz gebeizter Esche mit Leiter-Rückenlehne und Polstersitz
Cassina

10 **Walter Gropius** 1910 Germany ▷

Bench "D51/2" and armchair "D51" of black stained ashwood with loose cushions
Sitzbank »D51/2« und Armstuhl »D51« aus schwarz gebeizter Esche mit losen Sitz- und Rückenkissen
Tecta Möbel

7 **Josef Hoffmann** 1903 Austria
  Armchair "Purkersdorf" with frame of wooden laths in white high-gloss finish, spanned with black and white straps, loose seat cushion
  Armstuhl »Purkersdorf« mit Holzlattengestell in weißem Schleiflack, bespannt mit schwarzen und weißen Gurten, loses Sitzkissen
  Franz Wittmann

8 **Josef Hoffmann** 1908 Austria
  Armchair "Armlöffel" of chalked and ebonized ashwood with loose seat cushion
  Armstuhl »Armlöffel« aus gekalkter und schwarz gebeizter Esche mit losem Sitzkissen
  Franz Wittmann

9 **Josef Hoffmann** 1909 Austria
  Armchair "Fledermaus" of beech bentwood with upholstered seat and back
  Armstuhl »Fledermaus« aus Bugholz in Buche, Sitz und Rückenlehne gepolstert
  Franz Wittmann

11 Gerrit Thomas Rietveld 1918 Netherlands

Lounge chair "Red and Blue" of beechwood, frame with black and yellow aniline finish, seat and back with blue and red lacquer finish
Sessel »Rot und Blau« in Buche, Gestell schwarz und gelb anilingebeizt, Sitz und Rückenlehne blau und rot lackiert
Cassina

12 Gerrit Thomas Rietveld 1934 Netherlands

Chair "Zig-Zag" of elm and table "Crate 4" of solid unfinished beechwood
Stuhl »Zickzack« in Ulme und Tisch »Crate 4« in Buche massiv natur
Cassina

13 Mogens Koch 1932 Denmark

Folding table "MK" of ashwood and folding chair "MK" of beechwood, seat and back covered with canvas or leather, stitched arm-
straps in leather
Klapptisch »MK« in Esche und Klappsessel »MK« in Buche, Sitz
und Rückenlehne mit Leinen oder Leder bespannt, Armriemen aus
Naturleder
Rud. Rasmussens Snedkerier

14 Kaare Klint 1933 Denmark

"Safari chair" with detachable frame of ash, held together with
leather straps; seat, back and loose cushion in oxhide or canvas;
also stool available
»Safari-Stuhl« mit zerlegbarem Gestell in Esche, das mit Lederriemen zusammengehalten wird; Sitz, bewegliche Rückenlehne und
loses Kissen in Rindleder oder Segeltuch; dazu Fußbank
Rud. Rasmussens Snedkerier

15 **Le Corbusier, Charlotte Perriand, Pierre Jeanneret** 1928
France

Table "LC6" with steel base and top of ash or glass
Tisch »LC6« mit Stahlgestell und Platte aus Esche oder Glas
Cassina

16+17 **Le Corbusier, Charlotte Perriand, Pierre Jeanneret** 1928
France

"Fauteuil grand confort LC2, LC3" with chrome-plated, black or
colored tubular steel frame; loose cushions with polyurethane and
Dacron padding, fabric or leather upholstery
»Fauteuil grand confort LC2, LC3« mit verchromtem, schwarzem
oder farbigem Stahlrohrgestell; lose Kissen mit Polyurethan und
Dacron gepolstert und mit Stoff oder Leder bezogen
Cassina

18 **Le Corbusier, Charlotte Perriand, Pierre Jeanneret** 1928
France

Revolving armchair "LC7" with tubular steel frame, back and seat
cushion padded with polyurethane and fabric or leather upholstery
Drehstuhl »LC7« mit Armlehnen, Gestell aus Stahlrohr, Rückenlehne und Sitzkissen mit Polyurethan gepolstert und mit Stoff oder
Leder bezogen
Cassina

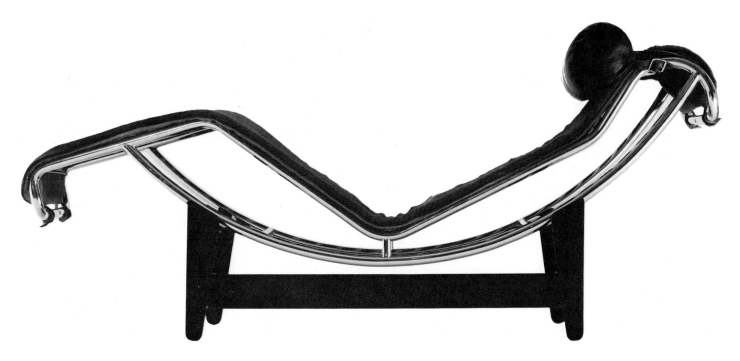

19 Le Corbusier, Charlotte Perriand, Pierre Jeanneret 1928
France

Lounge chair ''LC4'' with adjustable polished chrome-plated or
matte black enamel steel frame and matte black or colored enamel
steel base. Mat of skin, leather, or fabric; headrest padded with
Dacron and leather cover
Stufenlos verstellbare Liege »LC4« mit poliertem verchromten oder
schwarz matt lackiertem Stahlrohrrahmen und schwarz matt oder
farbig lackiertem Stahluntergestell. Auflage aus Fell, Leder oder
Stoff; Nackenrolle mit Dacronfüllung und mit Leder bezogen
Cassina

20+21 Le Corbusier, Charlotte Perriand, Pierre Jeanneret 1928
France

Easy chair ''LC1'' with adjustable back. Frame of chrome-plated
or matte black enamel tubular steel, arm rests of leather straps,
seat and back covered in skin, leather, or fabric
Sessel »LC1« mit beweglicher Rückenlehne. Gestell aus verchromtem oder matt lackiertem Stahlrohr, Armlehnen aus Ledergurten,
Sitz und Rückenlehne mit Fell, Leder oder Stoff bespannt
Cassina

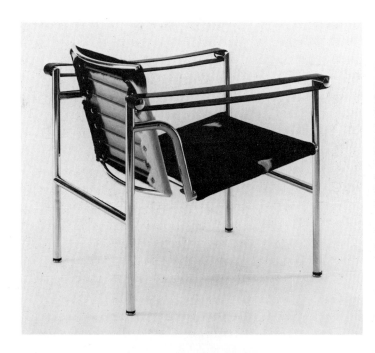

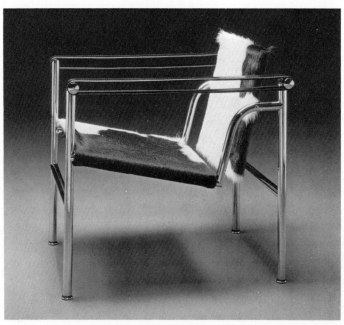

22 **Mart Stam** 1926 Netherlands

Chair "S 33" with chrome-plated tubular steel frame, seat and back of leather
Stuhl »S 33« mit verchromtem Stahlrohrgestell, Sitz und Rücken-lehne mit Leder bespannt
Thonet

23 **Marcel Breuer** 1928 Germany

Cantilevered chair with or without armrests; base of chrome-plated tubular steel, seat and back with bentwood frame and cane
Hinterbeinloser Stuhl mit oder ohne Armlehnen; Gestell aus ver-chromtem Stahlrohr, Sitz und Rückenlehne mit Bugholzrahmen und Rohrgeflecht
Gavina

24 + 25 **Hans Corey, Hans Fischli** 1939 Switzerland

Stacking chair "Landi" of light metal alloy
Stapelstuhl »Landi« aus Leichtmetall-Edellegierung
MEWA P. + W. Blattmann

26 Marcel Breuer 1927 Germany

Easy chair "D4" with demountable frame of chrome-plated tubular steel; seat, back, and armrests of iron thread straps
Sessel »D4« mit zerlegbarem Gestell aus verchromtem Stahlrohr; Sitz, Rücken- und Armlehnen mit Eisengarngurten bespannt
Tecta Möbel

27 Marcel Breuer 1925/26 Germany

Coffee table "Laccio" with chrome-plated tubular steel frame and top of wood or plastic laminate
Couchtisch »Laccio« mit verchromtem Stahlrohrgestell und Platte aus Holz oder laminiertem Kunststoff
Knoll International/Thonet

28 Marcel Breuer 1925 Germany

Easy chair "Wassily" with demountable frame of chrome-plated tubular steel; seat, back, and armrests of leather slings
Sessel »Wassily« mit zerlegbarem Gestell aus verchromtem Stahlrohr; Sitz, Rücken- und Armlehnen mit Leder bespannt
Gavina

29 Marcel Breuer 1928 Germany

Easy chair "S35L" with chrome-plated tubular steel frame, seat and back of leather
Sessel »S35L« mit Gestell aus verchromtem Stahlrohr, Sitz und Rückenlehne mit Leder bespannt
Thonet

30 Marcel Breuer c. 1928 Germany

Desk "S286" with chrome-plated tubular steel frame, top and drawers of wood
Schreibtisch »S286« mit Gestell aus verchromtem Stahlrohr, Platte und Schubfächer aus Holz
Thonet

	26
27	28
29	30

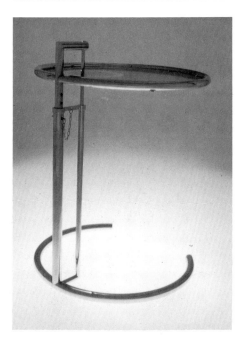

31 Ludwig Mies van der Rohe 1930
Germany

Day bed "258" with foam rubber upholstery and leather cover, frame of teak in oiled finish, chrome-plated metal legs
Liege »258« mit Schaumgummipolsterung und Lederbezug; Gestell geöltes Teakholz mit verchromten Metallfüßen
Knoll International

32 Ludwig Mies van der Rohe 1926
Germany

"MR" chair "S 533 LF" with chrome-plated tubular steel frame, seat and back of leather
»MR«-Stuhl »S 533 LF« mit Gestell aus verchromtem Stahlrohr, Sitz und Rückenlehne mit Leder bespannt
Thonet

33 Ludwig Mies van der Rohe 1929
Germany

"Barcelona" table "252" with frame of chrome-plated spring steel and glass top
»Barcelona«-Tisch »252« mit Gestell aus verchromtem Spezialfederstahl und Platte aus Kristallspiegelglas
Knoll International

34 Ludwig Mies van der Rohe 1927
Germany

Coffee table "259" with frame of chrome-plated tubular steel and top of smoked glass
Couchtisch »259« mit Gestell aus verchromtem Stahlrohr und Platte aus Rauchglas
Knoll International

35 Eileen Gray 1927 USA

Occasional table "E 1027" with chrome-plated tubular steel frame and glass top
Beistelltisch »E 1027« mit Gestell aus verchromtem Stahlrohr und Platte aus Kristallglas
Images

31	32
33	34
	35

36 Ludwig Mies van der Rohe 1926, 1930, 1929 Germany

"MR" chair "S 533" with tubular steel frame and canework seat and back; "Brno" chair "245" with frame of spring steel and fabric or leather-covered upholstery; "Barcelona" chair "250" with frame of special spring steel, loose seat and back cushions covered with leather (from left to right)
»MR«-Stuhl »S 533« mit Stahlrohrgestell und Korbgeflecht; »Brno«-Stuhl »245« mit Gestell aus Spezialfederstahl und lederbezogener Polsterung; »Barcelona«-Sessel »250« mit Gestell aus Spezialfederstahl und abnehmbaren Sitz- und Rükkenkissen mit Schaumgummifüllung und Lederbezug (von links nach rechts)
Knoll International/Thonet

37 Ludwig Mies van der Rohe 1930 Germany

"Tugendhat" chair "254" with frame of chrome-plated special spring steel and loose cushions covered with leather
»Tugendhat«-Sessel »254« mit Gestell aus verchromtem Spezialfederstahl und losen, mit Leder bezogenen Kissen
Knoll International

38 Ludwig Mies van der Rohe 1931 Germany

Chaise longue "241" with chrome-plated steel tube frame, continuous roll and pleat cushion with linen cover supported by rubber straps
Liegesessel »241« mit Gestell aus verchromtem Stahlrohr und durchgehend quergestepptem Kissen mit Stoffbezug auf Gummibändern
Knoll International

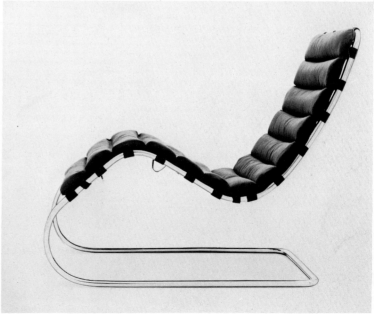

39 **Bruno Mathsson** 1933–35 Sweden

Lounge chair and ottoman "Pernilla" with laminated beech frame, seat and back of webbed straps or with canvas or leather upholstery
Sessel und Hocker »Pernilla« mit Gestell aus Buchen-Schichtholz, Sitz und Rückenlehne mit Gurtenbespannung oder mit Stoff oder Leder gepolstert
Dux

40+41 **Alvar Aalto** 1947 Finland

Coffee tables with bases of molded laminated wood and tops of plywood or glass
Couchtische mit Gestell aus verformtem Schichtholz und Sperrholz- oder Glasplatten
Artek

42 **Alvar Aalto** 1954 Finland

Coffee table with base of molded laminated wood and top of wooden slats or glass
Couchtisch mit Gestell aus verformtem Schichtholz und Platte aus Holzlamellen oder Glas
Artek

43 **Alvar Aalto** c. 1947 Finland

Stools with frame of laminated birchwood and seat with webbed straps or cane-work
Hocker mit Schichtholzgestell in Birke und Sitz mit Gurtenbespannung oder Rohrgeflecht
Artek

44 **Alvar Aalto** 1954 Finland

Stool of bent, solid wood, construction with fanned bends
Hocker aus gebogenem Massivholz, Konstruktion mit gefächerter Biegung
Artek

40	41	42
43		44

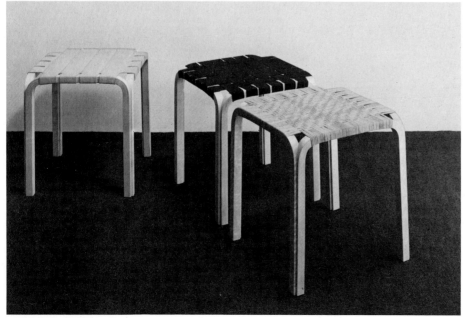

45 **Alvar Aalto** 1929–35 Finland

Stacking stools and chairs of birchwood
Stapelbare Hocker und Stühle aus Birken-
holz
Artek

46 **Alvar Aalto** c. 1947 Finland

Armchair with frame of molded laminated
wood, seat and back of cane
Armstuhl mit Gestell aus verformtem
Schichtholz, Sitz und Rückenlehne aus
Rohrgeflecht
Artek

	45	
46	47	48
	49	

47 **Alvar Aalto** 1929–33 Finland

Armchair with frame of molded laminated
wood and seat of molded plywood
Sessel mit Gestell aus verformtem Schichtholz und Sitz aus verformtem Sperrholz
Artek

48 **Alvar Aalto** 1935–39 Finland

Armchair with frame of molded laminated
wood and seat of webbed straps
Sessel mit Gestell aus verformtem Schichtholz und Sitz mit Gurtenbespannung
Artek

49 **Alvar Aalto** 1929–33 Finland

"Paimio" armchair with frame of molded
laminated birchwood, seat and back of
molded plywood
»Paimio«-Sessel mit Gestell aus verformtem
Schichtholz in Birke, Sitz und Rückenlehne
aus verformtem Sperrholz
Artek

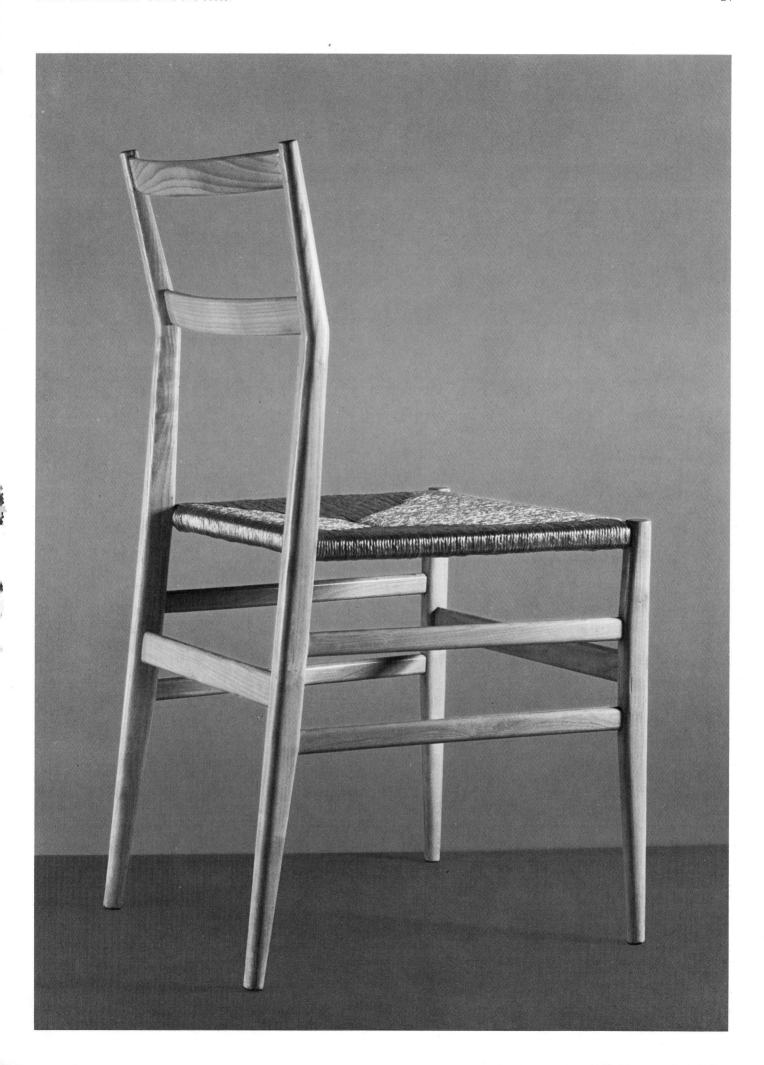

When someone sits down in a chair, the way he sits allows conclusions to be drawn about his psyche and character. The choice of a chair is also to a large extent self-presentation; it can range from occupying a throne to meekly sitting around on a foot stool. Whether a person leans back in a chair or sits nervously on the edge, whether he relaxes across the whole seat or sits bolt upright, whether he stretches his legs out or winds them nervously round the chairlegs, whether his hands are placed on the arms or in his lap–hardly any other piece of furniture permits such an array of gestures as the chair. Of all similar articles we probably have our most intimate and revealing relationship with it.

The variety of different kinds of chairs there has always been has greatly helped this behavioural phenomenon of course, but nowadays it occurs more than in the past. Because of the numerous examples in existence, the 20th century could be called the age of the chair–a fact that is probably connected with the growing trend towards individuality in this century. To each his own unmistakable chair, that he may be recognised.

The choice ranges from traditional wooden chairs to ones made of steel tubing combined with wood or plastic and ones made entirely of synthetic materials. The change in forms was also a change in materials, or rather, new materials produced forms different from previous ones. One must note, however, that the latest designs are not necessarily the best. The various kinds are about equal.

We like to remember the early wooden chairs by Max Bill (ill. 61), Georg Leowald (ills. 56, 62), Egon Eiermann (ills. 69, 109) and Finn Juhl (ill. 83) and do not feel they are old-fashioned compared with the grille or plastic shells by Harry Bertoia (ills. 209–211) and Charles Eames (ills. 263, 264), and decidedly not so compared with the plastic and cushion designs by Verner Panton (ills. 394, 395) and Olivier Morgue (ills. 410–412).

A "conventional" chair such as Gio Ponti's (ill. 50) is still valid today; in fact, despite its twenty-five years it appears almost avant garde today. After all the ups and downs we have had since then with modern chair design, some of which were very unfortunate, our appreciation of such an economical, disciplined, yet lively solution has been heightened. The traditional design of the Chiavari chair has been assimilated by Ponti with a logically modern interpretation. The original form has not been lost, but in rendering it more concise its earlier multiplicity of form has been replaced by a general spiritualisation. Here, a chair is still a chair and nothing but a chair, yet in an incomparable way. Ponti's design also shows us how severe a product was able to look, approaching the typical postures of the 1950s but not becoming their slave.

As convincing as the Italian chair is the Danish one by the designer Hans J. Wegener (ill. 80). It, too, is now over thirty years old. It is unmistakably "Scandinavian" in every detail, but so subtly so that it is capable of overcoming our exhaustion caused by a surfeit of teak furniture. So far as the use made of wood is concerned, this chair represents possibly the quintessence of the Scandinavian style, its most perfect product. When one sees this chair in a shop–it is still being produced completely unchanged–it is like meeting an old person whose wisdom quite naturally arouses our adoration.

It is quite amazing that almost at the same time, and "right next door" so to speak, such a completely different chair could be created as Arne Jacobsen's (ill. 170), probably the most successful combination of a shaped wooden seat and steel tube legs. The differences in the materials used make it hard for us to see the affinity of spirit and attitude the two Scandinavian chairs possess. Strictly speaking, they are not very far apart. Their high formal discipline is in both cases the result of a responsibility that still considered itself so close to the rudiments of modern development that it was not capable of being superficial or precipitous. Younger generations of designers became visibly bolder, but also presumptuous and effect-seeking. The American counterpart to the chair by Arne Jacobsen is the one Charles Eames designed in 1946 (ill. 166). Its use was, however, somewhat limited as it presented itself primarily as an office chair. This impression was caused by the back, which did not form a whole with the rest of the chair and was only joined to it in the middle. This is a detail that is also suitable for a chair for home use, but it was easy to see that the office chair had been used as a model. A successor to the lightness and perfection of this chair first appeared in David Rowland's metal stacking chair (ill. 202).

The principle of the skeletonised separation of supports and shell-shaped seats was continued by Charles Eames in the lounge chair (ill. 51), which is one of the most striking pieces of furniture of our time. This chair is both functionally and in its choice of form and material a product capable of presenting extremely frugally and precisely the spirit and ability of our time. This object bears unmistakable witness to technical design–it reminds one of a car or aeroplane seat, although neither exists in this form. It betrays such brilliant intelligence that it is impossible to observe this chair only as what it is designed to be. One has to see in it a fragment of a realised ideal. Here, industrial requirements and human designing capability have come together in an incomparable way.

The chair that Dieter Rams designed some years afterwards (ills. 378, 379) could be regarded as the "younger brother" of the lounge chair. In this case the combination of individual shell-shapes and cushioned parts is almost conventional, except that the solid elements are now made of plastic and not moulded wood. Nevertheless, despite the obvious details, the German example's more bourgeois attitude compared with the free thinking of the American cannot be overlooked.

50 Gio Ponti 1957 Italy

Chair "Superleggera" with frame of ash-wood and rattan seat
Stuhl »Superleggera« mit Gestell aus Eschenholz und Sitz aus Spanischem Rohr
Cassina

Wer einen Stuhl »besitzt«, tut das in zweifacher Weise. Er meldet seinen Anspruch als Eigentümer an und er legt zugleich eine Haltung vor, die Rückschlüsse auf Psyche und Charakter des Agierenden zuläßt. Die Wahl eines Stuhles ist zu einem guten Teil Selbstdarstellung; sie kann von der Thronbesteigung bis zum demütigen Herumrutschen auf der Fußbank reichen. Ob die Person sich zurücklehnt oder beklommen auf der Kante hockt, ob der Körper schräg und lässig quer über den ganzen Sitz gereckt ist oder kerzengerade ausharrt, ob die Beine vorgeschoben sind oder sich ängstlich mit denen des Stuhles verklammern, ob die Hände auf den Lehnen liegen oder im Schoß – kaum ein anderes Möbel läßt Gestisches in einem solchen Maße zu wie der Stuhl. Er ist unter allen ähnlichen Requisiten wahrscheinlich das, mit dem wir den intimsten und verräterischsten Umgang pflegen.

Nun wird dieses Verhalten allerdings sehr gefördert durch die Vielzahl von Typen, die es schon immer unter den Stühlen gegeben hat, in unserer Zeit aber noch mehr als früher. Das 20. Jahrhundert könnte dank seiner zahlreichen Beispiele zum Zeitalter des Stuhles ernannt werden – ein Umstand, der vermutlich zu tun hat mit der zunehmenden Individualisierung in diesem Säkulum. Jedem sein unverwechselbar eigner Sitz, auf daß man ihn erkenne.

Die Möglichkeiten reichen dabei von traditionellen Stühlen in Holz über solche aus Stahlrohr, kombiniert mit Holz oder Kunststoff, bis hin zu Exemplaren, die ganz aus synthetischem Material bestehen. Die Wandlung der Formen war auch eine der Werkstoffe, beziehungsweise neue Materialien erzeugten andere Formen als die bisherigen. Dabei ist zu beobachten, daß die letzten Modelle nicht etwa die besten sind, vielmehr stehen die verschiedenen Typen ziemlich gleichrangig nebeneinander.

Wir erinnern uns gern der frühen Holzstühle von Max Bill (Abb. 61), Georg Leowald (Abb. 56, 62), Egon Eiermann (Abb. 69, 109) und Finn Juhl (Abb. 83) und empfinden sie nicht als altmodisch neben den Gitter- oder Kunststoffschalen von Harry Bertoia (Abb. 209–211) oder Charles Eames (Abb. 263, 264) und erst recht nicht neben den Kunststoff- und Polsterformen von Verner Panton (Abb. 394, 395) und Olivier Mourgue (Abb. 410–412).

Ein so »konventioneller« Stuhl wie der von Gio Ponti (Abb. 50) ist bis heute überzeugend geblieben, ja, trotz seines Alters von nunmehr fünfundzwanzig Jahren wirkt er heute geradezu avantgardistisch. Nach vielen Wechselfällen mit zum Teil recht unglücklichen Ergebnissen, die wir inzwischen bei der modernen Stuhlgeschichte erleben mußten, ist unser Auge sehr für eine so ökonomische, disziplinierte und trotzdem animierend bewegte Lösung geschärft worden. Die traditionelle Form des Chiavari-Stuhles ist von Ponti einer konsequent modernen Auffassung assimiliert worden, die ursprüngliche Gestalt ist dabei nicht verloren gegangen, aber die Straffung hat den früheren Formenreichtum ersetzt durch eine generelle Vergeistigung. Ein Stuhl ist hier immer noch ein Stuhl und nichts als ein Stuhl, das jedoch in unvergleichlicher Weise. Pontis Entwurf lehrt auch, wie ernsthaft ein Produkt auszusehen vermochte, das typischen Haltungen der fünfziger Jahre nahe war, ihnen aber nicht verfiel.

Ähnlich überzeugend wie der italienische Stuhl ist der dänische des Entwerfers Hans J. Wegner (Abb. 80). Auch er ist inzwischen über dreißig Jahre alt. In allen Einzelheiten ist er unverkennbar »skandinavisch«, aber das in einer so subtilen Art, daß er unsere Ermüdung vor zuviel Teakholzmobiliar mühelos zu überwinden vermag. Der Stuhl könnte – was die Behandlung des Holzes angeht – geradezu die Quintessenz des skandinavischen Stiles sein, dessen am meisten vollendetes Produkt. Trifft man heute auf diesen Stuhl in einem Geschäft – er wird unverändert hergestellt –, dann ist das wie die Begegnung mit einer Person, deren Altersweisheit ganz selbstverständlich unsere Adorierung herausfordert.

Daß fast zur gleichen Zeit und sozusagen »unmittelbar nebenan« ein so ganz andersartiger Stuhl entstehen konnte wie der von Arne Jacobsen (Abb. 170), der die wohl gelungenste Verbindung eines verformten Holzsitzes mit Stahlrohrfüßen darstellt, ist heute kaum noch zu fassen. Die Unterschiede im Material machen dabei aber blind für die Verwandtschaft in Geist und Haltung, die beiden skandinavischen Stühlen zu eigen ist. Genaugenommen sind sie gar nicht weit voneinander entfernt. Ihre hohe formale Disziplin ist jeweils das Ergebnis einer Verantwortung, die sich den Anfängen der modernen Entwicklung noch so nahe fühlte, daß sie nie oberflächlich oder vorschnell zu sein vermochte. Jüngere Entwerfergenerationen wurden dann zusehends kühner, aber auch vorlaut und effekthascherisch.

Das amerikanische Gegenstück zu dem Stuhl von Arne Jacobsen ist der, den Charles Eames schon 1946 entworfen hat (Abb. 166). Seine Verwendung war jedoch etwas eingeschränkt, weil er sich in erster Linie als Arbeitsstuhl auswies. Dieser Eindruck entstand durch die abgelöste und nur in der Mitte gehaltene Rückenlehne – ein Detail, das auch für einen privat zu nutzenden Stuhl passend ist, dessen Vorbild sich nun aber einmal deutlich identifizieren ließ. In seiner leichten und formvollendeten Art fand dieser Stuhl erst in dem stapelbaren und ganz aus Metall gebildeten von David Rowland (Abb. 202) eine Nachfolge.

Das Prinzip der skelettierten Trennung von Stützgliedern und schalenförmigen Sitzteilen ist von Charles Eames dann weitergeführt worden an dem Lounge Chair (Abb. 51), der zu den charaktervollsten Möbeln unserer Zeit gehört. Dieser Sessel ist sowohl funktionell wie auch der Form und Materialwahl nach ein Produkt, in dem Zeitgeist und Zeitvermögen sich äußerst verknappt und sehr präzise darzustellen vermochten. Das unverkennbar technisch konzipierte Möbel – es erinnert an einen Auto- oder Flugzeugsitz, obgleich es weder das eine noch das andere in dieser Form gibt – verrät eine so bestechende Intelligenz, daß man diesen Sessel unmöglich nur als das wahrnehmen kann, was er dem Zweck nach ist, sondern in ihm auch ein Stück realisiertes Idealbild sehen muß. Industrielle Voraussetzung und menschliches Gestaltungsvermögen haben sich hier in unvergleichlicher Weise zusammengefunden.

Als den »jüngeren Bruder« des Lounge Chair konnte man dann einige Jahre später den Sessel ansehen, den Dieter Rams entworfen hat (Abb. 378 + 379). In einer schon fast wieder konventionellen Art sind auch hier einzelne Schalenformen mit Polsterteilen verbunden worden – nur daß die festen Elemente jetzt bereits aus Kunststoff sind statt aus Formholz. Jedoch bei aller Sinnfälligkeit im einzelnen: die eher bürgerliche Attitüde des deutschen Beispiels gegenüber dem amerikanischen Freigeist ist unübersehbar.

51 **Charles Eames** 1957 USA

Lounge chair "670" and ottoman on cast aluminum swivel base, rosewood veneer molded plywood frame with leather-covered polyfoam and down upholstery (cf. ill. 343)
Sessel »670« und Hocker mit Drehgestell aus Aluminiumguß, Sitzschale und Lehnen aus geformtem, mit Palisander furniertem Sperrholz, Schaumstoff- und Daunenpolsterung, mit Leder bezogen (vgl. Abb. 343)
Herman Miller

52 **Bengt Akerblom** c. 1950 Sweden

Chair in birch
Stuhl in Birke
Nässjo Stolfabrik

53 **Karl Erik Ekselius** 1953 Sweden

Chair with beech frame and upholstered
seat
Stuhl mit Buchenholzgestell und Polstersitz
Carlsson

54 **Works Design** 1952 Denmark

Stacking chair in beech
Stapelstuhl in Buche
Fritz Hansen

57+58 Jørgen Høj 1955 Denmark

Chair in fumed oak or teak, seat with fabric slings
Stuhl in geräucherter Eiche oder Teak, Sitz mit Stoffbespannung
Lindegård

◁◁ **55 Nanna and Jørgen Ditzel** 1955 Denmark

Chair with teak frame, seat of wicker-work
Stuhl mit Teakgestell, Sitz aus Weidengeflecht
Kolds Savværk

◁ **56 Georg Leowald** 1954 Germany

Chair with wooden frame and seat of wickerwork
Stuhl mit Holzgestell und Sitz aus Weidengeflecht
Wilkhahn

59 Paul M. Volther c. 1953 Denmark

Stacking chair of wood
Stapelstuhl aus Holz
F.D.B. Møbler

60 Grete Jalk 1957 Denmark

Collapsible chair "3-2" of fumed oak
Zerlegbarer Stuhl »3-2« in geräucherter Eiche
P. Jeppesen

63 **Ejner Larsen, A. Bender Madsen** 1955
Denmark
Chair with teak frame, seat and back of
leather
Stuhl mit Teakgestell, Sitz und Rückenlehne
aus Leder
Willy Beck

64 **Ejner Larsen, A. Bender Madsen** 1957/58
Denmark
Chair "1652/1653" with teak frame, seat in
cane or upholstered
Stuhl »1652/1653« mit Teakgestell, Sitz ge-
flochten oder gepolstert
Næstved

65 **Børge Mogensen** 1947 Denmark
Chair with oak or beech frame, seat in
cane
Stuhl mit Eiche- oder Buchengestell, Sitz ge-
flochten
F.D.B. Møbler

◁◁ 61 **Max Bill** c. 1950 Switzerland

Chair with wooden frame, seat and back of molded plywood
Stuhl mit Holzgestell, Sitz und Rückenlehne aus verformtem Sperrholz
Horgen-Glarus

◁ 62 **Georg Leowald** 1954 Germany

Chair with beech frame, seat and back of molded plywood, also
with plastic-covered polyfoam upholstery
Stuhl mit Buchengestell, Sitz und Rückenlehne aus verformtem
Sperrholz, auch mit kunststoffüberzogener Schaumstoffpolsterung
Wilkhahn

66 **Børge Mogensen** 1954 Denmark

Chair with oak frame, seat and back of teak
Stuhl mit Gestell in Eiche, Sitz und Rückenlehne in Teak
Søborg

67 **Carl Auböck** 1960 Austria

Stacking chair "4906" of beech
Stapelstuhl »4906« in Buche
Pollack

68 **Hans J. Wegner** 1952 Denmark

Stacking chair of wood
Stapelbarer Stuhl aus Holz
Fritz Hansen

69 **Egon Eiermann** c. 1950 Germany

Chair of molded plywood
Stuhl aus verformtem Schichtholz
Wilde & Spieth

70 **Works Design** c. 1951 Sweden

Armchair of molded plywood
Armstuhl aus verformtem Sperrholz
Nordiska Kompaniet

71 **Niko Kralj** 1954 Yugoslavia

Demountable chair with frame of molded
laminated wood, seat and back of molded
plywood
Zerlegbarer Stuhl mit Gestell aus verformtem Schichtholz, Sitz und Rückenlehne aus
verformtem Sperrholz
Stol Kamnik

72 **Ilmari Tapiovaara** 1959 Finland

Stacking chair "Alak" with frame of molded
laminated wood, seat and back of molded
plywood
Stapelstuhl »Alak« mit Gestell aus verformtem Schichtholz, Sitz und Rückenlehne aus
verformtem Sperrholz
Asko

73 **Charles Eames** 1946 USA
   Chair of molded and bent birch plywood
   Stuhl aus gebogenem und verformtem Birkensperrholz
   Herman Miller

74 **Poul Kjaerholm** 1952 Denmark
   Chair of molded laminated wood
   Stuhl aus verformtem Schichtholz
   Fritz Hansen

75 **Sori Yanagi** 1956 Japan
   Collapsible stool "Butterfly" of molded plywood
   Zerlegbarer Hocker »Butterfly« aus verformtem Sperrholz
   Akane Shokai

◁ ◁ 76 **Peter Hvidt, Orla Mølgaard Nielsen**
c. 1951 Denmark
Stacking armchair of wood
Stapelbarer Armstuhl aus Holz
Portex

◁ 77 **Ejner Larsen, A. Bender Madsen** 1949
Denmark
Armchair with wooden frame, seat and back
of molded plywood
Armstuhl mit Holzgestell, Sitz und Rücken-
lehne aus verformtem Sperrholz
Wilkhahn

80 **Hans J. Wegner** 1949 Denmark
"The chair (JH 501)" with teak frame and canework or upholstered seat
»Der Stuhl (JH 501)« mit Teakgestell und Sitz aus Rohrgeflecht oder gepolstert
Johannes Hansen

◁ ◁ 78 **Ejner Larsen, A. Bender Madsen** c. 1957
Denmark
Armchair "1656" in teak with upholstered
seat
Armstuhl »1656« in Teak mit Polstersitz
Næstved

◁ 79 **Ejner Larsen, A. Bender Madsen** 1959
Denmark
Armchair "2842/L" with teak frame, seat
and back of strong leather
Armstuhl »2842/L« mit Teakgestell, Sitz und
Rückenlehne aus starkem Leder
Willy Beck

81 **Ejner Larsen, A. Bender Madsen** 1957 Denmark

Armchair "1638/Tr" in teak with rattan seat
Armstuhl »1638/Tr« in Teak mit Sitz aus Rohrgeflecht
Willy Beck

82 **Ib Kofod-Larsen** 1958 Denmark

Armchair with rosewood frame, upholstered seat and back
Armstuhl mit Gestell in Palisander, Sitz und Rückenlehne gepolstert
Christensen & Larsen

83 **Finn Juhl** 1955 Denmark

Armchair with teak frame, upholstered seat and back
Sessel mit Teakgestell, Sitz und Rückenlehne gepolstert
Niels Vodder

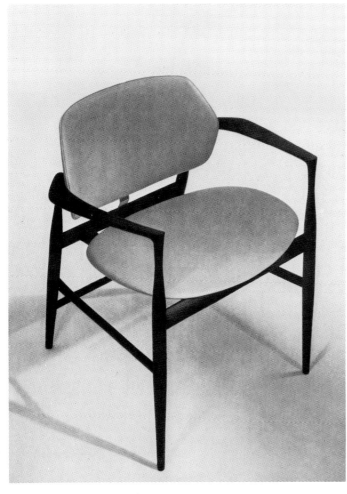

84 Georg Leowald 1954 Germany
Armchair "352 B" with frame of wood, seat
and back of molded plywood
Armstuhl »352 B« mit Gestell aus Holz, Sitz
und Rückenlehne aus verformtem Sperrholz
Wilkhahn

85 Finn Juhl 1964 Denmark
Stacking armchair "196" with teak frame,
seat and back upholstered
Stapelbarer Armstuhl »196« mit Teakgestell,
Sitz und Rücken gepolstert
France & Søn

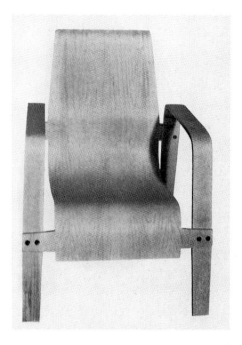

86+87 **Vittoriano Viganò** 1946 Italy

Collapsible stacking armchair "VV/46" of bent plywood, assembled with brass bolts
Zerlegbarer Stapel-Armstuhl »VV/46« aus gebogenem Sperrholz, zusammengefügt mit Messingbolzen
Compensati Curvi

88 **Roberto Mango** 1954 Italy

Collapsible chair with frame of wood, seat and back of molded plywood
Zerlegbarer Stuhl mit Massivholzgestell, Sitz und Rückenlehne aus verformtem Sperrholz

89 **Georg Leowald** 1954 Germany

Chair with wooden frame, seat and back of molded plywood
Stuhl mit Holzgestell, Sitz und Rückenlehne aus verformtem Sperrholz
Wilkhahn

90 **Carlo Bartoli** 1968 Italy

Chair "Mito" of ash in natural or lacquer finish
Stuhl »Mito« aus Esche natur oder lakkiert
Tisettanta

91 Gerd Lange 1973/74 Germany

Chair "2200" of solid oak, side parts of plywood, seat and back of plastic
Stuhl »2200« aus Buche massiv, Seitenteile aus Sperrholz, Sitz und Rückenlehne aus Kunststoff
Thonet

92+93 Sören Nissen, Ebbe Gehl 1979
Sweden

Stacking and linking chair "Jet" with frame of bent laminated oak, seat of molded oak, also upholstered
Stapel- und Reihenstuhl »Jet« mit Gestell in schichtverleimter Buche, Sitzschale in Buche formgepreßt, auch gepolstert
Skandi-Form

94 Wilhelm Ritz 1959 Germany

Chair "402" of laminated beech, seat and back upholstered
Stuhl »402« aus Schichtholz in Buche, Sitz und Rückenlehne gepolstert
Wilkhahn

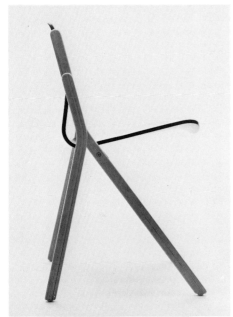  

95–97 **Niko Kralj** Yugoslavia
Chairs and armchairs with wooden frames,
seats and backs of perforated molded ply-
wood
Stühle und Armstühle mit Holzgestellen,
Sitze und Rückenlehnen aus durchbroche-
nem verformtem Sperrholz
Stol Kamnik

98 + 99 **Peter Hvidt, Orla Mølgaard Nielsen**
1950 Denmark
"AX" chair and armchair with laminated
beech frames, teak seats and backs
»AX«-Stuhl und Armstuhl mit Gestellen aus
Buchen-Schichtholz, Sitze und Rücken-
lehnen in Teak
Fritz Hansen

100 **Alberto Rosselli** 1954 Italy
Chair with laminated bent wood frame,
seat and back of molded plywood
Stuhl mit Gestell aus Bugholz, Sitz und
Rückenlehne aus verformtem Sperr-
holz
Cassina

101 Franco Albini, Luigi Colombini, Ezio Sgrelli c. 1950 Italy

Armchair with movable seat and back, foam-rubber padding
Armstuhl mit beweglichem Sitz und Rückenteil, Schaumgummipolsterung
La Rinascente

103 **Kai Kristiansen** 1960 Denmark   ▷

Chair "4110" with teak frame, upholstered
seat with leather or fabric cover
Stuhl »4110« mit Teakgestell, gepolsterter
Sitz mit Leder- oder Stoffbezug
Fritz Hansen

104 **Herbert Berry, Christopher Cattle** 1962 ▷
Great Britain

Chair in ash or mahogany with polyfoam
cushion on a base of molded plywood
Stuhl in Esche oder Mahagoni mit Sitz aus
verformtem Sperrholz und Schaumstoffkissen
Lucas

105 **Terence Conran** 1962 Great Britain   ▷

Dining chairs "Summa SU 22/23" in ash,
pine, or teak, backs in wood with or without upholstery
Stühle »Summa SU 22/23« in Esche, Kiefer
oder Teak, Rückenlehnen aus Holz mit
oder ohne Polsterung
Conran

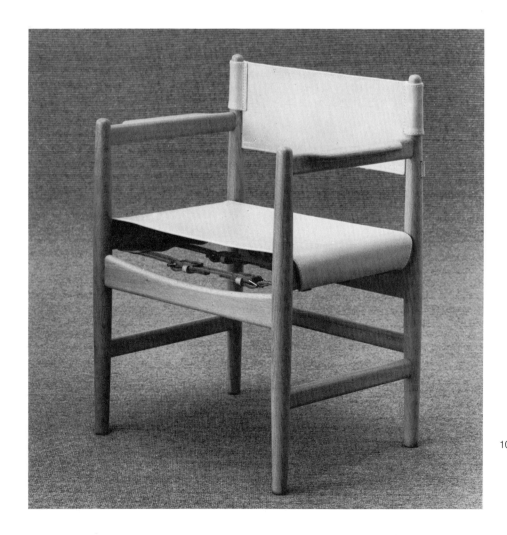

102 **Børge Mogensen** 1955 Denmark

Armchair "Øresund" in oak with removable leather slings
Armstuhl »Øresund« in Eiche mit abnehmbarer Lederbespannung
Karl Andersson

106 **Gio Ponti** 1964 Italy
Armchair "1215" in mat finished walnut
with rattan seat
Sessel »1215« mit Gestell in mattiertem
Nußbaum, Sitz aus Rohrgeflecht
Knoll International

103	106
104	
105	107

107 **Bruno Rey** 1972 Switzerland
Range of lacquer-finished stackable chairs
"2100" with seats and backs of high-pres-
sure-molded plywood, frames of solid
beech and die-cast aluminum joints. Also
with upholstery
Stapelstuhlprogramm »2100« mit Sitzen
und Rückenlehnen aus hochdruckver-
formtem Sperrholz, Stuhlbeinen aus Buche
massiv und Aluminiumdruckgußbeschlä-
gen, farbig lackiert. Auch mit Polsterung
Kusch

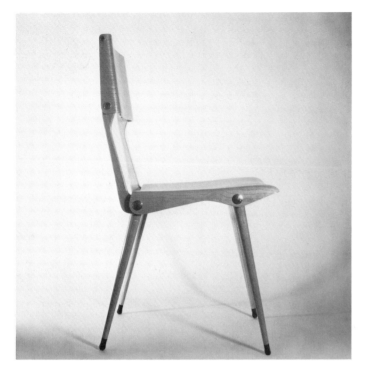

108 Carlo De Carli 1954 Italy

Collapsible chair "683" with ash frame, seat and back of molded plywood with chrome-plated metal fittings
Zerlegbarer Stuhl »683« mit Gestell in Esche, Sitz und Rückenlehne aus verformtem Sperrholz mit verchromten Metallbeschlägen
Cassina

109 Egon Eiermann 1952 Germany

Folding chair with beech frame, seat and back of molded plywood
Klappstuhl mit Buchenholzgestell, Sitz und Rückenlehne aus verformtem Sperrholz
Wilde & Spieth

110 Jack Ränge c. 1950 Sweden

Folding armchair with seat slings in canvas and leather straps
Klappstuhl mit Segeltuchbespannung und Lederriemen

111 Franco Albini c. 1950 Italy

Folding armchair with wooden frame, seat and back of plywood
Klappstuhl mit Holzgestell, Sitz und Rückenlehne aus Sperrholz

112 Marco Zanuso c. 1950 Italy

Folding armchair "Bridge" with wooden frame and polyfoam upholstery
Klappstuhl »Bridge« mit Holzgestell und Schaumstoffpolsterung
Arflex

113 Frei Otto 1967 Germany

Stackable knock-down chair with frame of beech, ash, or rosewood, canvas or leather slings
Zerlegbarer Stapelstuhl mit Gestell in Buche, Esche oder Palisander, Leder- oder Segeltuchbespannung
Karl Fröscher

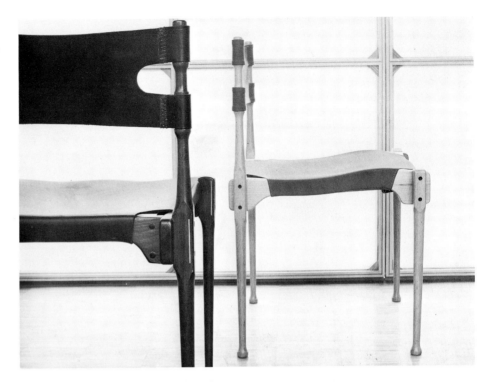

114+115 Jonathan De Pas, Donato D'Urbino, Paolo Lomazzi 1975 Italy

Demountable chair "Linda" and armchair "Lindapiù" with supple joints, frame of ash or beech, seat and back of canvas or cowhide
Zerlegbarer Stuhl »Linda« und Armstuhl »Lindapiù« mit beweglichen Gelenken, Gestell aus Esche oder Buche, Sitz und Rückenlehne mit Segeltuch oder Leder bespannt
Zanotta

116 Gerd Lange 1966 Germany

Furniture series "Bofinger Farmerprogramm" in knock-down construction. Wooden parts of ash in natural finish or stained are joined and then connected by means of canvas slings
Zerlegbares »Bofinger Farmerprogramm«; Holzteile in Esche natur oder gebeizt werden zusammengesteckt und durch die Segeltuchbespannung miteinander verbunden
Stoll

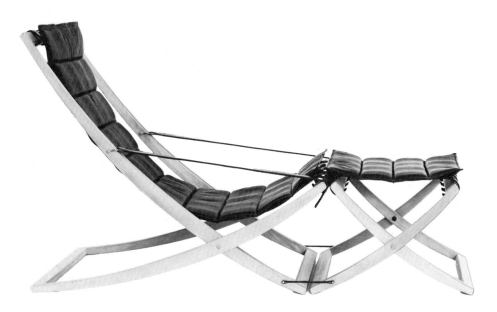

117 **Henrik Iversen, Harald Plum** 1964
Denmark

Lounge chair "PH 76" and stool "PH 77"
with frames of beech and fabric or leather
cover
Liegestuhl » PH 76 « und Hocker » PH 77 «
mit Buchenholzgestellen und Stoff- oder
Lederbezügen
Domus Danica

118 + 119 **Ernest Race** 1953 Great Britain

Stackable folding deck chair "Orient Neptune" of molded laminated beech in clear
lacquer finish, brass fittings, nylon belt-
ing
Stapelbarer Deckstuhl »Orient Neptune«
aus klarlackiertem verformtem Buchen-
schichtholz, Beschläge aus Messing, Ny-
lonbänder
Ernest Race

120 **Lauge Vestergaard** 1970 Denmark

Folding chair and stool "139" of beech
with canvas slings. Adjustable headrest
Klappsessel und Hocker »139« in Buche
mit Segeltuchbespannung. Kopfpolster
verstellbar
Cado

121 **Don Knorr** c. 1950 USA

Stool in birch with leather seat
Hocker in Birke mit Ledersitz
Kneedler-Fauchère

117	
118	119
120	121

122+123 **Jonathan De Pas, Donato D'Urbino, Paolo Lomazzi** 1975 Italy

Folding chair "Sanremo" with frame of ash, seat and back with canvas slings
Klappstuhl »Sanremo« mit Gestell aus Esche, Sitz und Rückenlehne mit Segeltuch spannt
Zanotta

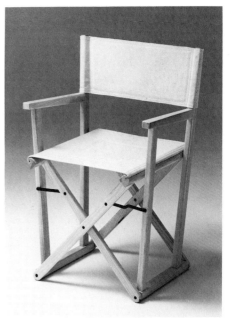

124 **Esko Pajamies** 1962 Finland

Folding chair "Finnsafari" with frame of molded beech veneer, seat, back, and side straps of leather
Klappsessel »Finnsafari« mit Gestell aus verformtem Buchenfurnier, Sitz, Rückenlehne und Gurte aus Leder
Kylmäkoski Oy

125+126 **Günter Sulz** 1971 Germany

"London Chair" with folding frame of beech, stained or lacquered, canvas slings. Matching table with plastic top
»London Chair« mit Klappgestell in Buche gebeizt oder lackiert und Segeltuchbespannung. Passender Tisch mit Kunststoff-platte
Behr+Sulz

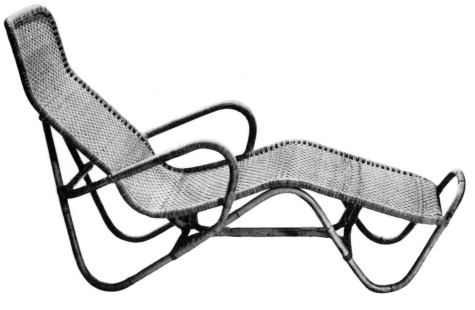

127 **Kolling Andersen** 1950 Denmark

Rattan lounge chair with seat of wicker-work
Liegestuhl mit Rohrgestell und Sitz aus Weidengeflecht
Laurids Løngborg

128 + 129 **Nanna and Jørgen Ditzel** 1950 Denmark

Chair with wooden base and rattan seat
Stuhl mit Holzgestell und Sitz aus Rohrgeflecht
L. Pontoppidan

130 **Franco Albini** 1951 Italy

Easy chair of rattan
Sessel aus Rohrgeflecht
BBB Bonacina

131 **Egon Eiermann** 1952 Germany

Easy chair of rattan
Sessel aus Rohrgeflecht
Friedrich Herr

132 **Egon Eiermann** 1957 Germany
   Easy chair of rattan
   Sessel aus Rohrgeflecht
   Heinrich Murrmann

133 **Nanna and Jørgen Ditzel** 1959
   Denmark
   Rattan hammock hanging on a chain
   Sitzkorb aus Rohrgeflecht, an einer Kette
   aufzuhängen
   Wengler

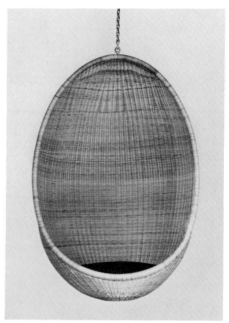

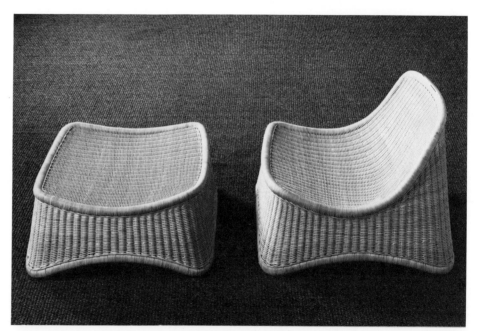

134 **Nanna Ditzel** 1961 Denmark
   Easy chair and footstool of rattan
   Sessel und Fußbank aus Rohrgeflecht
   Wengler

135 **Isamu Kenmochi** 1961 Japan
   Easy chair of rattan with loose cushion
   Sessel aus Rohrgeflecht mit losem Kissen
   Yamakawa Rattan Co.

136 **Albrecht Lange, Hans Mitzlaff** c. 1951
Germany

Easy chair with laminated wood frame,
rubber straps and loose cushions
Sessel mit Schichtholzgestell, Gummigurten und losen Kissen
Eugen Schmidt

137 **Pierre Jeanneret** c. 1951 France

Easy chair with wooden frame and polyfoam cushions on rubber straps
Sessel mit Holzgestell und Schaumstoffkissen auf Gummigurten
Knoll International

138 **Alf Svensson** c. 1953 Sweden

Easy chair with wooden frame and loose
cushions
Sessel mit Holzgestell und losen Sitzkissen
Ljungs Industrier

139 **Sonna Rosen** c. 1951 Sweden

Armchair in birch
Armstuhl aus Birke
Swedish Modern Furniture Co.

142 **Folke Ohlsson** c. 1953 Sweden ▷

Upholstered easy chair with wooden
frame
Polstersessel mit Holzgestell
Ljungs Industrier

143 **Florence Knoll** 1955 USA ▷▷

Lounge chair with teak frame and polyfoam upholstery
Sessel mit Teakgestell und Schaumstoffpolsterung
Knoll International

◁ 140 **Works Design** c. 1951 USA

Chairs and armchairs with wooden frames and seats with straps
or upholstery
Stühle und Armstühle mit Holzgestellen und Sitzen mit Gurtenbespannung oder Polsterung
Knoll International

▷ 141 **Otto Haupt** 1951 Germany

Easy chair with bentwood frame and fabric straps
Sessel mit Bugholzgestell und Stoffgurten
Pforzheimer Bugholzmöbel

144 **Eero Saarinen** c. 1950 USA

Upholstered armchair "61" with laminated birch frame and innerspring construction
Sessel »61« mit Gestell aus Birkenschichtholz und Feder-polsterung
Knoll International

145 **Arne Jacobsen** 1962 Denmark

Easy chair "4335" and ottoman "4533" in natural finished oak with fabric-covered polyfoam upholstery; stool may also be used as side table when cushion is removed
Sessel »4335« und Hocker »4533« in Eiche natur mit Schaumstoff-polsterung und Stoffbezug; ohne Polster ist der Hocker als Beistell-tischchen verwendbar
Fritz Hansen

146 **Joe Colombo** 1966 Italy

Easy chair "Supercomfort 1000" with frame of bent plywood in natural or white lacquer finish. Removable cushions covered with leather. Inserted tension springs of plastic may be relaxed or tightened
Sessel »Supercomfort 1000« mit Gestell aus naturfarbenem oder weiß lackiertem verformtem Schichtholz. Abnehmbare Kissen mit Lederbezug. Die Elastizität des Sessels ist durch eingelassene Kunststoffstäbe nach Wunsch regulierbar
Comfort

147 **Marco Zanuso, Richard Sapper** 1964 Italy/Germany

Easy chair "Woodline" with frame of molded laminated wood. Seat of wood with loose leather cushions
Sessel »Woodline« mit Gestell aus verformtem Schichtholz. Sitz aus Holz mit losen Lederpolstern
Arflex

148 **Poul Kjaerholm** 1971 Denmark

Lounge chair with frame of laminated wood and leather upholstery
Sessel mit Gestell aus Schichtholz und Lederpolster
E. Kold Christensen

149 **Kembo Team** 1978 Netherlands

Armchair "Eutektos" with frame of solid beechwood laminate, seat and back of plastic or upholstered and with leather or fabric covering
Sessel mit Gestell aus laminiertem Buchenmassivholz, Sitz und Rükkenlehne aus Kunststoff oder gepolstert und mit Leder oder Stoff bezogen
Kembo

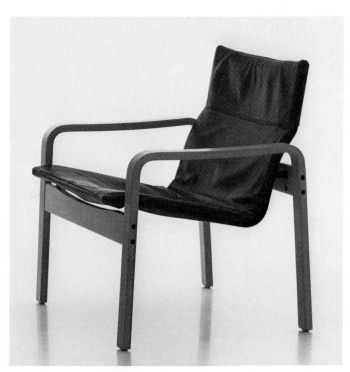

152 **Works Design** c. 1955 Denmark

Armchair "116" in teak with polyfoam
upholstery
Sessel »116« in Teakholz mit Schaumstoffpolsterung
France & Søn

153 **Ole Wanscher** c. 1955 Denmark

Armchair "119" in teak with polyfoam
upholstery
Sessel »119« in Teakholz mit Schaumstoffpolsterung
France & Søn

154 **Folke Ohlsson** 1953 Sweden

Armchair with wooden frame and polyfoam upholstery
Sessel mit Holzgestell und Schaumstoffpolsterung
Ljungs Industrier

150 **Finn Juhl** 1945 Denmark

Armchair with frame of oiled teak, upholstered seat and back, loose
seat cushion
Sessel mit Gestell aus geöltem Teakholz, Sitz und Rückenlehne
gepolstert, loses Sitzkissen
Niels Vodder

151 **Finn Juhl** 1958 Denmark

Armchair "136" in teak with polyfoam upholstery
Armstuhl »136« in Teak mit Schaumstoffpolsterung
France & Søn

150	152
151	153
	154

155 + 156 **Edvard Kindt-Larsen** 1954
Denmark

Armchair with beech or teak frame, seat
support of rubber straps, and loose cushions
Sessel mit Gestell in Buche oder Teak, Sitzunterlage aus Gummibändern und losen
Polstern
France & Søn

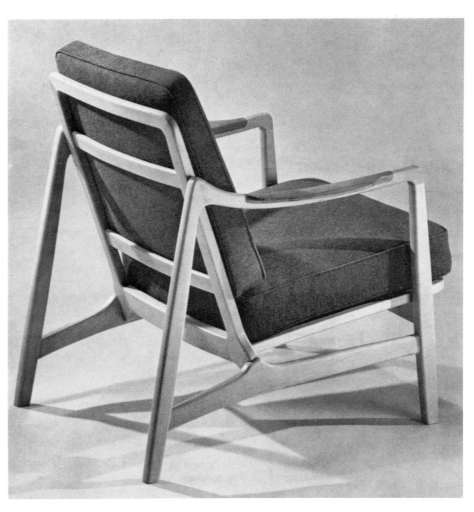

157 **Karl Erik Ekselius** 1953 Sweden

Armchair with wooden frame and polyfoam upholstery
Sessel mit Holzgestell und Schaumstoffpolsterung
Carlsson

158 **Folke Ohlsson, Alf Svensson** c. 1953
Sweden

Upholstered settee and armchair with
wooden frames
Polstersessel und Sofa mit Holzgestellen
Ljungs Industrier

162 **Franco Albini** 1954/55 Italy   ▷

Armchair with wooden frame, seat and
back of plywood, polyfoam upholstery
Sessel mit Gestell aus Massivholz, Sitz und
Rückenlehne aus Sperrholz mit Schaum-
stoffpolsterung
Carlo Poggi

163 **Herbert Hirche** 1957 Germany   ▷▷

Upholstered armchair with cherrywood or
teak frame
Polstersessel mit Gestell in Kirschbaum
oder Teak
Wilkhahn

159 **S.H. Vakassian** c. 1950 USA

Armchair with wooden frame and polyfoam upholstery
Sessel mit Holzgestell und Schaumstoffpolsterung
Vakassian & Sons

160 **Marco Zanuso** 1951 Italy

Armchair "Senior" with metal frame and
foam rubber upholstery
Sessel »Senior« mit Metallgestell und
Schaumgummipolsterung
Arflex

161 **Marco Zanuso** 1951 Italy

Armchair "Baby" with wooden frame and
foam rubber upholstery
Sessel »Baby« mit Holzgestell und
Schaumgummipolsterung
Arflex

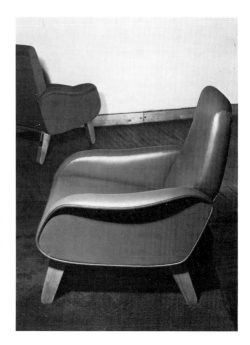

164 **Lewis Butler** c. 1956 USA

Armchair with beech frame, walnut back,
loose polyfoam cushions
Sessel mit Gestell in Buche, Rückenlehne
in Nußbaum, lose Schaumstoffkissen
Knoll International

165 **Roland Gibbard** 1963 Great Britain

Easy Chair "Q" with frame of beech, back of beech veneered plywood, seat supported on rubber webbing. Loose polyfoam cushions with detachable fabric covers
Sessel »Q« mit Gestell in Buche, Rückenlehne aus Sperrholz mit
Buchenfurnier, Sitz auf Gummigurten. Lose Schaumstoffkissen mit
abnehmbaren Stoffbezügen
Design Furnishing Contracts

169 **Arne Jacobsen** 1952 Denmark ▷

Three-legged stacking chair of molded
beech plywood and steel tube base
Dreibeiniger Stapelstuhl aus verformtem
Schichtholz in Buche und Stahlrohrge-
stell
Fritz Hansen

170 **Arne Jacobsen** 1955 Denmark ▷▷

Four-legged stacking chair of molded
beech plywood and steel tube base
Vierbeiniger Stapelstuhl aus verformtem
Schichtholz in Buche und Stahlrohrge-
stell
Fritz Hansen

166–168 **Charles Eames** 1946 USA

Dining chair and low side chair of molded
walnut plywood, steel rods, rubber shock-
mounts
Stuhl und niederer Stuhl aus geformtem
Nußbaum-Sperrholz; Stahlrohrgestell und
Gummipuffer
Herman Miller

171 **Søren Hansen** 1953 Denmark
   Stacking stool with steel tube frame and
   wooden seat
   Stapelhocker mit Stahlrohrgestell und
   Holzsitz
   Fritz Hansen

172 **Arne Jacobsen** 1955 Denmark
   Chair of molded plywood with steel tube
   base
   Stuhl aus verformtem Schichtholz und
   Stahlrohrgestell
   Fritz Hansen

173 **Arne Jacobsen** 1957 Denmark
   Chair of molded plywood with metal
   base
   Stuhl aus verformtem Schichtholz mit
   Metallgestell
   Fritz Hansen

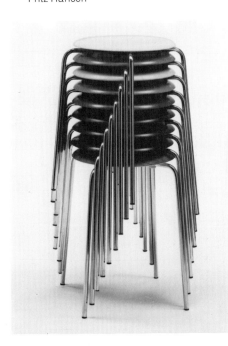

174 Egon Eiermann 1952 Germany

Chairs with steel tube frames and molded plywood seats and backs
Stühle mit Stahlrohrgestellen, Sitze und Rückenlehnen aus verformtem Sperrholz
Wilde & Spieth

175 Gastone Rinaldi 1955 Italy

Chair "DU66" with metal base, seat and back of molded plywood
Stuhl »DU 66« mit Metallgestell, Sitz und Rückenlehne aus verformtem Sperrholz
Rima

176 Friso Kramer 1954 Netherlands

Chair with metal frame, seat and back of molded plywood
Stuhl mit Metallgestell, Sitz und Rückenlehne aus verformtem Sperrholz
De Cirkel

177 Friso Kramer 1955 Netherlands

"Revolt" chair with steel frame, seat and back of molded plywood
Stuhl »Revolt« mit Stahlgestell, Sitz und Rückenlehne aus verformtem Sperrholz
De Cirkel

178 + 179 **Osvaldo Borsani** 1958 Italy

Folding chair "S88" with lacquered tubular steel frame, seat and back of molded plywood
Klappstuhl »S88« mit lackiertem Stahlrohrgestell, Sitz und Rückenlehne aus verformtem Sperrholz
Tecno

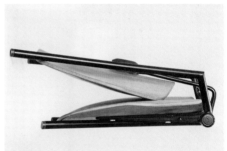

180 **Kurt Nordström** c. 1957 Sweden

Chair "145" with black lacquered tubular steel frame, seat and back of molded plywood
Stuhl »145« mit schwarz lackiertem Stahlrohrgestell, Sitz und Rückenlehne aus verformtem Sperrholz
Knoll International

181 **Theo Tempelman** 1960 Netherlands

Chair "41" with tubular steel frame, seat and back of teak or upholstered
Stuhl »41« mit Stahlrohrgestell, Sitz und Rückenlehne in Teak oder gepolstert
A. Polak's Meubelindustrie

182 **Gastone Rinaldi** 1960 Italy

Chair "S7" with tubular steel frame, seat and back of molded plywood veneered in various woods or upholstered
Stuhl »S7« mit Stahlrohrgestell, Sitz und Rückenlehne aus verformtem Sperrholz mit Edelholzfurnier oder Polsterung
Rima

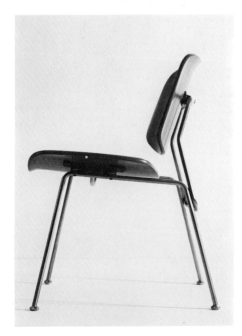

183 Robin Day c. 1953 Great Britain

Stacking chair with tubular steel frame, seat and back in molded plywood with plastic laminate
Stapelstuhl mit Stahlrohrgestell, Sitz und Rückenlehne aus verformtem Sperrholz mit Kunststoffbeschichtung
Hille

184 Eva and Nils Koppel 1949 Denmark

Stacking chair with steel tube frame and plastic-laminated molded plywood seat and back
Stapelstuhl mit Stahlrohrgestell, Sitz und Rückenlehne aus verformtem Sperrholz mit Kunststoffbeschichtung
Slagelse Møbelværk

185 Hans Bellmann c. 1952 Switzerland

Chair with chrome-plated steel tube base and birch seat
Stuhl mit verchromtem Stahlrohrgestell und Sitzschale in Birke
Wohnbedarf Zürich

186 Ray Komai c. 1950 USA

Chair with metal frame and seat of molded plywood
Stuhl mit Metallgestell und Sitz aus verformtem Sperrholz
JG Furniture

187 Hans Coray c. 1952 Switzerland

Chair with steel tube frame and molded plywood seat and back
Stuhl mit Stahlrohrgestell, Sitz und Rückenlehne aus verformtem Sperrholz
Hans Coray

188 W. Rietveld c. 1952 Netherlands

Chair with steel tube frame and molded plywood seat and back
Stuhl mit Stahlrohrgestell, Sitz und Rückenlehne aus verformtem Sperrholz
Gispen

189 Albert Rauch c. 1953 Switzerland

Chair with chrome-plated steel tube frame, seat and back of molded laminated wood
Stuhl mit verchromtem Stahlrohrgestell, Sitz und Rückenlehne aus verformtem Schichtholz
Werkgenossenschaft Wohnhilfe

187	188	189
	190	
	191	192

190 Peter Hjorth 1956 Denmark

Chair with tubular steel frame, seat and back in one piece of molded and perforated veneer wood
Stuhl mit Stahlrohrgestell, Sitz und Rückenlehne in einem Stück aus verformtem und ausgestanztem Furnierholz
Rosma

191 Friso Kramer, Jaap Penraat c. 1953 Netherlands

Upholstered armchair with steel tube frame
Gepolsterter Armstuhl mit Stahlrohrgestell
De Cirkel/Ahrend

192 Ilmari Tapiovaara 1952 Finland

Stacking armchair "Lukki" with steel tube frame and molded plywood seat and back
Stapelbarer Armstuhl »Lukki« mit Stahlrohrgestell, Sitz und Rückenlehne aus verformtem Sperrholz
Suomen Rautasänkytehdas

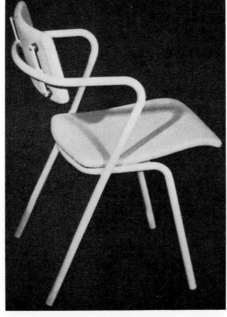

193 **Works Design** c. 1953 Sweden

Swivel chair with metal frame and adjustable back, seat in molded laminated wood with or without upholstery
Drehstuhl mit Metallgestell und verstellbarer Rückenlehne, Sitz aus verformtem Schichtholz mit oder ohne Polsterung
Nordiska Kompaniet

195 **Armin Wirth** c. 1953 Switzerland

Folding chair with aluminum frame, seat and back of molded plywood
Klappstuhl mit Aluminiumgestell, Sitz und Rückenlehne aus verformtem Sperrholz
Hans Zollinger Söhne

194 **Hillevi Sepponen** c. 1952 Finland

Swivel chair with metal frame, seat and adjustable back in molded wood
Drehstuhl mit Metallgestell, Sitz und verstellbare Rückenlehne aus verformtem Holz
Skanno

196 **Tokujiro Kaneko** c. 1952 Japan

Height-adjustable office chair with steel frame and upholstered seat and back
Höhenverstellbarer Bürostuhl mit Stahlgestell und gepolstertem Sitz und Rückenlehne
Okamura

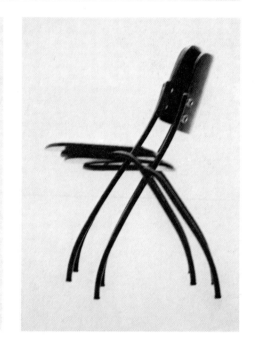

197 + 198 Nanna and Jørgen Ditzel 1958 Denmark

Stacking chair "150" with nickel-plated tubular steel frame with inlaid steel rod in all bendings.
Seat and back of plastic-laminated beech with edge and rail profiles of solid wood. The
chairs are linked by a steel bar which goes through the rails and is fastened with a rubber
ring
Stapelstuhl »150« mit vernickeltem Stahlrohrgestell mit Einlagen von Rundstahl in allen Krüm-
mungen. Sitz und Rückenlehne aus kunststoffbeschichteter Buche mit Kanten- und Zargen-
profilen aus Massivholz. Die Stühle werden mit einer Federstahlstange zusammengekoppelt,
die durch die Zargen geht und mit einem Gummiring befestigt ist
Kolds Savværk

199 + 200 Ilmari Tapiovaara 1958 Finland

Stacking chair "Nana" with lacquered tubular steel frame, seat and back of molded plywood
lacquered or covered with fabric. Linking chair with armrests
Stapelstuhl »Nana« mit lackiertem Stahlrohrgestell, Sitz und Rückenlehne aus verformtem
Sperrholz, lackiert oder mit Stoff bezogen. Reihenstuhl mit Armlehnen
J. Merivaara Oy

201 H.Th. Baumann 1956 Germany

Folding chair with chrome-plated tubular steel frame, seat and back of molded plywood
Klappstuhl mit verchromtem Stahlrohrgestell, Sitz und Rückenlehne aus verformtem Sperr-
holz
Formtex

204 **Achille and Pier Giacomo Castiglioni** ▷
1957 Italy

Stool "Mezzadro" with stem of chrome-plated steel, seat lacquered in various colors or chrome-plated, foot-rest of beech
Hocker »Mezzadro« mit Stützstange aus verchromtem Stahl, Sitz farbig lackiert oder verchromt, Fußstütze aus Buche
Zanotta

205 **Rodney Kinsman** 1974 Italy ▷ ▷

Chair "omkstack" with chrome-plated or lacquered steel tube frame, seat and back of sheet metal
Stuhl »omkstack« mit Gestell aus verchromtem oder thermolackiertem Stahlrohr, Sitz und Rückenlehne aus Metallblech
Bieffeplast

202 **David Rowland** 1964 USA

Stacking and linking chair "GF 40/4" of chrome-plated or plastic-laminated steel-rod. Seat and back panels of contoured sheet steel in plastic laminate. Clear plastic linking devices and gliders
Stapel- und Reihenstuhl »GF 40/4« aus verchromtem oder kunststoffbeschichtetem Rundstahl. Sitz und Rückenlehne aus gebogenem Stahlblech, mit Kunststoff beschichtet. Gleiter und Verbindungselemente aus glasklarem Kunststoff
The General Fireproofing Company

203 **Ernest Race** 1950 Great Britain

Chair "Antelope" with painted steel-rod frame and seat of molded plywood
Stuhl »Antelope« mit farbig lackiertem Stahlrohrgestell und geformtem Sperrholzsitz
Ernest Race

206 **James C. Witty** c. 1952 USA

Folding chair with metal frame and perforated metal seat and back
Klappstuhl mit Metallgestell, Sitz und Rükkenlehne aus ausgestanzter Metallfolie
Troy Sunshade Co.

207 **A.J. Milne** c. 1951 Great Britain

Garden chair with steel tube frame and
perforated metal seat and back
Gartenstuhl mit Stahlrohrgestell, Sitz und
Rückenlehne aus ausgestanzter Metallfolie

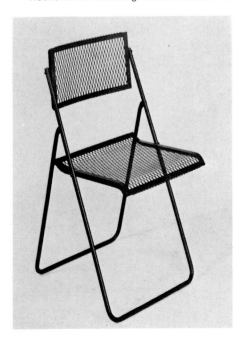

208 Charles Eames 1951 USA

Chair with formed wire seat, removable cushion, wire rod frame
Stuhl mit Sitz aus geformtem Draht, abnehmbarem Kissen und Gestell aus Metallgestänge
Herman Miller

209–211 Harry Bertoia 1952 USA

Lounge chair "423", stool "424", chairs "420" and "421" with steel rod bases, formed wire seats and removable polyfoam upholstery
Sessel »423«, Hocker »424«, Stühle »420« und »421« mit Gestellen aus Rundstahl, Sitzen aus geformtem Drahtgeflecht und abnehmbaren Schaumstoffpolstern
Knoll International

208	209
210	211

212 Warren Platner 1964/66 USA

Lounge chair "1705" and ottoman "1709"
with electronically welded steel wire bases,
copper- or nickel-plated. Polyfoam upholstery on plastic seat shells with loose
cushions
Sessel »1705« und Hocker »1709« mit Gestellen aus elektronisch verschweißtem,
verkupfertem oder vernickeltem Stahl-
draht; schaumstoffgepolsterte Kunststoff-
sitzschalen mit losen Kissen
Knoll International

213 Verner Panton 1960 Denmark

Deck chair "T-2" with base and seating
shell of steel wire with loose polyfoam
cushions
Liegestuhl »T-2« aus Drahtgeflecht mit
losen Schaumstoffkissen
Plus-linje

214 + 215 Verner Panton 1958/59 Denmark

Series of chairs in different heights and
shapes. Cone of wire, exterior in fabric, interior upholstered in polyfoam with fabric
cover, legs of stainless steel
Stuhlserie in verschiedenen Höhen und
Formen. Sitzkorb aus Draht, außen mit
Stoff bespannt, innen Schaumstoffpolsterung mit Stoffbezug, Fußgestell aus rostfreiem Stahl
Plus-linje

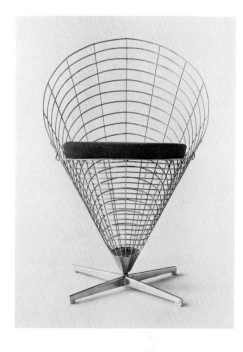
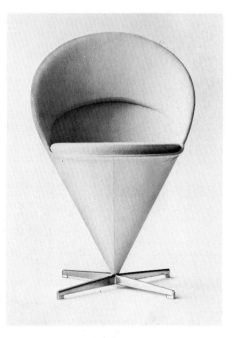

216 **Robin Day** 1963 Great Britain

Range of chairs with seat shells of injection-molded plastic and a great variety of additions: bases for multiple seating, for stacking and linking chairs, for swivel chairs, high bar stool frames, legs of beech, armrests, writing arm. Also with upholstery
Stuhlprogramm mit Sitzschalen aus formgespritztem Kunststoff und zahlreichen Kombinationsmöglichkeiten und Ergänzungen: Reihenbestuhlung, Gestelle für Reihen-, Stapel- und Drehstühle, hohe Gestelle für Barhocker, Beine in Buche, Armlehnen, Tablar. Auch mit Polsterung
Hille

217 **Ib Kofod-Larsen** 1955 Denmark

Chair with chrome-plated tubular steel base, seat of fiberglass with loose polyfoam cushion
Stuhl mit Gestell aus verchromtem Stahlrohr, Sitzschale aus Fiberglas mit losem Schaumstoffkissen
Vermund Larsen

218 **Esko Pajamies** 1961 Finland

Stacking chair "TU-520" with base of spring steel and seat shell of fiberglass-reinforced polyester, also with armrests and upholstery
Stapelstuhl »TU-520« mit Gestell aus Federstahl und Sitzschale aus glasfaserverstärktem Polyester, auch mit Armlehnen und Polsterung
Metalliteos Oy

219 **Don Albinson** 1965 USA

Stacking and linking chair "1601" with
cast-aluminum frame, seat and back of injection-molded plastic. Also with armrests,
writing arm, chrome-plated book rack, and
tabletops
Stapel- und Reihenstuhl »1601« mit Gestell
aus Aluminiumguß, Sitz und Rückenlehne
Kunststoff-Spritzguß. Zusätzlich Armlehnen, Schreibplatte, verchromte Buch-
ablage und Tischplatten
Knoll International

220 **Works Design** 1969 Germany

Linking and stacking chair "Multi" with
frame of chrome-plated or mat black
epoxy-finished tubular steel and plastic
seat and back
Reihen- und Stapelstuhl »Multi« mit Gestell
aus verchromtem oder mattschwarz epoxybeschichtetem Stahlrohr, Sitz und Rückenlehne aus Kunststoff
Fehlbaum

221 **Giancarlo Piretti** 1967 Italy

Stacking and linking chair "106" with cast-
metal frame and plastic-laminated legs of
tubular steel. Seat and back of molded
plywood in beech, walnut, rosewood, or
upholstered
Stapel- und Reihenstuhl »106« mit Rahmen aus Leichtmetall-Druckguß und
kunststoffbeschichteten Stahlrohrbeinen.
Sitz und Rückenlehne aus verformtem
Sperrholz in Buche, Nußbaum oder Palisander, auch gepolstert
Anonima Castelli

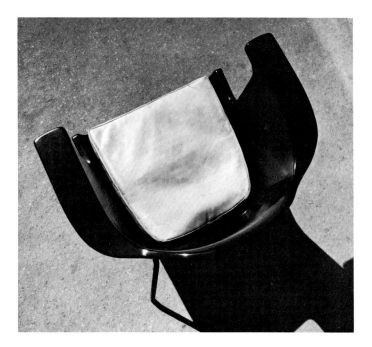

222 Angelo Mangiarotti 1949 Italy

Armchair of molded plastic with metal tube frame and loose cushion
Armstuhl aus Kunststoff mit Metallrohrgestell und losem Kissen

223 W. and E. Guhl c. 1950 Switzerland

Chair with plastic seat shell and metal legs
Stuhl mit Sitzschale aus Kunststoff und Metallbeinen
Scott Bader

224 Vermund Larsen 1956 Denmark

Stacking chair with chrome-plated tubular steel base and fiberglass
seat
Stapelstuhl mit Gestell aus verchromtem Stahlrohr und Sitzschale
aus Fiberglas
Vermund Larsen

225 Harry Bertoia 1955 USA

Chair "427 P" with black lacquered metal base and plastic seat shell
Stuhl »427 P« mit schwarz lackiertem Metallgestell und Kunststoff-
sitzschale
Knoll International

226 Kai Lyngfeldt Larsen, Steen Eiler Rasmussen 1960 Denmark

Chair "333" with tubular steel frame, seating shell of fiberglass
Stuhl »333« mit Gestell aus Stahlrohr, Sitzschale aus Fiberglas
Bovirke

222	223
	224
225	226

227–229 Charles Eames 1949–53 USA

Chairs of molded plastic with underframes of cast aluminum, metal
tube or wire rods
Stühle mit Kunststoffsitzschale, Gestelle aus Aluminiumguß, Stahlrohr oder Metalldraht
Herman Miller

230 + 231 George Nelson 1958 USA

Chairs with seat shells of molded reinforced plastic with fixed or
flexible back, curved tubular steel legs
Stühle mit Sitzschalen aus armiertem Kunststoff mit fester oder beweglicher Rückenlehne, Beine aus gebogenem Stahlrohr
Herman Miller

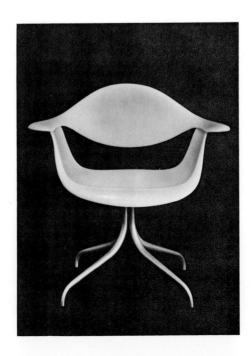 

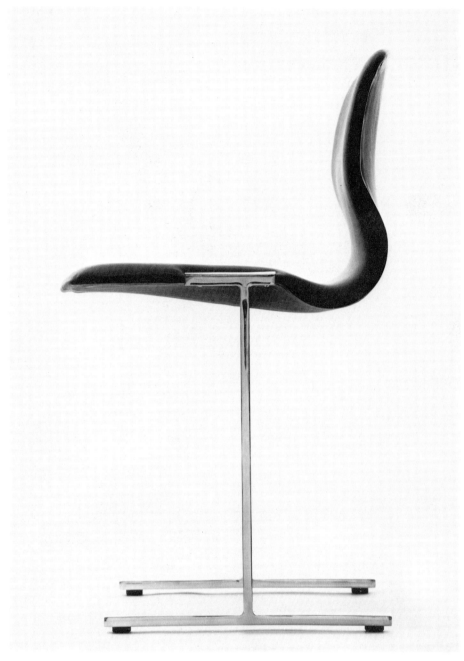

232 Antti Nurmesniemi 1959 Finland

Chair with steel frame, seat upholstered in polyfoam with leather cover
Stuhl mit Stahlgestell, schaumstoffgepolstertem Sitz und Lederbezug
J. Merivaara Oy

233 Hans Ell 1966 Germany

Stacking and linking chair "1000" with frame of chrome-plated or stove-enamelled steel tubing, seat and back of injection-molded plastic
Stapel- und Reihenstuhl »1000« mit Gestell aus verchromtem oder einbrennlackiertem Stahlrohr, Sitz und Rückenlehne Kunststoff-Spritzguß
Kusch

234 Gerd Lange 1971 Germany

Stacking and linking chair "SM 400 K Nova" with frame of chrome-plated tubular steel and seating shell of polyamid, also seat and back pads
Stapel- und Reihenstuhl »SM 400 K Nova« mit verchromtem Stahlrohrgestell und Sitzschale aus Polyamid, auch mit Sitz- und Rückenpolster
Drabert Söhne

235 **Marco Zanuso** 1970 Italy
Stacking and linking chair "Miniseat" with
seat shell of fiberglass-reinforced polyester
and chrome-plated steel tube base
Stapel- und Reihenstuhl »Miniseat« mit
Sitzschale aus glasfaserverstärktem Polyester und Gestell aus verchromtem Stahlrohr
Elam

236 **Ferdinando Buzzi** 1971 Italy
Chair "102" with frame of chrome-plated
tubular steel; seat and back of molded
plywood with polyfoam upholstery
Stuhl »102« mit Gestell aus verchromtem
Stahlrohr; Sitz und Rückenlehne aus formgepreßtem Sperrholz mit Schaumstoffpolsterung
Brunati

237 **Jørgen Kastholm** 1976 Denmark
Stacking chair "Serie 1500" with base of
chrome-plated tubular steel and seating
shell of plastic, also with removable upholstery
Stapelstuhl »Serie 1500« mit verchromtem
Stahlrohrgestell und Sitzschale aus Kunststoff, auch mit aufgelegten, auswechselbaren Sitz- und Rückenpolstern
Kusch

238 **Reiner Moll** 1978 Germany
Chair "Binar" with chrome-plated steel
tube frame and hollow body seating shell
of plastic
Stuhl »Binar« mit verchromtem Stahlrohrgestell und Hohlkörper-Kunststoffsitz-
schale
Wilkhahn

239 **Klaus Franck, Peter Beck** 1974 Germany

Chair "614/1" with chrome-plated tubular
steel frame, seat and back of molded
beech plywood
Stuhl »614/1« mit Gestell aus verchromtem
Stahlrohr, Sitz und Rückenlehne aus verformtem Sperrholz in Buche
Wilkhahn

242 **Arne Jacobsen** 1962 Denmark ▷

Armchair "3200" with chrome-plated metal
frame, upholstered seat, back in teak
Armstuhl »3200« mit verchromtem Metallgestell, gepolstertem Sitz und Rückenlehne
in Teak
Fritz Hansen

243 **Roland Rainer** 1960 Austria ▷

Chair "702" with nickel-plated steel frame
and upholstered seat; back upholstered or
veneered in various woods
Stuhl »702« mit vernickeltem Stahlgestell
und gepolstertem Sitz; Rückenlehne gepolstert oder mit Edelholzfurnier
Wilkhahn

244 **Dieter Waeckerlin** 1960 Switzerland ▷

Armchair "W55" with chrome-plated metal
frame, polyfoam upholstery covered in
leather or fabric
Armstuhl »W55« mit verchromtem Metallgestell, Schaumstoffpolsterung mit Stoff-
oder Lederbezug
Walter Knoll

240 **Robin Day** c. 1952 Great Britain

Armchair with chrome-plated steel tube
frame, seat of plywood with polyfoam
upholstery, back and armrests in one piece
of molded plywood veneered in walnut
Armstuhl mit verchromtem Stahlgestell, Sitz
aus Sperrholz mit Schaumstoffpolsterung,
Rücken- und Armlehnen in einem Stück
aus verformtem Sperrholz mit Nußbaumfurnier
Hille

241 **Carlo Santi** 1972 Italy

Chair "Santana" with frame of chrome-
plated tubular steel, upholstered seat
Stuhl »Santana« mit Gestell aus verchromtem Stahlrohr und gepolstertem Sitz
Zanotta

245 Poul Kjaerholm 1956 Denmark

Chair with chrome-plated tubular steel frame, seat and back of cane
Stuhl mit verchromtem Stahlrohrgestell, Sitz und Rückenlehne aus Rohrgeflecht
E. Kold Christensen

246 Verner Panton 1956 Denmark

Stacking chair with tubular steel frame, seat and back of plastic strings
Stapelstuhl mit Stahlrohrgestell, Sitz- und Rückenlehnenbespannung aus Plastikschnur
Fritz Hansen

247 Albrecht Lange, Hans Mitzlaff 1954 Germany

Armchair with tubular steel frame, innerspring seat and back upholstered in polyfoam, armrests in saran
Armstuhl mit Stahlrohrgestell, Sitz und Rückenlehne mit Federung und Schaumstoffpolsterung, Armlehnen in Sarangeflecht
Eugen Schmidt

248 Gastone Rinaldi c. 1950 Italy

Armchair with chrome-plated steel tube frame, seat and back with polyfoam upholstery
Armstuhl mit verchromtem Stahlrohrgestell, Sitz und Rückenlehne schaumstoffgepolstert
Rima

249 Dirk van Sliedregt 1953 Netherlands

Stacking chair with lacquered tubular steel frame, seat and back of rattan
Stapelstuhl mit lackiertem Stahlrohrgestell, Sitz und Rückenlehne aus Rohrgeflecht
Gebr. Jonkers

250 Hans Eichenberger 1955/56 Switzerland
Armchair with chrome-plated tubular steel
frame, cane-wrapped back and polyfoam
seat covered in leather
Armstuhl mit verchromtem Stahlrohrgestell, Rückenlehne mit Rohrwickelung,
schaumstoffgepolsterter Sitz mit Lederbezug
Hans Eichenberger

251 + 252 Poul Kjaerholm 1959 Denmark
Stool "33" with mat finished chrome-
plated steel frame, cushion covered with
oxhide
Hocker »33« mit matt verchromtem Stahlrohrgestell, Sitzkissen mit Rindsleder
bezogen
E. Kold Christensen

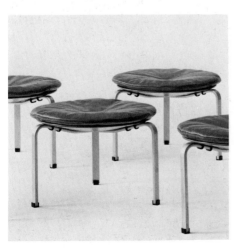

253 Achille and Pier Giacomo Castiglioni
1969 Italy
Chair "Castiglia" with frame of chrome-
plated or white lacquered steel tube and
leather or canvas slings
Stuhl »Castiglia« mit Gestell aus verchromtem oder weißlackiertem Stahlrohr
und Leder- oder Segeltuchbespannung
Zanotta

254 Marcello Minale, Brian Tattersfield 1969
Great Britain
Stackable armchair "MTP 1" with chrome-
plated tubular steel frame, seat and back
in rattan or with black leather slings
Stapelbarer Sessel »MTP 1« mit verchromtem Stahlrohrgestell, Sitz und Rückenlehne
aus Korbgeflecht oder mit Lederbespannung
Minale, Tattersfield, Provinciali Ltd.

255 **Poul Kjaerholm** 1961 Denmark
Folding stool "91" with mat finished
chrome-plated steel frame and oxhide or
canvas seat
Klapphocker »91« mit matt verchromtem
Stahlgestell und Bespannung aus Rinds-
leder oder Segeltuch
E. Kold Christensen

259 Giancarlo Piretti 1969 Italy

Folding chair "Plia" with frame of chrome-
plated steel, seat and back of transparent
plastic
Klappstuhl »Plia« mit Gestell aus verchromtem Stahl, Sitz und Rückenlehne aus
durchsichtigem Kunststoff
Anonima Castelli

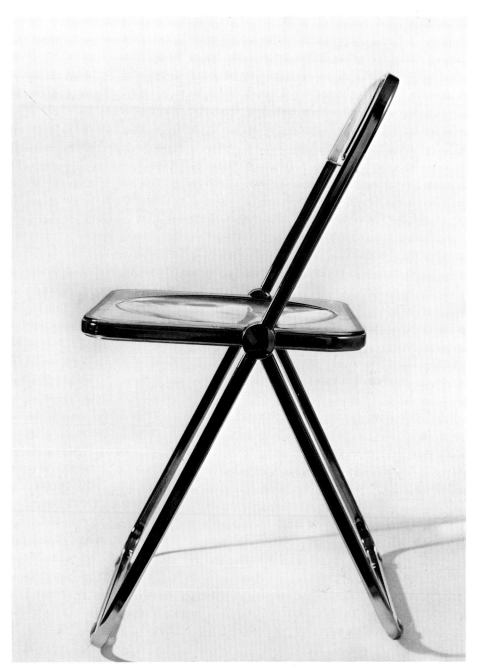

◁◁ **256 Gae Aulenti** 1971 Italy

Folding chair "April" with frame of stainless steel, seat and back with canvas or
leather slings
Klappstuhl »April« mit Gestell aus rostfreiem Stahl, Sitz und Rückenlehne mit Segeltuch oder Leder bespannt
Zanotta

◁ **257 Fred Tydor** c. 1950 USA

Folding armchair with aluminum tube
frame and canvas slings
Klappstuhl mit Aluminiumrohrgestell und
Segeltuchbespannung
Universal Converting Corp.

◁ **258 Olof Pira** c. 1952 Sweden

Folding chair with steel tube frame and
canvas slings
Klappstuhl mit Stahlrohrgestell und Segeltuchbespannung
Nordiska Kompaniet

260 Renato Zevi 1970 Italy

Folding chair "Z-15" with frame of chrome-
plated tubular steel. Seat of wood and
back of metal, plastic-covered
Klappstuhl »Z-15« mit Gestell aus verchromtem Stahlrohr. Sitz aus Holz und
Rückenlehne aus Metall, Kunststoffbezüge
Zevi

261 + 262 **Eero Saarinen** 1951 USA

Chairs "71" and "72" with polyfoam upholstered seat shells of
plastic, various steel frames
Stühle »71« und »72« mit schaumstoffgepolsterten Kunststoffsitz-
schalen, verschiedene Stahlgestelle
Knoll International

263 + 264 **Charles Eames** 1960 USA

"La Fonda" chairs with shells of fiberglass
and polyfoam upholstery, frames of
chrome-plated cast aluminum
Stühle »La Fonda« mit Sitzschalen aus
Fiberglas und Schaumstoffpolsterung,
Gestelle aus verchromtem Aluminiumguß
Herman Miller

265 **Poul Kjaerholm** 1960 Denmark   ▷
Chair "9" with mat finished chrome-plated
steel frame, seating shell covered in oxhide
Stuhl »9« mit matt verchromtem Stahlgestell, Sitzschale mit Rindsleder bezogen
E. Kold Christensen

▽ 266 **Gastone Rinaldi** 1953 Italy
Chair "DU 30" with lacquered tubular steel
base, polyfoam upholstery
Stuhl »DU 30« mit lackiertem Stahlrohrge-
stell, Schaumstoffpolsterung
Thema

▽ 267 **Giotto Stoppino** 1969 Italy
Stacking chair "Maya" with molded plastic
seat, without cover or covered in fabric or
leather; frame of chrome-plated tubular
steel
Stapelstuhl »Maya« mit Kunststoffsitzschale, ohne Bezug oder mit Stoff oder Leder
bezogen; Gestell aus verchromtem Stahlrohr
Bernini

268 **Pierre Paulin** 1961 France
Lounge chair "549" with chrome-plated
steel frame, seating shell of molded lami-
nated wood upholstered in polyfoam
Sessel »549« mit verchromtem Stahlgestell,
Sitzschale aus verformtem Schichtholz und
Schaumstoffpolsterung
Artifort

269 **Pierre Paulin** 1964 France
Easy chair "121" with chrome-plated metal
base; seat shell of molded laminated wood
with polyfoam upholstery covered in fabric,
loose seat cushion
Sessel »121« mit verchromtem Metallgestell. Sitzschale aus laminiertem verformtem Schichtholz mit Schaumstoffpolsterung und Stoffbezug, loses Sitzkissen
Artifort

270+271 **Georg Leowald, Friso Kramer**
1959/67 Germany/Netherlands
Range of height-adjustable swivel chairs
on aluminum pedestals with gliders or
casters; seat shells of fiberglass-reinforced
polyester with upholstered seat and
back
Drehstuhlprogramm mit höhenverstellbaren Aluminiumgestellen und Gleitern oder
Rollen; Sitzschalen aus glasfaserverstärktem Polyester mit gepolsterter Sitzfläche
und Rückenlehne
Wilkhahn

272 **Jørgen Rasmussen** 1967 Denmark
Swivel chairs "1904" and armchair "1908"
with height-adjustable base of die-cast
aluminum and plastic casters or gliders;
seat and back of injection-molded plastic,
polyfoam upholstery
Bürodrehstühle »1904« und Sessel
»1908« mit höhenverstellbarem Untergestell aus Aluminium-Druckguß und Gleitern oder Rollen aus Kunststoff. Sitz und
Rückenlehne Kunststoff-Spritzgußteile,
Schaumstoffpolsterung
Knoll International

273 **Arne Jacobsen** 1968 Denmark
Swivel office chair of plastic
Bürodrehstuhl aus Kunststoff

274 **Konrad Schäfer** 1969 Germany
Office swivel chair of fiberglass-reinforced
plastic with polyfoam upholstery covered
in leather or fabric
Bürodrehstuhl aus glasfaserverstärktem
Kunststoff mit Schaumstoffpolsterung und
Leder- oder Stoffbezug
Lübke

275 **Works Design** 1971 Italy

Seating shell "Modus" of injection-molded nylon with various frames of aluminum, also with armrests of black ABS and writing arm
Sitzschale »Modus« aus formgespritztem Nylon mit verschiedenen Gestellen aus Aluminium, auch mit Armlehnen aus schwarzem ABS und Tablar
Tecno

276 **Andrew Ivar Morrison, Bruce R. Hannah** 1970 USA

Swivel chair "2328" with height-adjustable steel base, armrests and legs on casters of die-cast aluminum; detachable polyfoam upholstery, fixed at the frame with plastic hoods
Drehstuhl »2328« mit höhenverstellbarem Stahlgestell, Armlehnen und Fußkreuz auf Rollen aus Aluminium-Druckguß; abnehmbare Schaumstoffpolsterung, mit Plastikkappen am Gestell befestigt
Knoll International

277 **Ettore Sottsass jr.** 1970/71 Italy

Office swivel chair of plastic, part of "Synthesis 45" office furniture system (see ills. 776–8). Polyfoam upholstery with covers of fabric. Back and seat height-adjustable
Bürodrehstuhl aus Kunststoff, aus dem Büromöbelsystem »Synthesis 45« (siehe Abb. 776–778). Polsterung aus Schaumstoff mit Stoffbezügen. Rückenlehne und Sitz höhenverstellbar
Olivetti

278 **Wilhelm Ritz** 1971 Germany

Office swivel chair "232" with upholstered seating shell in two parts of fiberglass reinforced polyester, height-adjustable, infinitely tilting back, casters, with or without armrests
Bürodrehstuhl »232« mit gepolsterter, zweigeteilter Sitzschale aus glasfaserverstärktem Polyester, höhenverstellbar, stufenlos neigbare Rückenlehne, Laufrollen, mit oder ohne Armlehnen
Wilkhahn

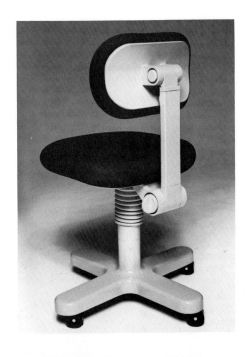

279 **Jorge Ferrari-Hardoy, Antonio Bonet, Juan Kurchan** 1938 USA

"Hardoy" lounge chair "198" with frame of steel rods and canvas or leather covering
»Hardoy«-Sessel »198« mit Gestell aus Rundstahl, Bezug aus Canvas oder Leder
Knoll International

280 **Germano Facetti, John Ollis** 1956 Great Britain

Lounge chair with spring steel frame and canvas slings, collapsible for transport
Liegestuhl mit federndem Stahlgestell und Segeltuchbespannung, für den Transport zusammenlegbar
The Wishbone Chair

281 **Works Design** c. 1952 Sweden

Stool with metal frame and seat slings in canvas or leather
Hocker mit Metallgestell und Sitzbespannung aus Segeltuch oder Leder
Nordiska Kompaniet

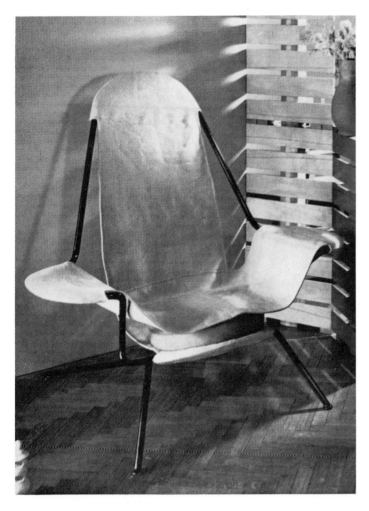

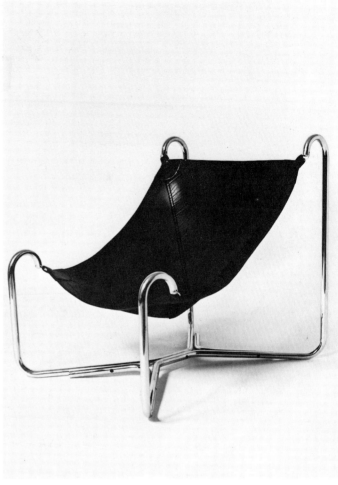

282 Paolo A. Chessa c. 1950 Italy

Armchair with metal frame, canvas slings and polyfoam cushion
Sessel mit Metallgestell, Segeltuchbespannung und Schaumstoff-
kissen
J.G. Furniture

284+285 Esko Pajamies 1965 Finland

Knock-down chair with frame of chrome-plated steel and seat
slings of canvas
Zerlegbarer Stuhl mit verchromtem Stahlrohrgestell und Sitzbespannung aus Segeltuch
Merva-Tuotanto

283 DAM (Designers Associati Milano) 1969 Italy

Chair "Baffo" with frame of chrome-plated tubular steel and sus-
pended leather seat
Stuhl »Baffo« mit verchromtem Stahlrohrgestell und eingehängtem
Ledersitz
Busnelli

286 **C. de Vries** c. 1950 Netherlands

Armchair with steel tube frame and seat slings in canvas
Sessel mit Stahlrohrgestell und Sitzbespannung aus Segeltuch

287 **Norman Cherner** c. 1953 USA

Lounge chair "120" with black steel frame and upholstery
Sessel »120« mit schwarzem Stahlgestell und Polsterung
Konwiser

288 **Otto and Ridi Kolb** c. 1953 USA

Armchair with steel tube frame and leather slings
Sessel mit Stahlrohrgestell und Lederbespannung
Kolb

289 **Pierre Paulin** 1955 France

Easy chair with tubular steel frame of two
components, seat slings of canvas or
leather
Sessel mit Stahlrohrgestell in zwei Teilen,
Sitzbespannung aus Segeltuch oder
Leder
Pierre Paulin

290 Pierre Paulin 1964 France

Folding chair "675" with frame of chrome-
plated metal and leather slings
Klappsessel »675« mit verchromtem Stahlrohrgestell und Lederbespannung
Artifort

291 Verner Panton 1956 Denmark

Lounge chair and foot stool with tubular
steel frame and canvas slings
Liegestuhl und Hocker aus Stahlrohr mit
Segeltuchbespannung
Fritz Hansen

292 Paulo Mendes da Rocha 1956 Brazil

Armchair with lacquered tubular steel
frame and leather slings
Sessel mit lackiertem Stahlrohrgestell und
Lederbespannung
Interiors Soc.

293 Rolf Gutmann 1954 Switzerland

Folding lounge chair with tubular steel
frame and canvas slings
Klappsessel mit Stahlrohrgestell und
Segeltuchbespannung
Wico

294 Poul Kjaerholm 1952 Denmark

Easy chair with steel frame, corded seat and back
Sessel mit Stahlgestell, Sitz und Rückenlehne mit Schnurbespannung
Fritz Hansen

295 Hendrick van Keppel, Taylor Green c. 1950 USA

Lounge chair and footstool with tubular steel frame and corded seat
Sessel und Hocker mit Stahlrohrgestell und schnurbespanntem Sitz
Van Keppel-Green

296 Hans Eichenberger 1957 Switzerland

Lounge chair with chrome-plated tubular
steel frame and rubber webbing
Sessel mit verchromtem Stahlgestell und
Gurtbespannung aus Gummi

297 Maija-Liisa Komulainen 1952 Finland

Easy chair with tubular steel frame and
fabric slings
Sessel mit Stahlrohrgestell und Stoffbespannung
Heteka Oy

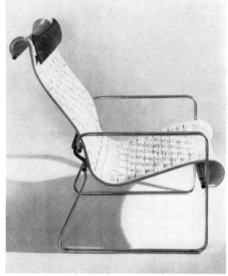

298 Marco Zanuso, Richard Sapper 1964
Italy/Germany

Easy chair "Fourline" with metal frame,
seat and back of fabric or leather joined
by hinges and equipped with sewed-in
metal springs. Seat is adjustable, allowing
four different body positions
Sessel »Fourline« mit Metallgestell. Durch
Scharnier verbundene Sitzfläche und Rükkenlehne aus Stoff oder Leder mit weichen
Metallfedern in eingenähten Taschen. Die
verstellbare Aufhängung der Sitzfläche erlaubt vier verschiedene Sitzpositionen
Arflex

299 Osvaldo Borsani 1961 Italy

Armchair with spring metal frame, foam-
rubber padding covered with fabric, plas-
tic, or leather
Sessel mit federndem Metallgestell,
Schaumgummipolsterung und Bezug aus
Stoff, Kunststoff oder Leder
Tecno

302 **Court Noxon** 1957 Canada

Easy chair "7957" with sectional steel frame, seat and back with rubber webbing and reversible cushions
Sessel »7957« mit Profilstahlgestell, Sitz und Rückenlehne mit Gummigurten, umdrehbare Polster
Metalsmiths Company

303 **Florence Knoll** c. 1954 USA

Easy chair "51" with metal base, seat and back with polyfoam upholstery
Sessel »51« mit Metallgestell, Sitz und Rückenlehne schaumstoffgepolstert
Knoll International

304 **Alf Svensson** c. 1951 Sweden

Easy chair with steel tube frame and loose cushions
Sessel mit Stahlrohrgestell und losen Sitzkissen
Dux

300	301
302	303
304	

◁ 300 **William Armbruster** c. 1950 USA

Easy chair with frame of square steel tubing, fabric straps and
loose leather-covered polyfoam cushions
Sessel mit Vierkantstahlrohrgestell, Stoffgurtbespannung und losen
lederbezogenen Schaumstoffkissen

◁◁ 301 **William Armbruster** 1958 USA

Easy chair "MS-951 B" with polished bronze frame and loose
cushions
Sessel »MS-951 B« mit poliertem Bronzegestell und losen Kissen
Edgewood Furniture

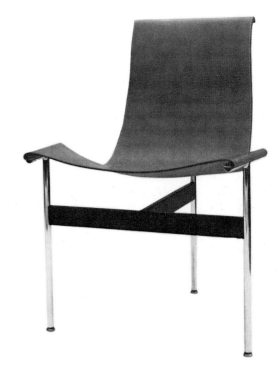

305 + 306 **William Katavolos, Ross Littell, Douglas Kelley** 1952/53
USA

Chairs with chrome-plated and black enameled steel frames and
leather seats
Stühle mit verchromten und schwarz lackierten Stahlgestellen und
Ledersitzen
Laverne

307 **William Katavolos, Ross Littell, Douglas Kelley** c. 1952 USA

Easy chair with chrome-plated steel frame and leather-covered
polyfoam upholstery on fabric straps
Sessel mit verchromtem Stahlgestell und lederbezogener Schaumstoffpolsterung auf Stoffgurtbespannung
Laverne

308 **Herbert Hirche** 1961 Germany

Easy chair "562", armchair "561", and stool "563" with square
tubular steel frames in lacquer finish, polyfoam upholstery
Sessel »562«, Sessel mit Armlehnen »561« und Hocker »563« mit
Gestellen aus lackiertem Vierkantstahlrohr, Schaumstoffpolsterung
Henkelwerke

309 **Herbert Hirche** c. 1950 Germany
Chair with frame of chrome-plated steel, fabric straps and loose
cushions
Sessel mit Gestell aus verchromtem Stahl, Stoffgurtbespannung
und losen Polstern
Rezila

310 **Robert Haussmann** 1955 Switzerland
Collapsible easy chair with flat steel spring frame, leather straps
and loose cushions covered in leather
Zerlegbarer Sessel mit Gestell aus federndem Flachstahl, Leder-
gurtbespannung und losen Lederpolstern
Haussmann & Haussmann

311 **Cees Braakman** c. 1952 Netherlands
Easy chair with frame of lacquered steel tube
Sessel mit lackiertem Stahlrohrgestell
Ums-Pastoe

312 **Herbert Hirche** 1953 Germany
Easy chair with steel tube frame and polyfoam upholstery
Sessel mit Stahlrohrgestell und Schaumstoffpolsterung
Stuttgarter Akademie-Werkstätten

313+314 George Nelson c. 1953 USA
Lounge chairs with chrome-plated steel
frames and polyfoam upholstery
Sessel mit verchromten Stahlrohrgestellen
und Schaumstoffpolsterung
Herman Miller

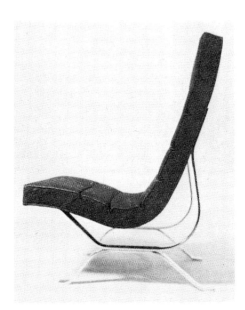

315 Nicos Zographos 1959 USA
Chair "301" with stainless steel frame, seat and back of plywood
with polyfoam upholstery and leather cover
Stuhl »301« mit Gestell aus rostfreiem Stahl, Sitz und Rückenlehne
aus Sperrholz mit Schaumstoffpolsterung und Lederbezug
Albano

316 Poul Kjaerholm 1956 Denmark
Easy chair "22" with chrome-plated flat steel frame, seat and back
of wickerwork or with leather slings
Sessel »22« mit Gestell aus verchromtem Flachstahl, Sitz und Rük-
kenlehne aus Weidengeflecht oder mit Lederbespannung
E. Kold Christensen

317+318 **Poul Kjaerholm** 1953 Denmark
Chair with steel spring frame and molded plywood seat
Stuhl mit federndem Flachstahlgestell und verformtem Sperrholzsitz
Fritz Hansen

319 **Poul Kjaerholm** 1968 Denmark
Easy chair "20" with base of chrome-plated steel and oxhide cover
Sessel »20« mit Gestell aus verchromtem Stahlrohr und Rindlederbezug
E. Kold Christensen

320 **Jan Dranger, Johan Huldt** 1972 Sweden
Easy chair "Stuns" with frame of lacquer-finished tubular steel. Slings and covers of the polyfoam upholstery in canvas or corduroy
Sessel »Stuns« mit Gestell aus lackiertem Stahlrohr. Sitzbespannung und Bezüge der Schaumstoffpolster aus Leinen oder Baumwollcord
Möbelmontage

321 Studio Tipi of Toffoloni-Palange 1971
Italy

Armchair "Z-22" with frame and seating
support of chrome-plated tubular steel.
Slings in leather
Sessel »Z-22« mit Gestell und Sitzrahmen
aus verchromtem Stahlrohr, Lederbespannung
Zevi

322 Esko Pajamies 1971 Finland

Easy chair "Juju" with frame of chrome-
plated or lacquer-finished tubular steel,
removable fabric slings and loose
cushions
Sessel »Juju« mit verchromtem oder farbig
lackiertem Stahlrohrgestell; abnehmbare
Stoffbespannung mit losen Kissen
Lepokalusto Oy

323 Giorgio Decursu 1971 Italy

Easy chair "Cetra" with frame of tubular
steel in mat or chrome-plated finish. Detachable upholstery with leather or fabric
covers
Sessel »Cetra« mit Gestell aus satiniertem
oder verchromtem Stahlrohr. Abnehmbare
Polsterung mit Leder- oder Stoffbezügen
IHF/ISA

324 Frank Mingis 1972 USA

Easy chair "Premier" with frame of
chrome-plated tubular steel. Covers of
polyfoam cushions and slings in canvas
or suede
Sessel »Premier« mit Gestell aus verchromtem Stahlrohr. Bezüge der Schaumstoffkissen und Sitzbespannung in Segeltuch oder Wildleder
Thonet

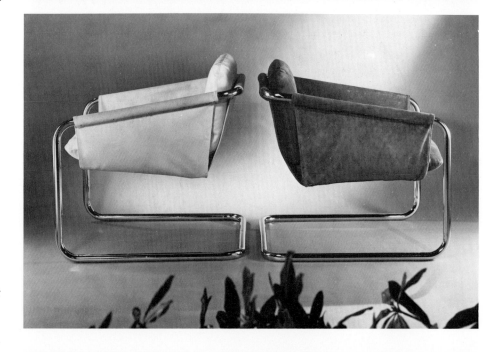

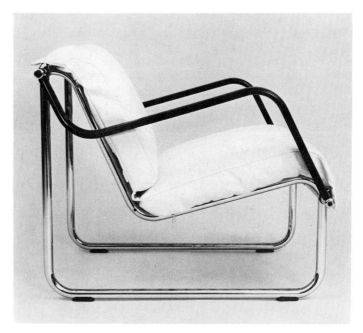

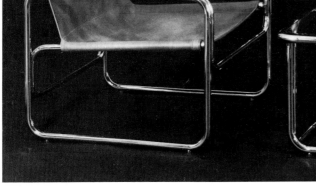

325 **Ueli Berger** 1960 Switzerland

Collapsible chair "BE 60" with chrome-plated steel tube frame and
leather or canvas slings
Zerlegbarer Stuhl »BE 60« mit verchromtem Stahlrohrgestell, Leder-
oder Segeltuchbespannung
Intraform E. Franz

327 **Antonello Mosca** 1970 Italy

Easy chair "Attico" with frame of chrome-plated tubular steel and
leather seat slings
Sessel »Attico« mit Gestell aus verchromtem Stahlrohr und Lederbespannung
Ellisse

326 **Yrjö Kukkapuro** 1971 Finland

Collapsible easy chair "Remmi" with frame of chrome-plated or
stove-enamelled tubular steel. Leather-covered cushions on rubber
straps. Chairs can be combined to sofas
Zerlegbarer Sessel »Remmi« mit verchromtem oder ofen-emaillier-
tem Stahlrohrgestell, auch zu Sofas zu verbinden. Lederbezogene
Polster auf Gummigurten
Haimi Oy

328 **Jan des Bouvrie** 1973 Netherlands

Easy chair "740" with frame of chrome-plated tubular steel and
canvas seat slings with polyfoam upholstery
Sessel »740« mit Gestell aus verchromtem Stahlrohr und Segeltuchbespannung mit Schaumstoffpolsterung
Meubelindustrie Gelderland

329 + 330 Arne Jacobsen 1971 Denmark

Seating range comprising single easy chairs, sofas composed of
several elements, and circular sofas; frames of chrome-plated
tubular steel, polyfoam upholstery with fabric covers
Sitzmöbelprogramm mit Einzelsesseln, Sofas aus mehreren Elementen und Rundsofas; Gestelle aus verchromtem Stahlrohr, Schaumstoffpolsterung mit Stoffbezügen
Fritz Hansen

331 Jonathan De Pas, Donato D'Urbino, Paolo Lomazzi 1970 Italy

Easy chair "Duecavalli" with frame of chrome-plated tubular steel
to which the canvas seat is fixed by rubber rings. Detachable upholstery with fabric covers
Sessel »Duecavalli« mit Gestell aus verchromtem Stahlrohr. Sitz
aus Segeltuch, durch Gummiringe mit dem Gestell verbunden. Abnehmbare Polster mit Stoffbezügen
Driade

332 Jürgen Lange 1972 Germany

Easy chair "1011" with frame of chrome-plated tubular steel. Seat
sling in black canvas, polyfoam upholstery
Sessel »1011« mit Gestell aus verchromtem Stahlrohr. Sitz mit
schwarzem Segeltuch bespannt, Posterauflage aus Schaumstoff
Behr

334 Conran Design Group 1969 Great Britain

Seating range "Terminus Seating" with seat-back unit of molded laminated plywood with polyfoam upholstery, frame of chrome-plated tubular steel. Single chairs, also with armrests and high back, can be linked to units of any length
Reihenbestuhlung »Terminus Seating«. Sitz und Rücken aus verformtem Schichtholz mit Schaumstoffpolsterung, Gestelle aus verchromtem Stahlrohr. Die Einzelstühle, auch mit Armlehnen und hohem Rückenteil, können zu beliebig langen Reihen verbunden werden
Conran

333 Gae Aulenti 1975 Italy

Armchair "54-S1" with frame of aluminum profiles, loose seat and back cushions with fabric or leather cover
Armlehnsessel »54-S1« mit Gestell aus gezogenen Aluminiumprofilen, lose Sitz- und Rückenkissen mit Bezug aus Stoff oder Leder
Knoll International

335 Sergio Asti 1968/70 Italy

Chair "Charlotte" of chrome-plated or lacquered steel tube with seat covered in velvet or oilcloth
Stuhl »Charlotte« aus verchromtem oder lackiertem Stahlrohr, Sitz mit Wachstuch oder Samt überzogen
Zanotta

336+337 Gae Aulenti 1963 Italy

Furniture series "Locus Solus" including lounge chair "P.G. 02", stool/table "P.G. 01", bench "D.G. 05", and table. Frames of steel tubing in lacquer finish, loose cushions with printed patterns
Möbelprogramm »Locus Solus« mit Sessel »P.G. 02«, Hocker/Tischchen »P.G. 01«, Bank »D.G. 05« und Tisch. Gestelle aus lackiertem Stahlrohr, lose Kissen mit aufgedruckten Mustern
Poltronova

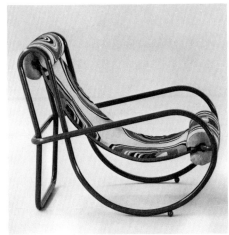

337

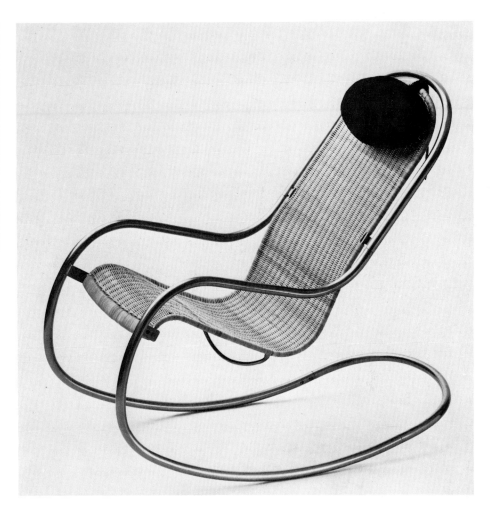

338 Sigurd Persson 1967 Sweden
Rocking chair with tubular steel frame and
rattan seat
Schaukelstuhl mit verchromtem Stahlrohr-
gestell und Sitz aus Rohrgeflecht
Åry Stålmöbler

339 Bartolucci, Waldheim c. 1950 USA
Lounge chair with aluminum tube frame and canvas slings
Liegestuhl mit Gestell aus Aluminiumrohr und Segeltuchbespan-
nung
Barwa

340 Pierre Guariche 1963 France
Collapsible lounge chair with frame of chrome-plated steel tubing
and black imitation leather slings
Zerlegbarer Liegestuhl mit Gestell aus verchromtem Stahlrohr und
schwarzer Kunstlederbespannung

342 George Nelson 1957 USA

Armchair with chrome-plated tubular steel frame, seat and high back of molded plywood with polyfoam cushions
Sessel mit verchromtem Stahlrohrgestell, Sitz und hohe Rückenlehne aus verformtem Sperrholz mit Schaumstoffpolstern
Herman Miller

341 Eero Saarinen 1945–48 USA

Armchair "Womb 70" and ottoman "74" with chrome-plated tubular steel frame and molded plastic shell, fabric-covered polyfoam upholstery, loose cushions
»Wannen«-Sessel »70« und Hocker »74« mit Gestell aus verchromtem Stahlrohr, Sitzschale aus geformtem Kunststoff, Schaumstoffpolsterung mit Stoff bezogen, lose Kissen
Knoll International

343 Charles Eames 1957 USA

Lounge chair "670" and ottoman "671" on cast aluminum swivel base, rosewood veneer molded plywood frame with leather covered polyfoam and down upholstery
Sessel »670« und Hocker »671« mit Drehgestell aus Aluminiumguß, Sitzschale und Lehnen aus geformtem, mit Palisander furniertem Sperrholz, Schaumstoff- und Daunenpolsterung, mit Leder bezogen
Herman Miller

344 **Jørn Utzon** 1969 Denmark
Easy chair "8101" and footstool "8110" of molded laminated wood; chrome-plated tubular steel frame, polyfoam upholstery with fabric cover
Sessel »8101« und Hocker »8110« aus verformtem Schichtholz mit verchromtem Stahlrohrgestell und Schaumstoffpolsterung mit Stoffbezug
Fritz Hansen

345 **Yrjö Kukkapuro** 1965 Finland
Lounge chair "Karuselli" with seat shell and swivel base of fiberglass; seat suspended by means of a steel spring. Polyfoam upholstery with leather cover
Drehsessel »Karuselli« mit Sitzschale und Fußgestell aus Fiberglas; der Sitz ist in einen Stahlbügel eingehängt. Schaumstoffpolsterung mit Lederbezug
Haimi Oy

346 Charles Eames 1960 USA

"Lobby Chair 675" with chrome-plated cast aluminum frame, black leather upholstery
»Lobby Chair 675«, Sessel mit verchromtem Aluminiumgußgestell, schwarze Lederpolsterung
Herman Miller

347 Charles Eames 1958 USA

Lounge chair "682" with cast aluminum frame and plastic-covered upholstery
Sessel »682« mit Gestell aus Aluminiumguß und kunststoffbezogener Polsterung
Herman Miller

348 Richard Sapper 1978/79 Germany ▷

"Sapper Collection" multiple seating system. Seat frames of molded steel profile, polyfoam upholstery covered with fabric or leather; steel bases, height adjustable, revolving and tipping devices, casters; with or without armrests
Sitzmöbelprogramm »Sapper Collection«. Sitzrahmen aus verformtem Stahlprofil, Schaumstoffpolsterung mit Stoff- oder Lederbezug; Stahlgestell, höhenverstellbar, mit Dreh- und Kippmechanik, Fußrollen; mit oder ohne Armlehnen
Knoll International

349 **Charles Pollock** 1965 USA

Armchair "1255" on aluminum pedestal with or without swivel. Black plastic seat shell, polyfoam upholstery
Armstuhl auf Aluminiumgestell, auch drehbar. Schwarze Kunststoff-Sitzschale, Schaumgummipolsterung
Knoll International

350 **Mauser – Hircheteam** 1976 Germany

Office chair "Serie 180", multiple seating system, with our without swivel, height adjustable; spring frames to be combined with different types of bases; polyfoam upholstery covered with leather or fabric
Bürostuhl aus dem Sitzmöbelprogramm »Serie 180«, auch drehbar und höhenverstellbar; federnde Sitzrahmen sind mit verschiedenen Gestelltypen kombinierbar; Schaumstoffpolsterung mit Leder- oder Stoffbezug
Mauser Waldeck

351 **Hircheteam – W. Müller-Limmroth** 1978 Germany

"Ergomat 190", office chair developed according to medical and ergonomical researches. Inside mechanism of hinges, each position can be fixed
»Ergomat 190«, nach medizinischen und ergonomischen Forschungen entwickelter Bürostuhl. Die Bewegungsmechanik ist durch innenliegende Gelenke gesteuert, jede Stellung ist durch Tastendruck fixierbar
Mauser Waldeck

352 + 353 Charles Eames 1962 USA

"Eames Tandem Seating 2600", multiple
seating system with two to ten seats for
single and double rows. Legs and seat
frames of polished cast aluminum; T-
shaped support beam and back spreader
of black painted steel. Suspended upholstery of black plastic
»Eames Tandem Seating 2600«, Reihenbestuhlung mit zwei bis zehn Sitzen in Einzel-
oder Doppelreihe. Fußstützen und Sitzrahmen aus poliertem Aluminiumguß; T-förmi-
ger Tragebalken und Schiene zur Rücken-
lehnenversteifung aus schwarz lackiertem
Stahl. Sitzbespannung aus schwarzem
Kunststoff
Herman Miller

354 Richard Sapper 1978/79 Germany

"Sapper Collection" multiple seating system. Seat frames of molded steel profile,
polyfoam upholstery covered with fabric or
leather; legs of polished cast aluminum,
support rails of black painted steel. Also
with armrests and matching table tops (see
also ill. 348)
Reihenbestuhlung »Sapper Collection« mit
Sitzrahmen aus verformtem Stahlprofil,
Schaumstoffpolsterung und Bezügen aus
Stoff oder Leder; Gestell aus poliertem Aluminiumguß mit schwarz lackierten Stahl-
stützen. Auch mit Armlehnen und passenden Tischplatten (vgl. Abb. 348)
Knoll International

356 Friso Kramer 1968 Netherlands   ▷

Seating system "1200" combined of two-
seated shells of glass-reinforced polyester
which can be linked to any length by
means of tubes incorporated in the cast
aluminum frames
Banksystem »1200« mit zweisitzigen
Schalen aus glasfaserverstärktem Polyester, die durch eine Rohrverbindung im
Gestell aus Aluminiumguß zu beliebig langen Reihen verbunden werden können
Wilkhahn

△ 355 **Geoffrey D. Harcourt** 1969 Great Britain

"Multiple Seating" range with seat shells of molded plywood and polyfoam upholstery, covers in leather or fabric. Anodized aluminum fixtures, support rails of black painted steel. Also with armrests and matching table tops
Reihenbestuhlung »Multiple Seating« mit Sitzschalen aus hochfrequenzgepreßtem Holz und Schaumstoffpolsterung, Bezüge aus Leder oder Stoff. Eloxierte Aluminiumhalterungen, Tragebalken aus schwarz lackiertem Stahl. Auch mit Armlehnen und passenden Tischplatten
Artifort

▽ 357 + 358 **Giancarlo Piretti** 1969 Italy

Seating system "Axis 3000" with frames of cast aluminum; seat and back veneered in oak, walnut, beech, rosewood, or with upholstery. Matching table tops. Elements are fixed to a supporting steel rail by means of clips and special screws
Reihenbestuhlung »Axis 3000« mit Gestellen aus Aluminiumguß; Sitze und Rückenlehnen in Eiche, Nußbaum, Birke oder Palisander furniert oder mit Polsterung; passende Ablageplatten. Die einzelnen Elemente werden mit Bügeln und Spezialschrauben an einer durchgehenden Stahlzarge befestigt
Anonima Castelli

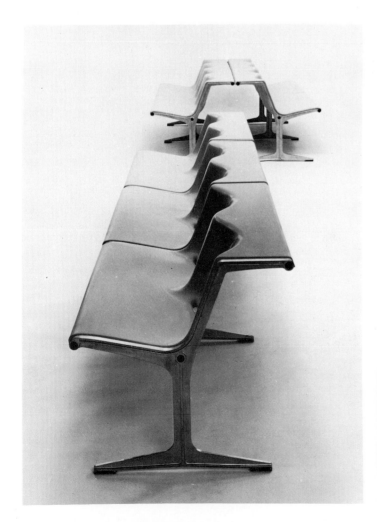

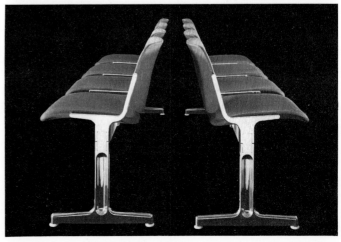

359 **George Kasparian** 1960 USA

Modular seating arrangement "Multalum" with frames of anodized aluminum, polyfoam upholstery. Seats with or without backs
Modulares Sitzmöbelprogramm »Multalum« mit Gestellen aus eloxiertem Aluminium und Schaumstoffpolsterung. Sitze mit und ohne Rückenlehnen
Kasparians

360 **George Kasparian** 1962 USA

Modular seating arrangement "X-ALUM" with cross-shaped frames of anodized aluminum, polyfoam upholstery over rubber webbing, loose cushions. Various components: seats with or without backs and armrests, table tops, and drop-in units
Modulares Sitzmöbelprogramm »X-ALUM« mit kreuzförmigen Gestellen aus eloxiertem Aluminium, Schaumstoffpolstern über Gummigurten, losen Schaumstoffkissen. Zahlreiche Elemente: Sitze mit und ohne Rückenlehnen und Armstützen, Tischplatten, Doppelplattenkästen
Kasparians

361 **Werner Heumann, George Kasparian** 1964 USA

"Kolum Series" multiple seating allowing a great variety of combinations. Bases of anodized aluminum, seat shells of fiberglass with polyfoam upholstery, loose cushions
Sitzmöbelprogramm »Kolum Series« mit zahlreichen Variationsmöglichkeiten. Gestelle aus eloxiertem Aluminium, Sitzschalen aus Fiberglas mit Schaumstoffpolsterung und lose eingelegten Kissen
Kasparians

362 Verner Panton 1959 Sweden

Seating range "853/854" with frames of chrome-plated flat steel and upholstery
Sitzgruppe »853/854« mit Gestellen aus verchromtem Flachstahl und Polsterung
Hans Kaufeld

363 Ernst Moeckl 1962 Germany

Range of combination furniture with bases of anodized flat oval aluminum tubing and linking devices. Wooden parts of walnut or rosewood, polyfoam upholstery over springs
Kombinationsprogramm mit Gestellen aus eloxiertem Aluminium-Flachovalrohr und Steckverbindungen. Holzteile in Nußbaum oder Palisander, Schaumstoffpolsterung auf Unterfederung
Lübke

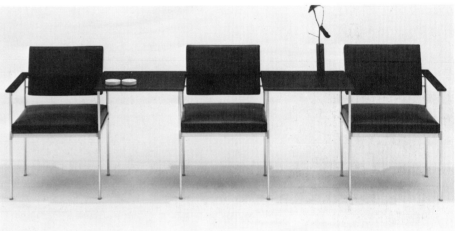

364 + 365 Andrew Ivar Morrison, Bruce R. Hannah 1971 USA

Seating range with four basic types: easy chairs with and without headrest, easy chair with a more upright position for offices, and stools. All models can be assembled to two-, three-, and four-seaters. Suspension seating held together by extruded aluminum edges with plastic-covered cast aluminum frame. Polyfoam upholstery with fabric or leather covers

Sitzmöbelprogramm mit vier Grundtypen: Sessel mit und ohne Nak-kenstütze, Sessel mit steilerer Rückenlehne für Büros und Hocker. Alle Elemente können zu maximal viersitzigen Einheiten verbunden werden. Die Sitze sind in querlaufende Zargen aus gezogenem Aluminium eingespannt und mit kunststoffbeschichteten Fußbügeln aus gegossenem Aluminium verschraubt. Polsterung aus Schaumstoff, mit Leder oder Stoff bezogen
Knoll International

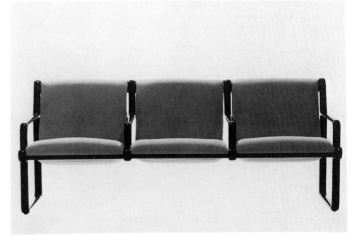

366 **Pierre Paulin** 1959 France

Easy chair "437" with chrome-plated steel
tube frame and double shell of molded laminated wood upholstered in polyfoam
Sessel »437« mit verchromtem Stahlrohrgestell und schaumstoffgepolsterter Dop-
pelschale aus verformtem Schichtholz
Artifort

367 **Poul Kjaerholm** 1953 Denmark

Chair with steel tube legs and aluminum
seat, also with polyfoam upholstery
Stuhl mit Stahlrohrbeinen und Sitzschale
aus Aluminium, auch mit Schaumstoffpolsterung
Chris Sørensen

368 **Herbert Hirche** 1957 Germany

Chair with tubular steel frame and plastic
seat with polyfoam upholstery
Stuhl mit Stahlrohrgestell und schaumstoffgepolsterter Sitzschale aus Kunststoff
Walter Knoll

369–371 **Arne Jacobsen** 1958 Denmark
"Egg" and "Swan" easy chairs with swivel
frames of aluminum or with teak veneered
wooden legs, shells of plastic upholstered
in polyfoam, covered with fabric, leather,
or plastic
Sessel »Ei« und »Schwan« mit Drehgestel-
len aus Aluminium oder Holzbeinen in
Teak, schaumstoffgepolsterte Sitzschalen
aus Kunststoff, mit Stoff, Leder oder Kunstleder bezogen
Fritz Hansen

372 **Arne Jacobsen** 1958 Denmark
"Bow" easy chair with tubular steel frame,
shell of plastic upholstered in polyfoam
and covered with leather
Sessel »Kuhle« mit Stahlrohrgestell, Sitzschale aus Kunststoff mit Schaumgummipolsterung und Lederbezug
Fritz Hansen

369		
370	371	372

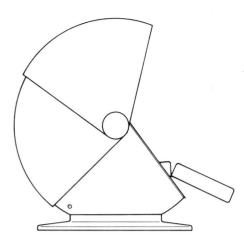

373+374 Günter Ferdinand Ris, Herbert Selldorf 1969/71 Germany

Easy chair "Sunball" for open-air use. The sphere which can be completely closed consists of two segments, easily movable by balance springs, and a basic shell of fiberglass-reinforced polyester. Seat for one or two persons of polyfoam with fabric cover, can be changed into a daybed. Clamp-on trays, built-in lamp and loudspeakers
Sessel »Sunball« zur Benützung im Freien. Die voll schließbare Kugel besteht aus zwei durch Ausgleichsfedern leicht beweglichen Segmenten und einer durch ein Teflon-Gleitlager mit dem Fußteil verbundenen Schale aus glasfaserverstärktem Polyester. Sitzfläche aus Schaumstoff für ein bis zwei Personen, mit Baumwollcord bezogen, zur Liege auszuklappen. Aufstecktabletts, eingebaute Lampe und Lautsprecher
Rosenthal

375 Pierre Paulin 1967 France

Easy chair "300" with glass-fibre shell and removable polyfoam upholstery covered with stretch fabric
Sessel »300« mit Fiberglas-Sitzschale und abnehmbarer, mit elastischem Stoff bezogener Schaumstoffpolsterung
Artifort

376 Angelo Mangiarotti 1961 Italy

Easy chair "1110" with cast metal base and shell of foamed polystyrole with fabric cover
Sessel »1110« mit gegossenem Metallgestell und Sitzschale aus aufgeschäumtem Polystyrol mit Stoffbezug
Cassina

377 Joe Colombo 1964 Italy

Swivel easy chair "Elda 1005" with plastic
shell molded in one piece, detachable
upholstery of black leather
Drehbarer, in einem Stück verformter
Schalensessel »Elda 1005« mit abnehmbarer Polsterung und schwarzem Lederbezug
Comfort

378+379 Dieter Rams 1962 Germany

Seating range "RZ 62" with shells of fiberglass-reinforced polyester in plastic laminate finish on casters. Loose down cushions with removable leather or fabric
covers
Sitzmöbelprogramm »RZ 62« mit Sitzschalen aus glasfaserverstärktem Polyester mit
Kunststoffbeschichtung, auf Rollen. Lose
Daunenkissen mit abnehmbaren Leder-
oder Stoffbezügen
Vitsoe + Zapf

380 **Estelle and Erwine Laverne** 1962
USA

"Champagne" chair and coffee table with
cast aluminum pedestals; swivel chair with
seat shell of clear transparent plastic and
loose cushion, table top of marble
Stuhl und Tischchen »Champagne« mit
Säulenfuß aus Aluminiumguß; Drehstuhl
mit Sitzschale aus glasklarem Kunststoff
und losem Kissen, Tischplatte aus Marmor
Laverne

381 + 382 **Estelle and Erwine Laverne** 1960
USA

Chairs "Daffodil", "Jonquil", "Buttercup",
and "Lily" of clear transparent plastic,
loose cushions
Sessel »Daffodil«, »Jonquil«, »Buttercup«
und »Lily« aus glasklarem Kunststoff, lose
Sitzkissen
Laverne

383–385 **Eero Saarinen** 1956/57 USA
Single pedestal armchair "150", chair "151", and stool "152" with
cast aluminum bases, seat shells of fiberglass-reinforced polyester
with polyfoam upholstery, loose cushions
Armstuhl »150«, Stuhl »151« und Hocker »152« mit Säulenfuß aus
Aluminiumguß, Sitzschalen aus glasfaserverstärktem Polyester mit
Schaumstoffpolsterung, lose Kissen
Knoll International

386+387 **Helmut Bätzner** 1964 Germany

Stacking and linking chair "BA 1171" of fiberglass-reinforced polyester
Stapel- und Reihenstuhl »BA 1171« aus glasfaserverstärktem Polyester
Menzolit-Werke

388+389 **André Vandenbeuck** 1967 France

Chair and easy chair "Unica I and II" of fiberglass
Stuhl und Sessel »Unica I und II« aus Fiberglas
Strässle

391+392 **Joe Colombo** 1965 Italy   ▷

Stacking and linking chair "4868" of plastic with added feet of several heights to meet varying needs
Stapel- und Reihenstuhl »4868« aus Kunststoff mit gesondert hergestellten Beinen in verschiedenen Längen für verschiedene Zwecke
Kartell

393 **Vico Magistretti** 1971 Italy   ▷▷▷

Chair "Gaudi" of reinforced resin
Stuhl »Gaudi« aus verstärktem Kunstharz
Artemide

390 **Vico Magistretti** 1968 Italy
Stacking chair "Selene" of fiberglass-rein-
forced polyester
Stapelstuhl »Selene« aus glasfaserver-
stärktem Polyester
Artemide

394 Verner Panton c. 1954 Denmark

Chairs "275/276" of molded laminated
wood, stained or lacquered
Stühle »275/276« aus verformtem Schichtholz, gebeizt oder lackiert
Thonet

395 Verner Panton 1960 Denmark

Stacking chair of fiberglass-reinforced
polyester
Stapelstuhl aus glasfaserverstärktem Polyester
Herman Miller

396 Walter Papst 1964 Germany

Stackable garden bench "1000" of fiberglass-reinforced polyester
Stapelbare Gartenbank »1000« aus glasfaserverstärktem Polyester
Wilkhahn

397 Eero Aarnio 1967 Finland

"Pastilli" chair of glass-reinforced poly-
ester
Sessel »Pastilli« aus glasfaserverstärktem
Polyester
Asko

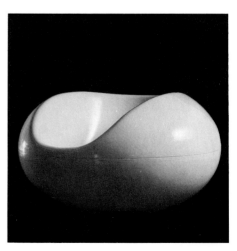

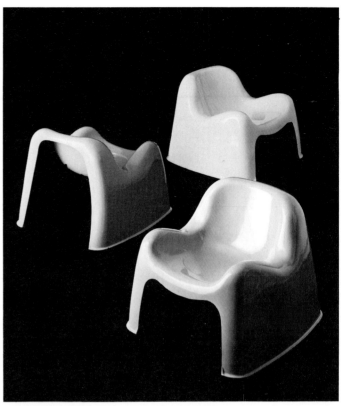

398 Pierre Paulin 1969 France

Polyester chair "305"
Polyestersessel »305«
Artifort

399 Sergio Mazza 1968 Italy

Easy chair "Toga" of fiberglass-reinforced
polyester
Sessel »Toga« aus glasfaserverstärktem
Polyester
Artemide

400 Sori Yanagi 1956 Japan

Stacking stool of plastic
Stapelbarer Kunststoffhocker

401+402 Stacy Dukes 1970 USA

Stool "Efebo" of plastic
Kunststoffhocker »Efebo«
Artemide

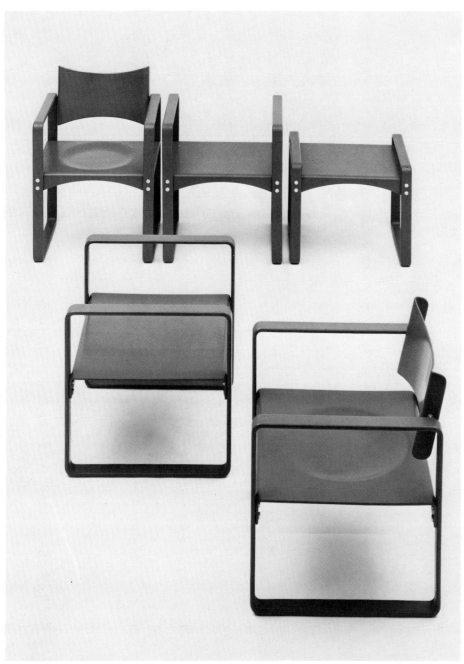

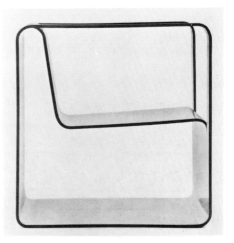

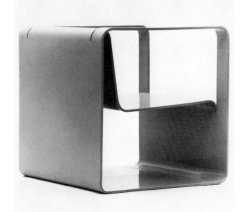

403 Verner Panton 1968 Denmark

Seating range "270/271" composed of identical parts of molded laminated plywood with lacquer finish which can be assembled as desired
Sitzmöbelprogramm »270/271« mit gleichen Bügel- und Sitzteilen aus lackiertem verformtem Sperrholz mit zahlreichen Kombinationsmöglichkeiten
Thonet

404+405 Heinz Witthoeft 1967 Germany

"Tail 13", a thermoplastic panel cut molded to form armchair or table
»Tail 13«, Sessel oder Tisch aus einer geschlitzten, thermoplastisch verformten Kunststoffplatte
Witthoeft

403	404
	405
406	

406 Grete Jalk 1963 Denmark

Chair of molded laminated oak, also upholstered
Stuhl aus verformtem Schichtholz in Eiche, auch gepolstert
P. Jeppesen

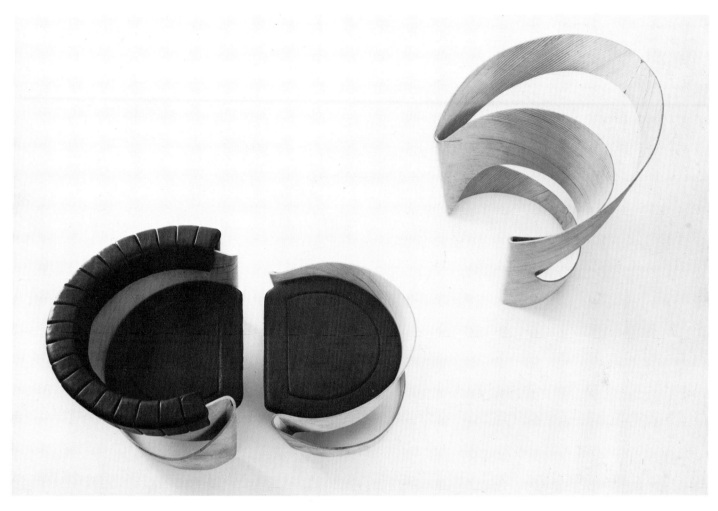

407 Grete Jalk 1963 Denmark
Armchairs and ottoman of molded laminated Oregon pine, uphol-
stered
Sessel und Hocker aus verformtem Schichtholz in Oregon Pine,
gepolstert
P. Jeppesen

408 Joe Colombo 1963 Italy
Easy chair "4801" assembled of three interlocking parts of molded
plywood
Sessel »4801«, zusammengesetzt aus drei ineinandergreifenden
Teilen aus verformtem Sperrholz
Kartell

409 Motomi Kawakami 1968 Japan
Lounge chair "Florenza" of molded plastic
Sessel »Florenza« aus verformtem Kunststoff
Alberto Bazzani

410–412 **Olivier Mourgue** 1965 France
Daybeds and easy chair "Collection Domino" with metal frames, polyfoam upholstery and detachable fabric covers
Ruhesofas und Sessel der »Collection Domino« mit Metallrahmen, Schaumstoffpolsterung und abnehmbaren Stoffbezügen
Airborne

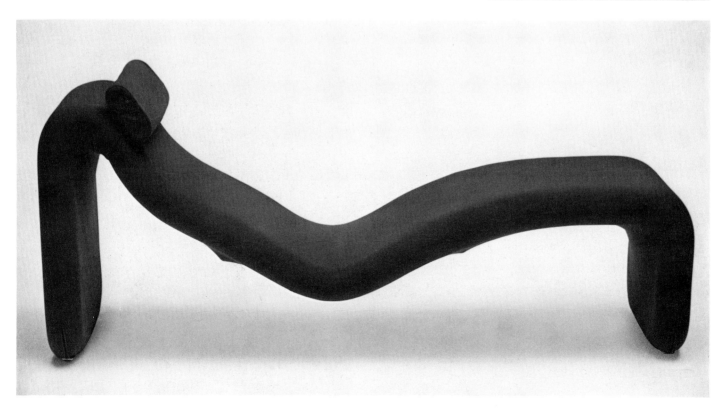

413+414 Pierre Paulin 1967 France
Easy chair "577" with frame of metal tubing and rubber straps, polyfoam upholstery
Sessel »577« mit Gestell aus Metallrohren und Gummigurten, Schaumstoffpolsterung
Artifort

415 Pierre Paulin 1972 France
Easy chair "598" with metal chassis and polyfoam upholstery, zip-fastened covers of stretch material. Foot glides in extruded aluminum couple the two elements of the chair. Linking device for connection of several chairs
Sessel »598« mit Metallchassis und Schaumstoffpolsterung, elastische Stoffbezüge mit Reißverschlüssen. Gleitschiene aus gezogenem Aluminium zur Verbindung der beiden Teile des Sessels. Kupplungsstück zur Aneinanderreihung von mehreren Sesseln
Artifort

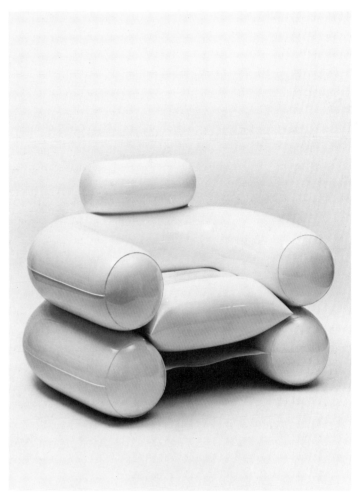

416 **Piero Gatti, Cesare Paolini, Franco Teodoro** 1969 Italy

Bag chair "Sacco" of leather, filled with plastic beads conforming to the body in any position
Sitzsack »Sacco« aus Leder. Der Sack ist mit Kunststoffperlen gefüllt, die sich jeder Sitzposition anpassen
Zanotta

417 **Carla Solari, Paolo Lomazzi, Jonathan De Pas, Donato D'Urbino** 1967 Italy

Inflatable armchair "Blow" of plastic with electronic welding, suspended seat and headrest
Aufblasbarer Sessel »Blow« aus Kunststoff, elektronisch geschweißt, mit eingehängtem Sitz und Kopfstütze
Zanotta

▽ 418 + 419 **Günter Sulz** 1973 Germany

Seating combination "Canvas" of inflatable plastic cushions with canvas covers. All parts are connected with cords and eye-lets
Sitzkombination »Canvas« aus luftgefüllten Kunststoffkissen mit Segeltuchbezügen, die zu größeren Einheiten zusammengeschnürt werden
Behr + Sulz

420 Gaetano Pesce 1969 Italy

"Serie UP" seating range consisting of six designs of polyurethene foam covered in stretch fabric. Seats come in a compressed air-tight container and instantly expand into their proper shape when case is opened

Sitzmöbel »Serie UP« in sechs verschiedenen Formen aus geschäumtem Polyurethan, Bezüge aus elastischen Stoffen. Die Sessel werden in flachen, luftdichten Verpackungen geliefert und dehnen sich an der Luft in kurzer Zeit zu ihrer Originalform aus

B & B Italia

421 + 422 Roger Dean 1968 Great Britain

"Sea Urchin", a truncated seating sphere of fabric-covered polyfoam

»Seeigel«, eine abgeflachte, mit Stoff bezogene Sitzkugel aus Schaumstoff

Hille

423 Gruppo A.R.D.I.T.I. 1972 Italy

Easy chair "Memoria" with basic structure of polyurethene foam and air-tight layer; inside air cavity can be regulated by adjusting valve for optimal sitting position. Various fabric covers

Sessel »Memoria« mit Kern aus Polyurethanschaum, der eine Luftkammer umschließt und luftdicht abgedeckt ist. Die Füllung der Luftkammer kann durch ein Ventil entsprechend der gewünschten Sitzposition geregelt werden. Zahlreiche Bezugsstoffe

Cassina

	420
421	423
422	

424 George Nelson 1963 USA

Sofa "Sling" with frame and base of chrome-plated steel. Sections of underframe are joined
by epoxy resin. Loose down and polyfoam cushions with leather cover
Sofa »Sling« mit Schlingenrahmen für die Polsterung und Gestell aus verchromtem Stahl.
Die einzelnen Abschnitte des Gestells sind mit Epoxyharz dauerhaft verbunden. Lose Kissen
aus Daunen und Schaumstoff mit Lederbezug
Herman Miller

In the past three decades the sofa has changed from the familiar classic model into a seating landscape. This means that it has developed from the exactly contoured piece of furniture on four legs into an amorphous and variable collection of elements that can be grouped according to one's needs and mood. No other type of furniture has experienced a comparable metamorphosis. More important than the changes in construction and materials that can be noticed here is the completely different use that one of the oldest items of furniture we know has been put to. The change in lifestyle during recent years can be seen very clearly in the sofa. Like the table but unlike the chair, the sofa is an object meant for use by several people; it is therefore a "communal piece of furniture". A sofa only fulfils its purpose properly when at least two people are using it at the same time. New customs are reflected in such a piece of furniture faster than elsewhere. The preference for a more relaxed attitude and for less constrained behaviour, but also the sacrificing of "conversation" in favour of free attitudes–all this can been seen in the example of the sofa. Because the seating height has been reduced, we have placed ourselves lower, and the item of furniture naturally as well. It is no longer the symbol of an important ritual activity that it once was. On the contrary, its new form represents a very direct expression of modern customs. The interchangeable order of movable seating elements can be interpreted as being a result of the increasing dismantling of hierarchies ·and as a simile of continuous change in our society. Even if one does not want to go that far, it must be admitted that the way we deal with each other in private is different from what it used to be and this aspect of our lives is characterised in the furniture we use.
The sofa designed by George Nelson in 1963 (ill. 424) was still very much indebted to the classic form. For a long time it was exhibited in the Museum of Modern Art in New York as one of the very few modern articles of furniture. The object is without doubt beautiful and, as regards its structure, logical as well. It expresses convincingly that it is a technically conceived object. Its aesthetics are those of an object coupling two sorts of sensuality: the cold, dominating sensuality of steel tubes with the warm sensuality of dark leather. However, the large, encompassing bow form, which subordinates everything, not without strictness, to a structural idea, remains dominant. It is a matter for consideration whether this is really a good idea and if it does not give the impression of being superimposed. This design is, however, a clear attempt at connecting the traditional idea of a sofa with modern preferences and ways of thinking. At the same time it was not possible for it to avoid giving the impression that the basic idea behind this piece of furniture came from elsewhere, from architecture and car design for instance. The example of the adjustable car seat has had a stimulating effect; several items indicate this clearly (ills. 485, 486, 499, 501, 502).
The seating snake by Jørn Utzon (ills. 466, 467) was a new departure for the sofa. The principle of serial arrangement surprises at first but it also makes sense. The idea that a piece of furniture can grow and decrease in size and that it can behave like an organic being was unusual and led to a revision of old attitudes. Organic associations had already been included covertly, but never as directly as here.

Das Sofa hat sich im Lauf der letzten drei Jahrzehnte vom vertrauten klassischen Modell zur Sitzlandschaft gewandelt, das heißt, die Entwicklung ging hier vom genau konturierten Möbel auf vier Beinen hin zu einer amorphen und variablen Ansammlung von Einzelteilen, die je nach Bedürfnis und Laune gruppiert werden können. Wohl kein zweiter Möbeltyp hat eine vergleichbare Metamorphose erlebt. Wichtiger nun als die Änderungen in Konstruktion und Material, die hier feststellbar sind, ist die ganz andere Handhabung eines Einrichtungsgegenstandes, der zu den ältesten gehört, die wir kennen. Der Wandel im Lebensgefühl, der sich in jüngerer Zeit vollzogen hat, ist am Sofa recht deutlich abzulesen. Ähnlich wie der Tisch, aber anders als der Stuhl, ist das Sofa ein Objekt, das zur Benutzung durch mehrere bestimmt ist, es handelt sich also um ein »Gemeinschaftsmöbel«. Ein Sofa erfüllt seinen Sinn erst richtig dann, wenn es von mindestens zwei Personen besetzt ist. Neue Sitten spiegeln sich nun in einem solchen Gegenstand schneller als anderswo. Die Vorliebe für legerere Haltungen und ein ungezwungenes Benehmen, aber auch die Opferung der »Konversation« zugunsten einer freien Haltung – das alles läßt sich am Beispiel Sofa erkennen. Mit der reduzierten Sitzhöhe haben wir uns selber tiefer gesetzt, aber das Möbel natürlich auch. Die Haupt- und Staatsaktion, die es früher gern gewesen ist, ist es heute nicht mehr. Dagegen stellt seine neue Form einen sehr unmittelbaren Ausdruck moderner Gewohnheiten dar. Die austauschbare Anordnung mobiler Sitzelemente kann interpretiert werden als eine Folge des zunehmenden Abbaues von Hierarchien und als Gleichnis für die permanente Wandlung in unserer Gesellschaft. Auch wenn man nicht so weit gehen will, so steht doch wohl fest, daß unser privater Umgang heute anders ist als früher und sich das in dafür charakteristischen Möbeln abzeichnet.
Noch sehr der klassischen Urform verpflichtet war das Sofa, das George Nelson 1963 entworfen hat (Abb. 424) und das lange im Museum of Modern Art in New York als eines der ganz wenigen modernen Möbel ausgestellt war. Der Gegenstand ist zweifellos schön und, was die Konstruktion anbetrifft, auch logisch. Er bringt überzeugend zum Ausdruck, ein technisch konzipiertes Objekt zu sein. Seine Ästhetik ist die eines Gegenstandes, in dem sich zweierlei Sinnlichkeit paart: die kalte und beherrschende des Stahlrohrs mit der warmen des dunklen Leders. Dominierend bleibt jedoch die große umgreifende Form des Bügels, die nicht ohne Rigorosität alles einer konstruktiven Idee unterordnet. Ob sie an diesem Gegenstand tatsächlich sinnvoll ist und ob sie nicht zu aufgesetzt wirkt, wäre noch zu prüfen. Mit diesem Entwurf ist jedenfalls deutlich versucht worden, die traditionelle Vorstellung von einem Sofa mit den heutigen Vorlieben und Denkweisen zu verbinden. Wohl nicht zu vermeiden war dabei, daß man leicht das Gefühl vermittelt bekommt, dieses Möbel habe seine Grundidee von woanders her bezogen, etwa aus der Architektur und dem Fahrzeugbau. Das Vorbild des verstellbaren Autositzes hat übrigens in vieler Hinsicht anregend gewirkt, die Beispiele zeigen das deutlich (Abb. 485 + 486, 499, 501 + 502).
Ein erster Aufbruch in neue Sofawelten war die Sitzschlange von Jørn Utzon (Abb. 466 + 467). Das Prinzip der seriellen Anordnung wirkte im ersten Moment überraschend, aber auch einleuchtend. Die Vorstellung, daß ein Möbel wachsen und schrumpfen kann und daß es sich wie ein organisches Wesen gibt, war ungewöhnlich und brachte die alten Ansichten tatsächlich »ins Laufen«. Assoziationen, die auf Organisches zielten, waren auch früher schon immer einmal versteckt eingebracht worden, aber noch nie so direkt wie hier.

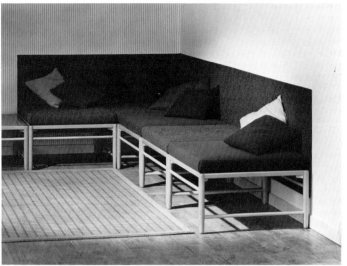

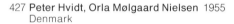

425 **Peter Hvidt, Orla Mølgaard Nielsen**
c. 1952 Denmark

Sofa with wooden frame and polyfoam
upholstery
Sofa mit Holzgestell und Schaumstoffpolsterung
France & Søn

426 **Alf Svensson** c. 1953 Sweden

Ottomans "Corner", also to be used as
tables, with wooden frame and polyfoam
upholstery
Hocker »Corner«, auch als Tischchen zu
verwenden, mit Holzgestell und Schaumstoffpolstern
Ljungs Industrier

427 **Peter Hvidt, Orla Mølgaard Nielsen** 1955
Denmark

Sofa with frame of wood and seat support
of rubber straps, metal fittings, seat and
back upholstered, removable arm-rests
Sofa mit Gestell aus Holz und Sitzunterlage
aus Gummibändern, Metallbeschläge, Sitz
und Rückenlehne gepolstert, abnehmbare
Armlehnen
France & Søn

428 **Karl Erik Ekselius** c. 1957 Sweden

Sofa with wooden frame, can be converted
to a bed
Sofa mit Holzgestell, kann in ein Bett verwandelt werden
J.O. Carlsson

429 George Kasparian c. 1951 USA
Sofa/bed "700" with wooden legs, upholstered seat and back of wood
Sofa/Bett »700« mit Holzbeinen, Polstersitz und Rückenlehne aus Holz
Kasparians

430 + 431 Hans Olsen 1955 Denmark
Bench system with removable polyfoam upholstered seats and table tops
Banksystem mit abnehmbaren Schaumstoffsitzen und Tischplatten
N.A. Jørgensens Møbelfabrik

432 Edward J. Wormley c. 1951 USA
Sofa with detachable legs of brass or aluminum, polyfoam upholstery
Sofa mit abnehmbaren Messing- oder Aluminiumbeinen und Schaumgummipolsterung
Dunbar

433 Florence Knoll c. 1950 USA
Settee and sofa with black lacquered metal tube frame and poly-
foam upholstery
Sessel und Sofa mit schwarz lackiertem Metallrohrgestell und
Schaumstoffpolsterung
Knoll International

436 George Nelson c. 1957 USA ▷
"Modular Combination" with chrome-plated metal bases and interchangeable inserts: upholstered chairs, table tops of white plastic,
chests of drawers in walnut or rosewood
»Modular Combination«, Sitzkombination mit verchromten Fußge-
stellen und auswechselbaren Elementen: Polstersitze, Tischplatten
mit weißer Kunststoffbeschichtung, Kasteneinheiten in Nußbaum
oder Palisander
Herman Miller

434 Norman Cherner c. 1951 USA
Sofa/bed "300" with metal frame and polyfoam upholstery
Sofa/Bett »300« mit Metallgestell und Schaumstoffpolsterung
Konwiser

435 Florence Knoll c. 1955 USA
Sofa "67" and lounge chair "65A" with chrome-plated square steel
frame, polyfoam cushions over springs
Sofa »67« und Sessel »65A« mit verchromtem Stahlrohrgestell,
Schaumstoffpolsterung auf Unterfederung
Knoll International

▷ 437 **George Nelson** 1952 USA

Seating range with metal bench frame and interchangeable elements: seats with rubber webbing and loose cushions, table tops with plastic laminate
Sitzmöbelprogramm mit Bankgestell aus Metall und auswechselbaren Elementen: Sitze mit Gummigurtenbespannung und losen Polstern, Tischplatten mit Kunststoffbeschichtung
Herman Miller

▽ 438 **Nanna and Jørgen Ditzel** 1961 Denmark

Modular seating range with benchlike frames of wengé and black square tubular steel legs. Polyfoam upholstery, L-shaped seating elements on fiberglass frames, detachable trays of wengé
Modulares Sitzmöbelsystem mit bankförmigen Untergestellen aus Wengé mit schwarzen Vierkantstahlrohrfüßen, Schaumstoffpolster, L-förmige Lehnenteile auf Glasfaserrahmen, abnehmbare Serviertabletts aus Wengé
Kolds Savværk

439 Edward J. Wormley 1949 USA

Sofa "4907 A" with frame of maple, metal legs, loose cushions with silk covers
Sofa »4907 A« mit Ahorngestell, Metallfüßen und losen Polstern mit Seidenbezug
Dunbar

440 William Katavolos, Ross Littell, Douglas Kelley c. 1952 USA

Sofa with frame of chrome-plated steel, black-enamelled steel rail and polyfoam upholstery
Sofa mit Stahlgestell, schwarz emaillierter Zarge und Schaumstoffpolsterung
Laverne

441 Hans J. Wegner 1957 Denmark

Sofa "A.P. 35/3 S" with steel legs, polyfoam upholstery and woolen fabric cover
Sofa »A.P. 35/3 S« mit Stahlbeinen, Schaumstoffpolsterung und Wollstoffbezug
A.P. Stolen

442 George Kasparian 1960 USA

Sofa "KM/108", three- or four-seater, metal
or wood frame, loose cushions
Sofa »KM/108«, drei- oder viersitzig, mit
Metall- oder Holzgestell und losen Kis-
sen
Kasparians

443 Theo Tempelman 1959 Netherlands

Sofa "18" with frame of square steel or
in teak, loose polyfoam cushions with
cover in leather or fabric
Sofa »18« mit Gestell aus Vierkantstahlrohr oder in Teak, lose Schaumstoffpolster
mit Leder- oder Stoffbezügen
A. Polak's Meubelindustrie

444 Pierre Paulin 1962 France

Sofa "442" with wooden frame on chrome-
plated metal base. Loose polyfoam cushions covered in leather or fabric over
springs
Sofa »442« mit Untergestell aus verchromtem Metall. Sitzrahmen aus Holz mit Unterfederung, lose Schaumstoffpolster mit Le-
der- oder Stoffbezügen
Artifort

445 Charles Eames 1954 USA

Sofa with folding back and chrome-plated steel base
Sofa mit umklappbarer Rückenlehne und Gestell aus verchromtem Stahl
Herman Miller

446 Charles Eames 1962 USA

Sofa "RE-204" with base of polished cast aluminum, polyfoam upholstery with black plastic cover
Sofa »RE-204« mit Gestell aus poliertem Aluminiumguß, Schaumstoffpolsterung mit schwarzem Kunststoffbezug
Herman Miller

447 Poul Kjaerholm 1958 Denmark

Sofa "31" with frames of chrome-plated steel, leather-covered seat, back, and armrests, loose down cushions
Sofa »31« mit Gestell aus verchromtem Stahl, Sitz, Rücken- und Armlehnen lederbezogen, lose Daunenkissen
E. Kold Christensen

448 Estelle and Erwine Laverne 1962
USA

"Philharmonic Suspension Bench" with
polished steel frame, polyfoam upholstery
with leather or plastic cover
»Philharmonic Suspension Bench«, Bank
mit poliertem Stahlgestell, Schaumstoffpolsterung und Leder- oder Kunststoffbezug
Laverne

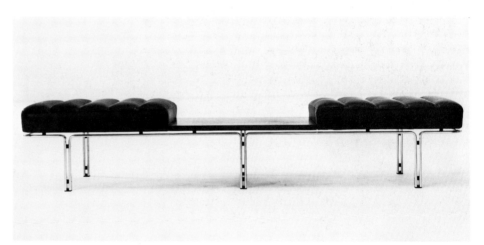

449+450 Horst Brüning 1969 Germany
Sofa "6915" and bench "Systembank"
with frames of chrome-plated flat steel
hoops, upholstery covered in leather or
fabric, table tops in marble, glass, wood,
or white plastic laminate. Seats and table
tops can be combined to units of various
lengths
Sofa »6915« und »Systembank« mit Gestellen aus verchromten Flachstahlbügeln,
Polster mit Leder- oder Stoffbezug, Tischplatten in Marmor, Glas, Holz oder mit weißer Kunststoffbeschichtung. Sitzpolster
und Tischplatten können zu beliebig langen Einheiten verbunden werden
Kill

451 Horst Brüning 1968 Germany

Range of furniture, including easy chair "6910", two- and three-seater sofas "6912/6913" and tables, with frames of chrome-plated flat steel hoops in mat finish, upholstery covered in leather or fabric
Möbelprogramm mit Sessel »6910«, zwei- und dreisitzigem Sofa »6912/6913« und Tischen; Gestelle aus matt verchromten Flachstahlbügeln, Polster mit Leder- oder Stoffbezug
Kill

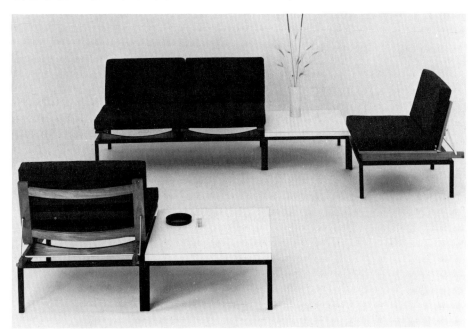

452 Frank Gullie 1963 Great Britain

"Duo Seating, 300 Group" with seating unit which can be converted to form single or double bed; white plastic-laminated coffee table tops. Seat frames of afrormosia on black metal underframes, upholstered cushions over rubber webbing
»Duo Seating, 300 Group«, Sitzelemente, die mit zurückgeklappter Lehne auch zu Einzel- oder Doppelbetten zusammengestellt werden können; Tischplatten mit weißem Kunststoff beschichtet. Stuhlgestelle Afrormosia auf schwarzen Metallrahmen, Polsterkissen auf Gummigurten
A.F. Buckingham

455 **Arne Jacobsen** 1957 Denmark

Armchair "3000" and sofa "3003" with chrome-plated tubular steel frames and upholstery
Sessel »3000« und Sofa »3003« mit verchromten Stahlrohrgestellen und Polsterung
Fritz Hansen

456 **Jørn Utzon** 1968 Denmark

Modular furniture system in knockdown construction. Basic structure of nine sizes of U-shaped hoops of triangular-shaped aluminum tubing. Cushions of polyfoam with covers in oxhide or fabric, table tops of plastic laminate. Pieces can be used separately or linked
Modulares Möbelsystem mit Gestellen aus U-Bügeln (Aluminium-Dreieckrohr in neun Größen), Schaumstoffpolstern mit Leder- oder Stoffbezügen, Tischplatten mit Kunststoffbeschichtung. Alle Elemente können einzeln aufgestellt oder zu Reihen verbunden werden
Fritz Hansen

◁◁ 453 **Roland Rainer** c. 1956 Austria

Armchair "460S" and sofa "462S" with chrome-plated steel frames, loose seat and back cushions
Sessel »460S« und Sofa »462S« mit verchromten Stahlgestellen, lose Sitz- und Rückenpolster
Wilkhahn

◁ 454 **Alain Richard** 1960 France

Sofa with chrome-plated square steel frame and upholstery
Sofa mit verchromtem Vierkantstahlrohrgestell und Polsterung
Meubles T.V.

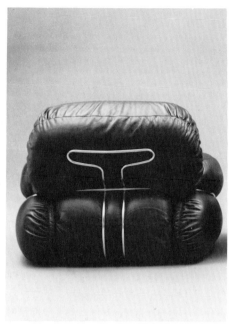

457 + 458 **Adriano Piazzesi** 1970 Italy

Seating group "Okay" with frame structure of chrome-plated tubular steel into which cushions of soft foam are inserted; covers of fabric, leather or plastic. Ottoman converts into a table when glass top is clipped on
Sitzgruppe »Okay« mit Gestell aus verchromten Stahlrohrbügeln, das die weichen Schaumstoffkissen zusammenhält; Bezüge aus Stoff, Leder oder Kunststoff. Der Hocker kann mit einer aufgesteckten Glasplatte in einen Tisch verwandelt werden
Tre D

459 **Gianfranco Frattini** 1970 Italy

Sofa and easy chair "Sesann" with upholstery of polyfoam on wooden base, covers of leather or fabric, and chrome-plated steel tube base
Sofa und Sessel »Sesann« mit Schaumstoffpolsterung auf Holzunterlage, Leder- oder Stoffbezügen und verchromtem Stahlrohrrahmen
Cassina

460 **Gianni Songia** 1963 Italy

Convertible sofa "GS 195" with frame of rosewood and fittings of brass. Polyfoam upholstery covered in leather or fabric
Sofa/Bett »GS 195« mit Gestell aus Palisander und Beschlägen aus Messing. Schaumstoffpolsterung mit Leder- oder Stoffbezügen
Sormani

461 **Tobia Scarpa** 1971 Italy

Easy chair and Sofa "Bonanza" with dacron fibres upholstery on plastic seating shell, covers in leather or fabric
Sessel und Sofa »Bonanza« mit Polsterung aus Dacronfasern auf Kunststoffsitzschale, Bezüge aus Leder oder Stoff
B & B Italia

462 Afra and Tobia Scarpa 1970 Italy
Seating group "Soriana" with polyfoam
upholstery and leather or fabric covers,
frame of chrome-plated steel
Sitzgruppe »Soriana« mit Schaumstoffpolsterung und Leder- oder Stoffbezügen,
verchromte Stahlbügel
Cassina

463–465 Works Design 1971 Italy
Sofa "Anfibio" with substructure of steel and polyfoam upholstery, covers in fabric or leather.
Frame and mattress are kept in folded position by nylon zippers and leather straps, by
opening it changes to a bed
Sofa »Anfibio« mit innerer Struktur aus Profilstahl, Schaumstoffpolsterung und Stoff- oder
Lederbezügen. Rahmen und Matratze sind mit Nylonreißverschlüssen und Lederriemen zu-
sammengehalten und können durch Aufklappen in ein Bett verwandelt werden
Giovannetti

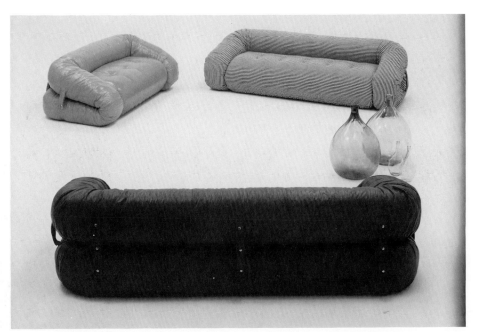

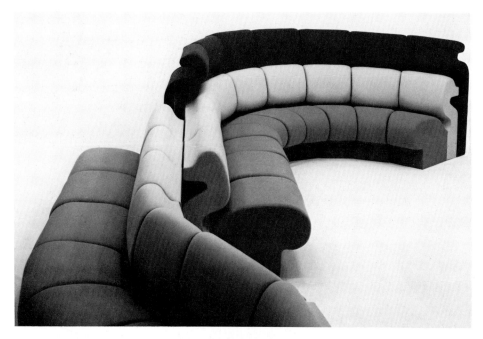

466	467
468	
469	

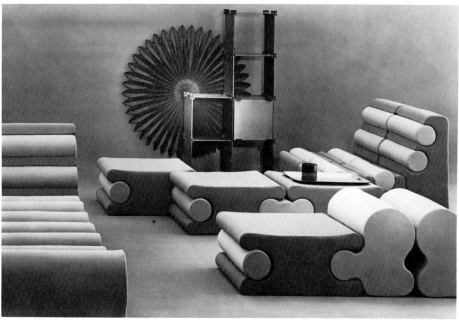

468 Dieter Schempp 1968 Germany

Polyfoam elements that may be combined to form all kinds of seating units and furniture landscapes, removable covers with zippers
Schaumstoffelemente, die sich zu Sitzmöbeln und ganzen Wohnlandschaften zusammensetzen lassen, abnehmbare Bezüge mit Reißverschlüssen
Co-Produktion Schempp

469 Burkhard Vogdherr 1970/71 Germany

Seating system "VarioPillo" for straight or curved arrangements. Five different elements of polyfoam with varying density on plastic shells with handles. Elements are linked by plastic coupling devices, clamp-on trays
Sitzmöbelsystem »VarioPillo« für gerade oder gebogene Sitzreihen. Fünf verschiedene Elemente aus Schaumstoff in verschiedenen Härtegraden auf L-Schalen aus Kunststoff mit Griffmulde, Verbindung der Elemente durch Kupplungsstücke aus Kunststoff, passendes Aufstecktablett
Rosenthal

472+473 Pierre Paulin 1969 France ▷

Easy chair and ondulating sofa of three fiberglass units which are separately upholstered in polyfoam and are then joined and mounted on a base with casters
Sessel und Wellensofa aus drei Fiberglaselementen, die unabhängig voneinander mit Schaumstoff gepolstert, dann verbunden und auf einem Rollengestell montiert werden
Artifort

474+475 Joe Colombo 1969 Italy ▷▷

"Additional System", a seating program consisting of upholstered polyfoam segments in six different sizes, each covered in stretch fabric and mounted on a steel rail to form chairs and sofas of any desired length and shape
Sitzmöbelprogramm »Additional System« aus sechs verschiedenen, scheibenförmigen Schaumstoffteilen mit elastischem Stoffbezug, die an einer Stahlschiene befestigt werden und Sessel oder Sofas beliebiger Form und Länge bilden
Sormani

◁ 466+467 **Jørn Utzon** 1968 Denmark
Seating system consisting of three basic elements of polyfoam with
fabric covers for arrangements in straight or curved lines
Sitzelementsystem mit drei Grundeinheiten aus Schaumstoff mit
Stoffbezügen, die sich zu geraden oder gebogenen Reihen zusam-
menstellen lassen
Ken Muff Lassen

470+471 **Marco Zanuso** 1967 Italy   ▷
Seating element "Lombrico" with units of fiberglass-reinforced
polyester upholstered in polyfoam and covered in fabric may be
combined to any length
Sitzelementsystem »Lombrico« mit Grundeinheiten aus glasfaserverstärktem Polyester mit Schaumstoffpolsterung und Stoffbezügen, die sich zu beliebiger Länge zusammenstellen lassen
B & B Italia

470	471
472	473
474	475

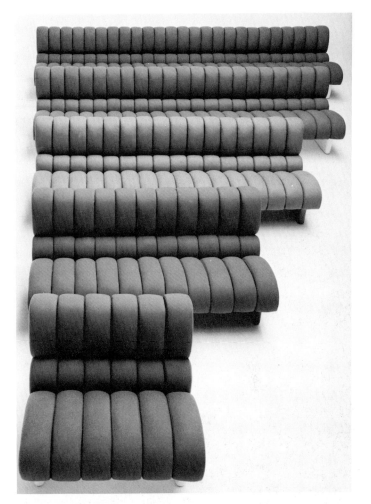

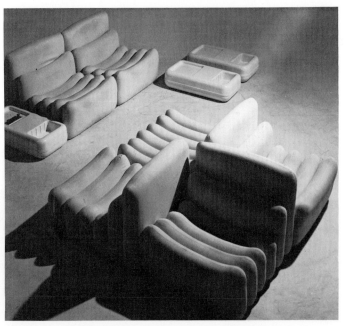

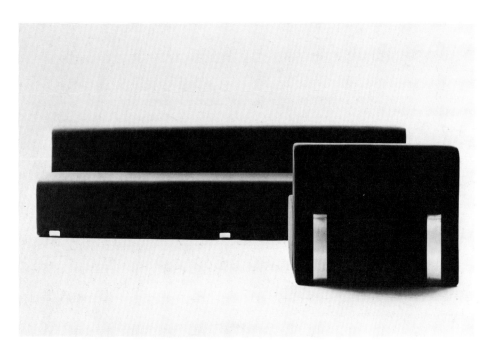

476 **Kazuhide Takahama** 1965 Italy

Easy chair and sofa "Marcel" with polyfoam cushions on aluminum frame
Sessel und Sofa »Marcel« aus Schaumstoffkissen mit Aluminiumgestell
Knoll International

477 **Kazuhide Takahama** 1965 Italy

Easy chair "Suzanne" of polyfoam cushions with base of chrome-plated steel;
matching sofa and single chair
Sessel »Suzanne« mit Gestell aus verchromtem Stahlrohr und Schaumstoffkissen; passendes Sofa und Einzelsessel
Knoll International

478 **Works Design** 1970 Great Britain

"F" range of chairs and ottomans of polyfoam with removable plastic covers.
Chairs can be linked by special zipping
device
Sessel und Hocker »F« aus Schaumstoff
mit abnehmbaren Kunststoffbezügen. Die
Sessel können durch ein spezielles Reiß-
verschlußsystem verbunden werden
OMK

480+481 **Rodolfo Bonetto** 1971 Italy ▷

Linking easy chair "Boomerang" with
chrome-plated steel frame, polyfoam
upholstery and covers in fabric
Reihensessel »Boomerang« mit verchromtem Stahlgestell, Schaumstoffpolsterung
und Stoffbezug
Flexform

479 Hughes Steiner 1969 France

Sofa complex "Swany" of three units of polyfoam allowing a wide
variety of arrangements, covered in plastic or fabric
Sofa »Swany« aus drei Grundelementen, die sich zu verschiedenen
Gruppierungen zusammenstellen lassen. Schaumstoff mit Stoff-
oder Kunststoffbezügen
Steiner

482 Ueli Berger 1968 Switzerland

"Multi-Soft" seating unit of polyfoam with fabric cover; can be
used as chair, sofa, bed, or daybed
Sitzmöbel »Multi-Soft« aus Schaumstoff mit Stoffbezug; als Sessel,
Sofa, Liege oder Bett zu verwenden
Victoria-Werke

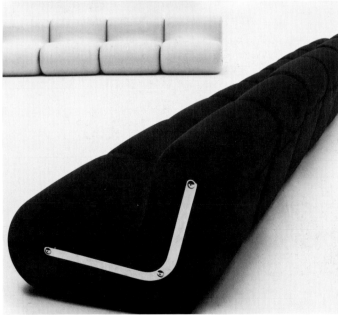

483 Luigi Colani 1970/71 Germany

Living pad "Pool" consisting of square ground, border, and corner elements of polyfoam
with detachable covers in various fabrics. Supplementary cushions and black or white slide-
tables
Wohnmulde »Pool«, zusammengesetzt aus quadratischen Boden-, Rand- und Eckelementen
aus Schaumstoff mit abnehmbaren Bezügen aus verschiedenen Stoffen. Als Ergänzung Stütz-
polster sowie Tischschlitten aus schwarzem oder weißem Kunststoff
Rosenthal

484 Bernard Govin 1967 France

Furniture elements "Asmara"; four basic elements of polyfoam with removable fabric covers
can be combined to form seating units or landscapes
Sitzelemente »Asmara« aus Schaumstoff mit abnehmbaren Stoffbezügen. Vier Grundelemente lassen sich zu beliebigen Sitzmöbeln und Wohnlandschaften zusammenstellen
Roset

485 + 486 Joe Colombo 1971 Italy

Furniture range "Livingcenter" consisting of daybeds with angular cushions, a "dinner element" and a "service element". Daybed with frame of chrome-plated tubular steel with gliders and casters, plastic-laminated extensible shelves. The angular cushions can be used as foot- or headrest or be put on the daybed as raised seat during the meals. Polyfoam upholstery with fabric covers.
Cabinet elements plastic-laminated in various colors, on casters. Dinner element with electric plate-warmer and refrigerator, extensible lids and pull-out sides to enlarge table top. Service element with shelves behind grey plastic tambour doors and built-in loudspeakers
Möbelsystem »Livingcenter« mit Sitzliegen und zugehörigen Winkelpolstern, einem »Dinnerelement« und einem »Serviceelement«. Die Liege auf verchromtem Stahlrohrgestell mit Kufen und Rollen hat seitlich ausziehbare Ablagebretter und ein Fach am Kopfende; das Winkelpolster dient als Fuß- und Kopfstütze oder, auf eine Liege gestellt, als erhöhte Sitzfläche beim Essen. Polster aus Schaumstoff mit Stoffbezügen.
Kastenmöbel in verschiedenen Farben kunststoffbeschichtet, auf Rollen laufend. Beim Dinnerelement mit eingebauter Warmhalteplatte, Kühlbox und Fächern für Geschirr sind die Seitenteile hochzuklappen, um die Tischfläche zu vergrößern. Das Serviceelement hat zahlreiche Fächer, die durch graue Kunststoffjalousien verschlossen werden, und eingebaute Lautsprecher
Rosenthal

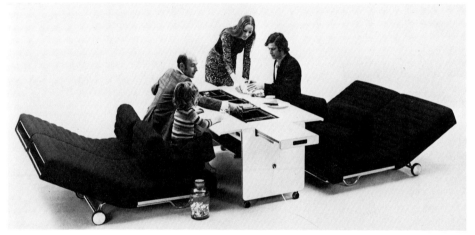

487 Jonathan De Pas, Donato D'Urbino, Paolo Lomazzi 1972 Italy

Cushion system "Ali Baba" consisting of square seat and back cushions with removable canvas covers, additional table top
Polsterkombination »Ali Baba« mit viereckigen Bodenkissen und Rückenpolstern, abnehmbare Segeltuchbezüge, passende Tischplatte
BBB Bonacina

488 + 489 **Torsten Johansson** 1953 Denmark

Seating furniture with wooden frame and
various polyfoam elements, can be combined as desired
Sitzmöbel mit Holzrahmen und verschiedenen Schaumstoffelementen, die beliebig
kombiniert werden können
A.J. Iversen

488	
489	
490	492
491	493

▽ 490 + 491 **Verner Panton** 1962 Denmark

Modular seating range with chests of
wengé or teak with hinged lids and casters,
fabric-covered polyfoam cushions
Zerlegbares Sitzmöbelsystem mit Kastenelementen aus Wengé oder Teak mit auf-
klappbaren Deckeln und Rollen, stoffbezo-
gene Schaumstoffpolster
France & Søn

▽ 492 + 493 **Roland Gibbard** 1963
Great Britain

Knockdown "Plus Unit Seating" of plywood panels veneered in larch, joined by
anodized aluminum angles and fixed by
bolts to any desired combination. Loose
polyfoam cushions with detachable fabric
covers
Zerlegbares Sitzmöbelsystem »Plus Unit
Seating« aus Sperrholzplatten mit Lär-
chenfurnier, verbunden durch Winkel aus
eloxiertem Aluminium mit Bolzenbefesti-
gung, beliebig kombinierbar. Lose
Schaumstoffkissen mit abnehmbarem
Stoffbezug
Design Furnishing Contracts

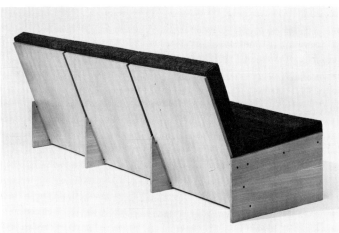

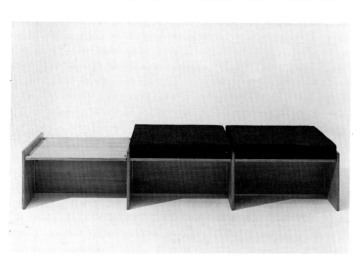

494 Heinz Witthoeft 1959–70 Germany

Modular furniture system "Tail 4" with
frames of pinewood and inserted panels;
seat slings of canvas or leather. An earlier
designed group has been considerably ex-
panded and now comprises chairs, tables,
beds, and shelving, all easily assembled
and suited for living rooms, studios, children's rooms, students' hostels, among
others
Möbelsystem »Tail 4« mit Fichtenholzrah-
men und lose eingelegten Platten; einge-
hängte Sitze aus Leder oder Leinen. Das
Programm eines früheren Entwurfes wurde
wesentlich erweitert und umfaßt jetzt
Stühle, Tische, Betten und beliebig kombinierbare Regale. Geeignet für Wohn- und
Arbeitsräume, Kinderzimmer, Studenten-
wohnheime u.a.
Witthoeft

495 Rolf Heide 1975 Germany

Terrace furniture. An easily assembled
construction of wood with canvas covers,
which can be used either indoors or
out
Terrassenmöbel. Leicht zusammenbau-
bare Konstruktion aus Holz mit Segeltuchbespannung, für innen und außen
Wohnbedarf Hamburg

496–498 Studio B.B.P.R. 1950 Italy

Daybed with movable frame of metal tubes and wood, polyfoam mattress
Ruhebett mit verstellbarem Rost aus Metallrohr und Holz, Schaumstoffmatratze

499 Hans Gugelot c. 1951 Switzerland

Easy chair with wooden frame and movable seat
Liegesessel mit Holzgestell und verstellbarem Sitz
Wohnbedarf Zürich

500 Friso Kramer, Jaap Penraat c. 1952 Netherlands

Adjustable lounge chair with steel tube frame and polyfoam upholstery
Verstellbarer Liegestuhl mit Stahlrohrgestell und Schaumstoffpolsterung
Ahrend

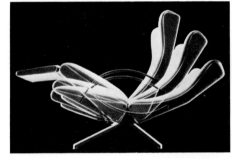

501 + 502 **Osvaldo Borsani** 1956 Italy

Adjustable lounge chair "P 40" with metal
frame, elastic armrests and polyfoam
upholstery, hinged footrest
Liegesessel »P 40« mit Metallgestell, elastischen Armlehnen und Schaumstoffpolsterung, Sitz und Rückenlehne verstellbar,
ausklappbare Fußstütze
Tecno

503–505 **Osvaldo Borsani** 1957 Italy

Adjustable daybed "L 77" with metal frame
and polyfoam mattress on straps
Verstellbare Liege »L 77« mit Metallgestell
und Schaumstoffmatratze auf Gurtenbespannung
Tecno

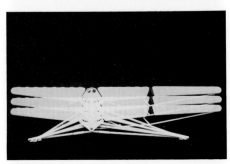

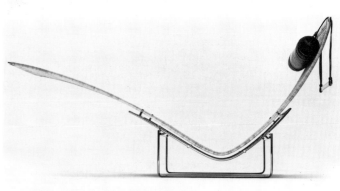

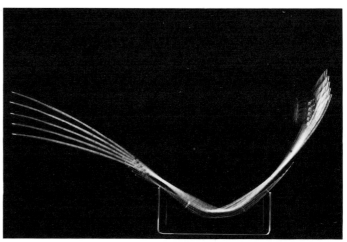

506+507 **Hendrik van Keppel, Taylor Green** c.1952 USA

Daybed with adjustable frame of wood and polyfoam mattress
Ruhebett mit verstellbarem Holzgestell und Schaumstoffmatratze
Van Keppel-Green

508+509 **Poul Kjaerholm** 1966 Denmark

Adjustable lounge chair "24" of rattan with base of stainless steel,
neck-cushion covered in leather
Verstellbarer Liegestuhl »24« aus Peddigrohrgeflecht mit Gestell
aus rostfreiem Stahl und lederbezogener Nackenstütze
E. Kold Christensen

510 **Julien Hébert** 1951 Canada

Lounge chair "Sun-Lite" with aluminum
tube frame and nylon slings
Liegestuhl »Sun-Lite« mit Gestell aus Aluminiumrohr und Nylonbespannung
Siegmund Werner

511 **George Nelson** c. 1953 USA

Chaise "5490" with base of chrome-plated
steel and polyfoam upholstery
Liegesessel »5490« mit Gestell aus verchromtem Stahl und Schaumstoffpolsterung
Herman Miller

512 Charles Eames 1969 USA

Chaise "ES 106" from "Soft Pad" group. Black base of epoxy-coated aluminum; six soft, foam-padded, leather-covered cushions joined by zippers
Liege »ES 106« aus der »Soft Pad«-Gruppe mit schwarzem Unter-gestell aus epoxybeschichtetem Aluminium; sechs weiche, mit Schaumstoff gefüllte und durch Reißverschlüsse verbundene Kis-sen mit Lederbezug
Herman Miller

513 Richard Schultz 1966 USA

"Outdoor Program", for indoor use as well, including chair and easy chair with or without arms, lounge chair, tea and dining tables. Frames of cast and profile aluminum in mat white lacquer finish with white plastic gliders. Seats of a special white synthetic fabric with side strips of brown plastic
»Outdoor Programm«, Innen- und Außenraumgruppe mit Stühlen und Sesseln mit und ohne Armlehnen, Liegesesseln, Couch- und Eßtischen. Gestelle aus mattweiß lackiertem Aluminiumguß- und -Profilteilen, weiße Kunststoffgleiter. Sitze aus weißem syntheti-schem Spezialgewebe mit seitlicher Einfassung aus braunem Kunststoff
Knoll International

514 George Nelson c. 1950 USA

Upholstered easy chair and stool with
metal legs, small removable table
Polstersessel und -Hocker mit Metallbeinen, kleines abnehmbares Tischchen
Herman Miller

515 Edward J. Wormley c. 1950 USA

Daybed with wooden frame, detachable
brass legs and polyfoam mattress
Liegesofa mit Holzrahmen, abnehmbaren
Messingbeinen und Schaumstoffma-
tratze
Dunbar

516 Works Design c. 1951 USA

Hotel bed "Tourinns" on metal legs with
casters, innerspring mattress, upholstered
headboard
Hotelbett »Tourinns« mit Metallbeinen auf
Rollen, Federkernmatratze, gepolstertes
Kopfteil
Knoll International

517 **Harvey Probber** c. 1951 USA

Beds with frame and matching corner cabinet of wood
Betten mit Rahmen und passendem Eckschrank für Bettzeug aus Holz
Harvey Probber

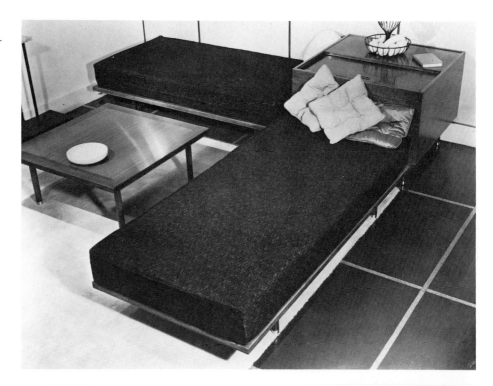

518 **Carlo Pagani** c. 1952 Italy

Bed with frame of wood and cabinet section
Bett mit Holzgestell und Schrankteil
La Rinascente

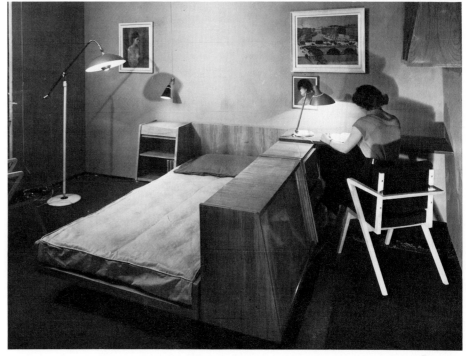

519 + 520 **Hans Olsen** 1955 Denmark

Daybed with one or two frame parts of wood and adjustable polyfoam cushions
Ruhebett mit ein- oder zweiteiligem Holzgestell und verstellbaren Schaumstoffpolstern
Werner Birksholm

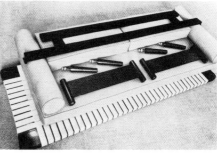

521 + 522 **Eduard Ludwig** c. 1953 Germany
Demountable daybed with innerspring
mattress
Auseinandernehmbares Liegesofa mit
Federkernmatratze
Domus

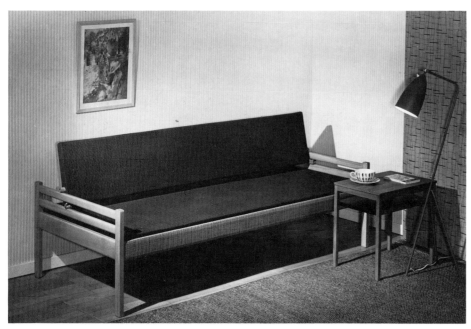

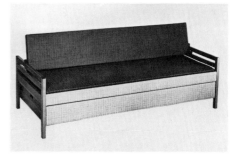

523–525 **Erik Berglund, Uno Swalen** 1956/57 Sweden
Daybed with convertible back upholstered in polyfoam, beech frame
Liegesofa mit abnehmbarer Rückenlehne und Schaumstoffpolsterung, Gestell aus Buche
Eilas

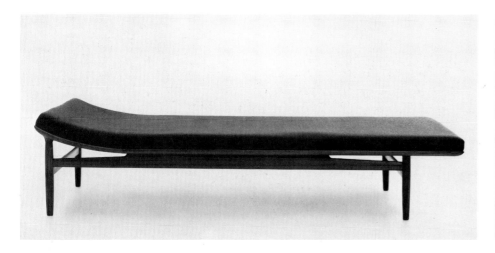

528 **Herta-Maria Witzemann, Wolfgang Stadelmaier** 1960 Germany
Bed "Dagmar" with frame of teak
Bett »Dagmar« mit Rahmen aus Teak
Femira-Werk

529 **Carl Bjørn** 1960 Sweden
Bed "Triva-Snark" with oak frame, foam rubber upholstery over No-sag springs
Liege »Triva-Snark« mit Rahmen in Eiche, Nosag-Federung mit Schaumgummimatratze
Nordiska Kompaniet

530 **Pertti Aalto** 1963 Finland
Bed "Silja" with frame of white lacquered wood, head- and footboards covered in black imitation leather
Bett »Silja« mit Rahmen aus weiß lackiertem Holz, Kopf- und Fußblende mit schwarzem Kunstleder bezogen
Femira-Werk

◁◁ 526 **Kurt Østervig** 1958 Denmark
Bed "311" with teak frame, rubber webbing, and polyfoam mattress
Bett »311« mit Teakgestell, Schaumstoffmatratze auf Gummigurten
Jason

◁ 527 **Robin Day** 1962 Great Britain
"MK II" bed settee with steel frame, legs and armrests of afrormosia, polyfoam upholstery over rubber webbing
Sofaliege »MK II« mit Untergestell aus Stahl, Beine und Armlehnen in Afrormosia, Schaumstoffpolsterung auf Gummigurten
Hille

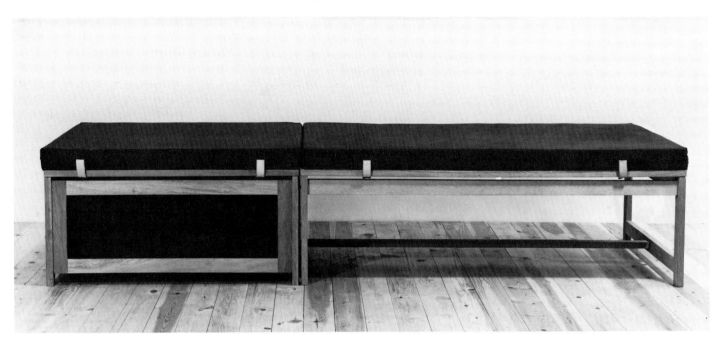

 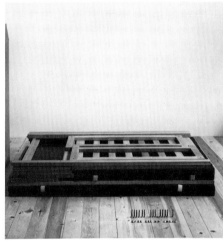

531–533 **Peter Hjorth, Arne Karlsen** 1958
Denmark

Collapsible bed consisting of two parts
and a case for bedclothes, with oak
frames, panels of the case black lacquered
Zerlegbares Bett, bestehend aus zwei Teilen und einem Bettzeugkasten, Rahmen
aus Eiche, Füllungen des Kastens schwarz
lackiert
Interna

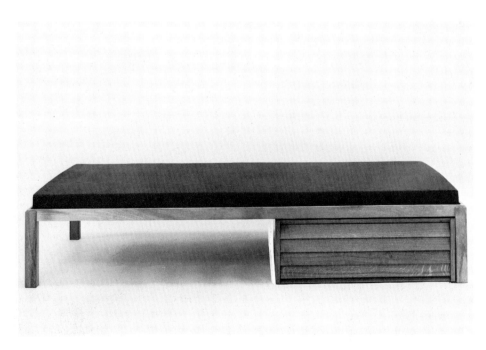

534 **Reino Ruokolainen** 1958 Finland

Bed "H" and attached wood case for bedclothes, polyfoam mattress on perforated
plywood plank
Liege »H« mit Bettzeugkasten aus Holz,
Schaumstoffmatratze auf gelochter Sperrholzplatte
Haimi Oy

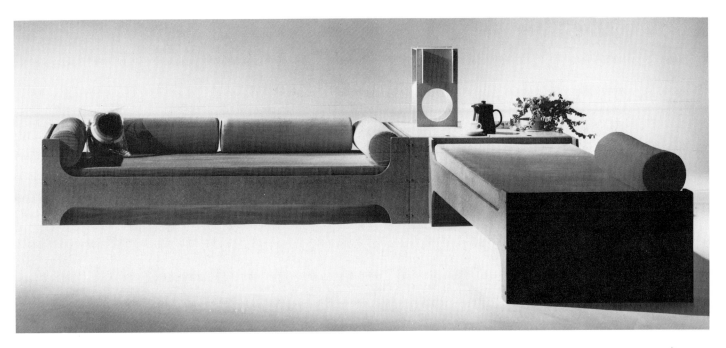

535+536 **Bård Henriksen** 1970 Denmark
Reversible sofa/bed with attached chest
for bedclothes serving as bedside table;
frames of chipboard stained in various
colors
Umkehrbares Sofa/Bett mit angehängtem
Bettzeugkasten, der als Nachttisch oder
Beistelltisch dient; Gestelle aus farbig ge-
beizten Spanplatten
Møbel-Fiske

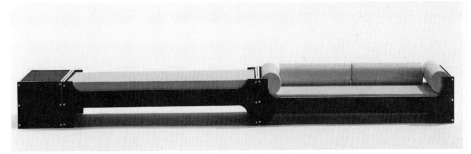

537 **Rolf Heide** 1969 Germany
Stacking beds "3001–3006" (in different sizes) and matching chest "3007" for bedclothes,
made of laminated wood stained in various colors or of chipboard laminated in white
plastic
Stapelbetten »3001–3006« (in verschiedenen Größen) und passender Bettzeugkasten
»3007« aus farbig gebeiztem Schichtholz oder Spanplatten mit weißer Kunststoffbeschichtung
Wohnbedarf Hamburg

538 Fred Ruf c. 1951 Switzerland

Bed of wood with metal legs
Bett aus Holz mit Metallbeinen
Wohnbedarf Zürich

539–541 Hans Gugelot 1955/56 Switzerland

Bed with wooden frames and polyfoam
mattress on metal base; convertible into
twin-beds by pulling out the single
beds
Bett mit Holzrahmen und Schaumstoffma-
tratzen auf Metalluntergestell; kann durch
Herausziehen der Einzelbetten in ein Dop-
pelbett verwandelt werden
Wohnbedarf Zürich

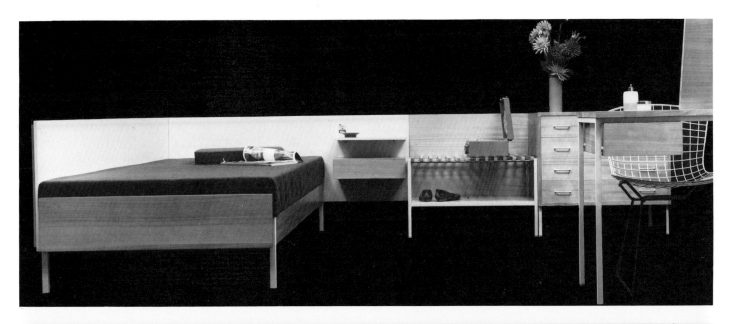

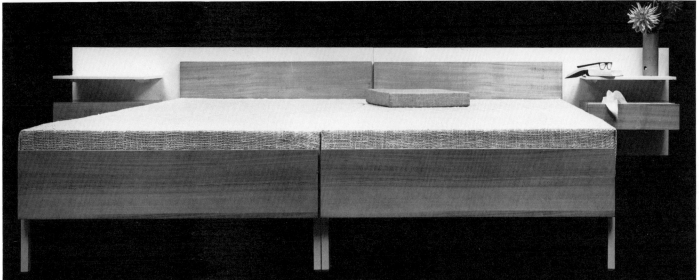

542+543 **Herbert Hirche** 1961 Germany

"MOL" bedroom furniture series of cherrywood, interiors white maple, white lacquered steel frames, headboard of white plastic
Schlafzimmer »MOL« in Kirschbaum, innen weiß Ahorn, Gestelle aus weiß lackiertem Stahl, Kopfbrett weißer Kunststoff
Christian Holzäpfel

544 **Rudolf Lübben** 1963 Germany

Bed with matching case for bedclothes and chest, made of oak and white plastic with aluminum edgings and cubical linking devices
Bett mit passendem Bettzeugkasten und Kommode in Eiche und weißem Kunststoff, mit Rahmen aus Aluminiumprofilen und würfelförmigen Verbindungselementen
Kalderoni

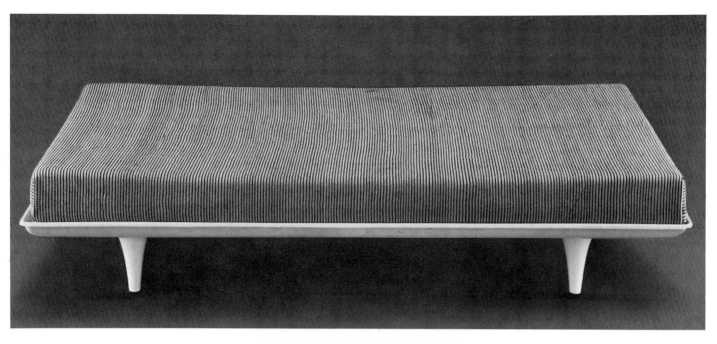

545 + 546 **Andreas Christen** 1960 Switzerland

Stacking bed of polyester
Stapelbett aus Polyester
H.P. Spengler

547 **Wolfgang Feierbach, Manfred Vitt** 1967 Germany

Daybed "fg 2003" with frame of fiberglass and polyfoam mattress
Liege »fg 2003« mit Gestell aus Fiberglas und Schaumstoffmatratze
Wolfgang Feierbach

548 **Anna Castelli Ferrieri, Ignazio Gardella** ▷ 1969 Italy

Bed "4550" with two identical parts of fiberglas-reinforced polyester in red or white, mounted on casters
Bett »4550« mit zwei gleichen Teilen aus glasfaserverstärktem Polyester in rot oder weiß, auf Rollen
Kartell

549 + 550 **Vittorio Parigi, Nani Prina** 1972 ▷ Italy

Bed of vacuum-formed ABS in various colors, metal grill resting on two chests for bedclothes. The chests can be pulled out
Bett mit Metallrost auf zwei ausziehbaren Bettkästen aus durchgefärbtem, vakuumverformtem ABS
Linea B

551 **Ennio Chiggio** 1971 Italy ▷

Bed "Luka" with frame of chrome-plated steel tube
Bett »Luka« mit verchromtem Stahlrohrgestell
Arrmet

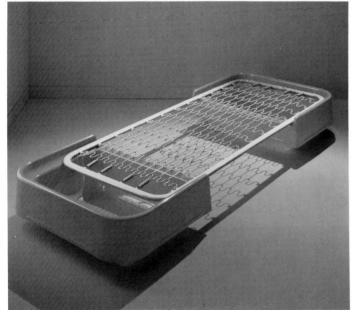

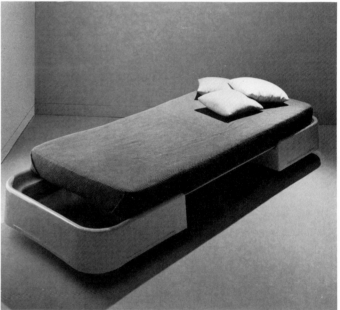

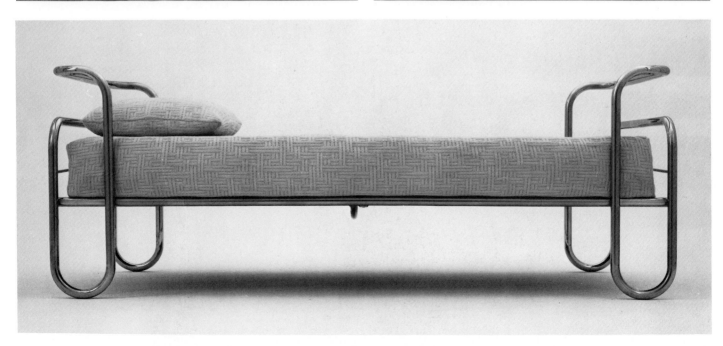

552 **Mogens Koch** 1960 Denmark
Folding table "ambassade" with beech frame, top in teak, legs held by leather straps
Klapptisch »ambassade« mit Gestell aus Buche, Platte in Teak, Beine mit Lederriemen
befestigt
Interna

One should really start the chapter on tables by stating that there are no longer any normal, sensible tables. By this is meant a robust wooden top with a veneered edge on four sturdy legs, connected by a frame. Basically the construction of this piece of furniture is one of the simplest in the world, but this seems to be exactly the reason why it can no longer be applied. Instead, what one comes across are examples that have dimensions that are much too weak, giving the impression of being delicate mixtures made out of squared iron and wood set on extremely thin legs. The only tables that have looked in any way convincing recently have come from the Ikea range. A reason for this shabby treatment may be the fact that there are hardly any separate dining-rooms these days and the "classic" dining tables have been condemned to extinction. Their modest successors seem to suffice for the eating areas in today's living space. If one happens to come across a decent table, one can be sure that it is an old one. It may be that a solid design does not correspond with the requirements and expectations of the furniture trade, which would like to sell furniture that is light and can be taken apart. But a basic model could be developed which, despite its robust dimensions, could be delivered in pieces. The suspicion remains that tables of a normal height have become cinderellas among furniture.

The folding table developed by the Danish designer Mogens Koch (ill. 552) to go with his previous folding chair (ill. 13) is excellent proof that it is worth rethinking a traditional form. This is a resurrection of the classic garden table, although the iron frame has been replaced by a wooden one. The process has not produced a hybrid–that is, a piece of furniture that is neither really simple nor sufficiently convincing as regards its worth–but just the best appearance this kind of table can attain. What is also very sensible about it is the shape of the top, which does without curved edges where this would have been only possible with the help of an extra structure. One feels that one is looking at a traditional model, or at least at a table that can stand as a light-legged, movable substitute for its missing brothers.

The situation as regards coffee tables is better than for dining tables. By far the most intelligent model was designed by Harald Roth in 1958 (ills. 584, 585). It is inspired by the idea that by changing the position of the legs the height can be altered from low to middle height. To do this, all one has to do is raise the top gently and the frames forming the lower structure automatically do the rest. The pieces slide quietly and effortlessly from one position to the other. This ingenious mechanism, which is somewhat mysterious, has such a sensible form that it is always a pleasure to operate it.

The table looks "Japanese", although it is not directly based on a specific model; the effect is produced above all by its inner philosophy. It is, if one can express it like this, the result of meditation on the job of designing a table. Most of the other designers are merely satisfied with creating a table.

Das Kapitel Tische verdient mit der Feststellung eröffnet zu werden, daß es keinen vernünftigen normalen Tisch mehr gibt. Gemeint ist eine stabile Holzplatte mit umleimtem Rand auf vier massiven Beinen, die durch eine Zarge verbunden sind. Im Grunde ist die Konstruktion eines solchen Möbels etwas vom Einfachsten auf der Welt, aber gerade deswegen darf sie offensichtlich nicht mehr angewendet werden. Was man statt dessen antrifft, sind Beispiele, die viel zu schwach dimensioniert sind, zerbrechlich wirkende Mischformen aus Vierkanteisen und Holz auf übertrieben dünnen Beinen. Die einzigen Tische, die in letzter Zeit halbwegs überzeugen konnten, stammten aus dem Programm von Ikea. Ein Grund für diese stiefmütterliche Behandlung mag sein, daß es kaum noch selbständige Speisezimmer gibt und damit die »klassischen« Eßtische zum Aussterben verurteilt sind. Für die Eßecke im Wohnraum scheinen die bescheidenen Nachfolger zu genügen. Trifft man doch einmal auf einen anständigen Tisch, dann kann man sicher sein, daß es ein alter ist. Vielleicht widerspricht eine massive Konstruktion den Anforderungen und Erwartungen des Handels, der gern Zerlegbares und Leichtes verkaufen möchte. Aber ein profundes Modell könnte wohl auch so entwickelt werden, daß es trotz kräftiger Dimensionen in Teilen geliefert werden kann. Der Verdacht bleibt, daß Tische mit einer normalen Höhe zu Stiefkindern unter den Möbeln geworden sind.

Einen schönen Beleg dafür, daß es sich lohnen kann, eine überlieferte Form neu zu überdenken, bildet der Klapptisch, den der dänische Entwerfer Mogens Koch passend zu seinem älteren Faltstuhl (Abb. 13) entwickelt hat (Abb. 552). Der klassische Gartentisch hat hier Wiederauferstehung gefunden, allerdings ist jetzt das eiserne Gestell durch ein hölzernes ersetzt worden. Die Veredelung hat nun aber keinen Zwitter hervorgebracht – also ein Möbel, das weder richtig einfach noch überzeugend kostbar ist –, sondern die wohl beste Gestalt, die diese Art von Tisch erringen kann. Sehr sinnvoll ist an ihm auch die Form der Platte, die dort auf die Rundung verzichtet, wo sie nur mit Hilfe einer zusätzlichen Konstruktion einzuhalten wäre. Man meint, ein Ur-Modell vor sich zu haben, einen Tisch zumindest, der einen leichtfüßigen, mobilen Ersatz bilden kann für die fehlenden stabileren Brüder.

Besser als bei den Eßtischen sieht es bei den Couchtischen aus. Das mit Abstand intelligenteste Modell hatte Harald Roth 1958 entworfen (Abb. 584 + 585). Es lebt von dem Einfall, daß durch Umlegen der Beine die Höhe von niedrig auf halbhoch verwandelt werden kann. Dazu genügt es, die Platte nur leicht anzuheben, die Rahmen, die die Unterkonstruktion bilden, folgen dann von alleine nach. Leise und mühelos gleiten die Teile von einer Lage in die andere. Diese ausgeklügelte Mechanik, die etwas Geheimnisvolles hat, ist so sensibel gestaltet, daß es immer wieder Lust bereitet, sie anzuwenden.

Der Tisch wirkt »japanisch«, obgleich es für ihn kein unmittelbares Vorbild gibt; er tut das vor allem auf Grund seiner inneren Kultur. Er ist, wenn das so ausgedrückt werden darf, das Resultat einer Meditation über die Aufgabe, einen Tisch zu gestalten. Für die meisten anderen Entwerfer genügt es, einfach einen Tisch zu machen.

553 **Børge Mogensen** 1952 Denmark
  Dining table "121" with oak frame, top in teak
  Eßtisch »121« mit Gestell aus Eiche, Platte in Teak
  Søborg Møbelfabrik

554 **Ejner Larsen** c. 1953 Denmark
  Coffee table of wood
  Couchtisch aus Holz
  Willy Beck

555 **Lewis Butler** 1954 USA
  Wooden table
  Tisch aus Holz
  Knoll International

556 **Works Design** 1953 Sweden

Table of wood
Tisch aus Holz
Nordiska Kompaniet

557 **Bruno Mathsson** c. 1952 Sweden

Table with teak top
Tisch mit Platte in Teak
Karl Mathsson

558 **Grete Jalk** 1957 Denmark

Teak table "03" with loose anodized aluminum plate
Teaktisch »03« mit lose eingelegtem,
schwarz eloxiertem Aluminiumtablett
Jeppesen

559 **Ib Kofod-Larsen** 1958 Denmark

Teak table
Tisch in Teak
Sella

560 **Hans J. Wegner** 1951 Denmark

Drop-leaf table of wood
Tisch mit Holzgestell und seitlichen Klappflächen
Andreas Tuch

561 **Basil Spence** c. 1951 Great Britain

Drop-leaf table
Tisch mit Klappfläche

562 **Folke Sundberg** 1952 Sweden

Drop-leaf table with red beech frame and teak top
Tisch mit Klappflächen, Gestell in Buche und Platten in Teak
Tengsjömöbler

564+565 **Michel Mortier** c. 1950 France   ▷

Extension top table of wood
Ausziehtisch aus Holz
Michel Mortier

566+567 **Fred Ruf** c. 1951 Switzerland   ▷

Extension table
Ausziehtisch
Wohnbedarf Zürich

568+569 **Roberto Mango** 1954 Italy   ▷

Extension double top dining table "T 48" of plywood with hinge-
joints, fittings of black lacquered metal
Ausziehtisch »T 48« mit Doppelplatte aus Sperrholz, durch Schar-
niere verbunden; Beschläge aus schwarz lackiertem Metall
Tecno

570+571 **Franco Albini** 1954/55 Italy   ▷

Folding table with wooden frame, top of polished wood with remov-
able woolen cloth cover
Klapptisch mit Holzgestell und polierter Holzplatte, abnehmbarer
Wollstoffüberzug
Carlo Poggi

563 **Arne Jacobsen** 1957 Denmark

Drop-leaf dining table "4606" with beech base and teak top
Tisch »4606« mit Klappfläche, Gestell in Buche, Platte in Teak
Fritz Hansen

575+576 Carl Auböck 1960 Austria

Stacking table in beech, grey plastic-laminated top
Stapeltisch in Buche, Platte mit grauer Kunststoffbeschichtung
Portois & Fix

577 Finn Juhl 1958 Denmark

Tables "533/531/536" of various sizes with one or two tops in teak.
Tables can be combined
Tische »533/531/536« in verschiedenen Größen mit einer oder zwei
Platten in Teak. Die Tische können beliebig aneinandergereiht wer-
den
France & Søn

578 Marco Zanuso 1974 Italy

Table "Forrestal" with top of solid ash or bay oak bands, glued
together at high frequency; removable legs
Tisch »Forrestal« mit Platte aus massiven Eschen- oder Steineiche-
leisten, mit Hochfrequenz verleimt; Beine abnehmbar
Zanotta

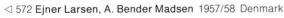

◁ **572 Ejner Larsen, A. Bender Madsen** 1957/58 Denmark

Extension table "1631" with teak top
Ausziehtisch »1631« mit Teakplatte
Næstved

◁ **573 Ejner Larsen, A. Bender Madsen** 1959 Denmark

Dining table "1636" in teak with one extension leaf
Eßtisch »1636« in Teak mit einer Ausziehplatte
Næstved

◁ **574 Ejner Larsen, A. Bender Madsen** 1962 Denmark

Dining table "1736" in oak or teak with extension leaf
Eßtisch »1736« in Eiche oder Teak mit Verlängerungsplatte
Næstved

579 + 580 **Mirko Romih** 1958 Yugoslavia

  Folding table in beech
  Klapptisch in Buche
  Stol Kamnik

581 + 582 **Franco Albini** 1954/55 Italy

  Folding table with wooden frame, top of polished wood with removable woolen cloth cover
  Klapptisch mit Holzgestell und polierter Holzplatte, abnehmbarer Wollstoffüberzug
  Carlo Poggi

583 **Jonathan De Pas, Donato D'Urbino, Paolo Lomazzi** 1976 Italy

  Folding outdoor table "Merenda" of solid bay oak
  Klappbarer Gartentisch »Merenda« aus massiver Steineiche
  Zanotta

584+585 **Harald Roth** 1958 Germany

"Mandarin" table in teak, height adjustable
Tisch »Mandarin« in Teak, Höhe verstellbar
Casa

586 **Franco Albini** c. 1951 Italy

Folding dining table of wood
Klappbarer Eßtisch aus Holz
La Rinascente

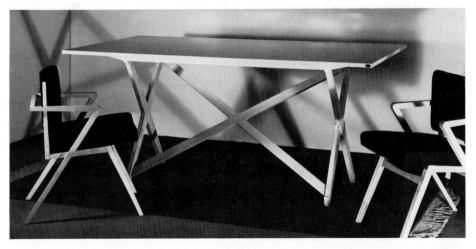

587 **Achille and Pier Giacomo Castiglioni**
1968 Italy

Working desk "Leonardo" with top of
white plastic laminate or glass
Arbeitstisch »Leonardo«, Platte mit weißer
Kunststoffbeschichtung oder aus Glas
Zanotta

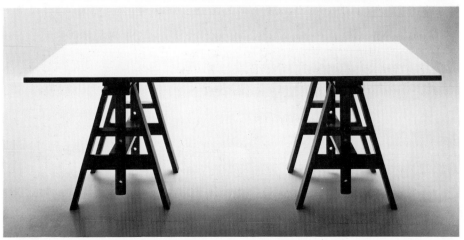

588 **Eduard Ludwig** c. 1951 Germany

Demountable shelves and coffee table of wood
Regal und Couchtisch aus Holz, zerlegbar
Domus

589 **Vico Magistretti** c. 1952 Italy

Coffee table with top in birch plywood and mahogany legs
Couchtisch mit Platte aus Birkensperrholz und Beinen aus Mahagoni

590 **Angelo Mangiarotti, Bruno Morassutti** 1955 Italy

Small tables and stools of molded plywood elements in birch with glass tops or cushions
Tischchen und Hocker aus verformten Sperrholzelementen in Birke mit Glasplatten oder Sitzkissen
Fratelli Frigerio

591 Hans Bellmann c. 1950 Switzerland

Demountable table of wood
Zerlegbarer Holztisch
Wohnbedarf Zürich

592 Jürg Bally 1952/57 Switzerland

Table with black lacquered metal base, adjustable height, black
plastic top with maple edges
Tisch mit schwarz lackiertem Metallgestell, höhenverstellbar,
schwarze Tischplatte mit Ahornkanten

593 Bruno Mathsson c. 1951 Sweden

Coffee table with base of bentwood and teak veneer top
Couchtisch mit Gestell aus Bugholz und Platte mit Teakfurnier
Larö Mathsson

594 Max Bill 1949/50 Switzerland

Table with three legs
Dreibeiniger Tisch
Wohnbedarf Zürich

595 **Ico Parisi** c. 1953 Italy

Table with steel tube frame and wooden top
Tisch mit Stahlrohrgestell und Holzplatte
Bega

596 **Florence Knoll** 1956 USA

Table with chrome-plated metal base and crystal glass top
Tisch mit verchromtem Metallgestell und Kristallglasplatte
Knoll International

597 **Alberto Rosselli** c. 1951 Italy

Table with steel tube frame and crystal glass top
Tisch mit Stahlrohrgestell und Kristallglasplatte

598 **Robin Day** c. 1952 Great Britain

Table with steel frame and plywood top
Tisch mit Stahlgestell und Sperrholzplatte
Hille

599 Florence Knoll 1961 USA

Conference and dining table "2480/81" with oval top of teak or rosewood and base of
chrome-plated steel
Konferenz- und Eßtisch »2480/81« mit ovaler Platte aus Teak oder Palisander; Gestell aus
verchromtem Stahl
Knoll International

600 Giancarlo Piretti 1974 Italy

"SBC" component system for tables. The
interchangeable components fit together
to provide unlimited possibilities for a vast
range of tables. Bases: columns of
chrome-plated steel tube, spider attache-
ments of die-cast metal enamelled white,
assembly rods of steel, blades available in
three lengths; tops in plastic laminate, walnut or rosewood veneer, treated with self-
hardening polyester resins (see also ill.
618)
»SBC« Tisch-Baukastensystem. Die aus-
tauschbaren Elemente ermöglichen zahlreiche Tischvariationen. Untergestell mit
Säule aus verchromtem Stahlrohr, Platten-
kreuz aus Leichtmetall-Druckguß mit weißer Kunststoffbeschichtung, Gewinde-
stange aus Stahl, Füße werden in drei Längen geliefert; Platten mit Kunststoffbeschichtung, in Nußbaum oder Palisander
mit mattem Schutzbelag aus farblosem Polyester (siehe auch Abb. 618)
Anonima Castelli

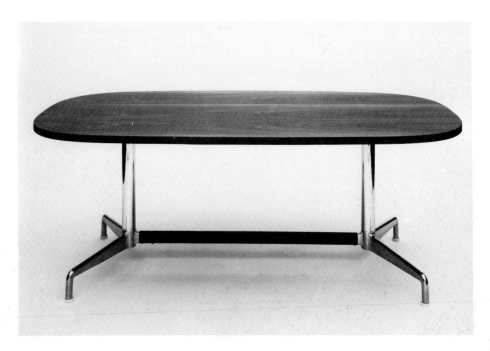

601 **Poul Kjaerholm** 1957 Denmark

Dining table "51" with frame of chrome-plated steel and wooden top
Eßtisch »51« mit Gestell aus verchromtem Stahl und Holzplatte
E. Kold Christensen

602+603 **Poul Kjaerholm** 1967 Denmark

Table with chrome-plated steel base and ash top
Tisch mit Gestell aus verchromtem Stahl und Platte in Esche
E. Kold Christensen

604 **Alfred Altherr** c. 1958 Switzerland

"Team" dining table with base of square tubular steel and plastic top
Eßtisch »Team« mit Gestell aus Vierkantstahlrohr und Kunststoff-platte
K.H. Frei

605 **Hans Eichenberger** 1956 Switzerland

Table with chrome-plated tubular steel base and plastic-laminated top
Tisch mit Gestell aus verchromtem Stahlrohr und kunststoff-beschichteter Platte
Teo Jakob

606 William Katavolos, Ross Littell, Douglas Kelley c. 1952 USA

Table with legs of chrome-plated steel tubes and marble top
Tisch mit Beinen aus verchromtem Stahlrohr und Marmorplatte
Laverne

607 J.M. Thomas 1959 Germany

Table "WR 194" with collapsible metal pedestal, adjustable height; top in various woods
Tisch »WR 194« mit zerlegbarem, höhenverstellbarem Säulen-Metallgestell; Platte in verschiedenen Edelhölzern
Wilhelm Renz

608 + 609 J.M. Thomas 1962 Germany

Double pedestal, height-adjustable table "WR 247" with charcoal lacquered steel tube columns and chrome-plated legs. Folding/sliding top of natural walnut, teak or rosewood
Zweisäulen-Verstelltisch »WR 247« mit Stahlrohrsäulen in Anthrazit und verchromten Füßen. Quer verschiebbare Klapp-Platte in Nußbaum natur, Teak oder Palisander
Wilhelm Renz

610 Hugh Acton 1962 USA

Round or oval table with chrome-plated steel base and walnut top
Runder oder ovaler Tisch mit Gestell aus verchromtem Stahl und Platte in Nußbaum
Hugh Acton

611 Knud Joos 1958 Denmark

Table "601" with collapsible chrome-plated steel frame, teak or rosewood top
Tisch »601« mit zerlegbarem Gestell aus verchromtem Stahl, Teak- oder Palisanderplatte
Jason

612 Jørgen Høj 1960 Denmark

Circular dining table "53" with three legs of mat finished anodized aluminum, top of laminated wood veneered in oak or rosewood
Runder Eßtisch »53« mit drei Beinen aus mattgeschliffenem, eloxiertem Aluminium; Platte aus Schichtholz, mit Eiche oder Palisander furniert
Niels Vitsøe

613 Arne Jacobsen 1962 Denmark

Table "3609" with aluminum base and top of teak
Tisch »3609« mit Gestell aus Aluminium und Platte in Teak
Fritz Hansen

614 Osvaldo Borsani 1964 Italy

Circular dining table "T 69" with top of teak, rosewood, or other woods. Base of nickel-plated steel
Runder Eßtisch »T 69« mit Platte in Teak, Palisander oder anderen Edelhölzern. Sockel aus vernickeltem Stahl
Tecno

610	
611	612
613	614

615	616 ▷
	617
618	619

615+616 Eugenio Gerli, Mario Cristiani 1961 Italy

Dining table "T92" with black lacquered or nickel-plated metal base. For extension the square wooden top is turned and the triangular drop-leaves are unfolded
Eßtisch »T92« mit schwarz lackiertem oder vernickeltem Gestell. Um den Tisch zu vergrößern, wird die quadratische Holzplatte gedreht und die dreieckigen Zusatzplatten nach außen geklappt
Tecno

617 Osvaldo Borsani 1958 Italy

Table "T41" with lacquered metal base, height adjustable, wooden top
Tisch »T41« mit höhenverstellbarem Gestell aus lackiertem Metall, Platte aus Holz
Tecno

618 Giancarlo Piretti 1974 Italy

"SBC" component system for tables (see ill. 600), round table
»SBC«-Tisch-Baukastensystem (vgl. Abb. 600), runder Tisch
Anonima Castelli

619 Works Design 1978 Italy

Folding table "Plano" with round or square top of rigid polyurethane in various colors, base of polished die-cast aluminum alloy with adjustable nylon glides. A patented locking mechanism ensures stability when table is erected, special hinges allow the table sections to be folded together
Klapptisch »Plano« mit runder oder quadratischer Platte aus Hart-Polyurethan in verschiedenen Farben, Gestell aus rostfreiem poliertem Aluminium-Druckguß mit verstellbaren Nylon-Gleitern. Ein patentierter Mechanismus sichert die Stabilität der Plattensegmente im ausgeklappten Zustand, spezielle Scharniergelenke ermöglichen das Zusammenklappen
Anonima Castelli

620+621 Robert Haussmann 1956 Switzerland

Drop-leaf dining table with base of black lacquered steel, top with linoleum cover
Eßtisch mit aufklappbarer Platte, linoleumbeschichtet; Gestell aus schwarz lackiertem Vierkantstahlrohr
Haussmann & Haussmann

625 Uli Wieser 1959 Switzerland ▷

Dining table "WI 1035" with extensible metal base and three-part walnut top. The central leaf can be stored in the frame
Eßtisch »WI 1035« mit ausziehbarem Metallgestell und dreiteiliger Platte in Nußbaum. Das mittlere Plattenstück kann zur Aufbewahrung in das Untergestell eingelegt werden
Bofinger

622+623 Fred Ruf c. 1952 Switzerland

Extension table with iron frame, top in maple with linoleum cover
Ausziehtisch mit Eisengestell, Platte in Ahorn mit Linoleumbeschichtung
Wohnbedarf Zürich

624 Ernst Kirchhoff 1959 Germany

Extension table "T-60" with square tubular steel frame, top in wood or plastic
Ausziehtisch »T-60« mit Gestell aus Vierkantstahlrohr und Platte in Holz oder Kunststoff
Casa

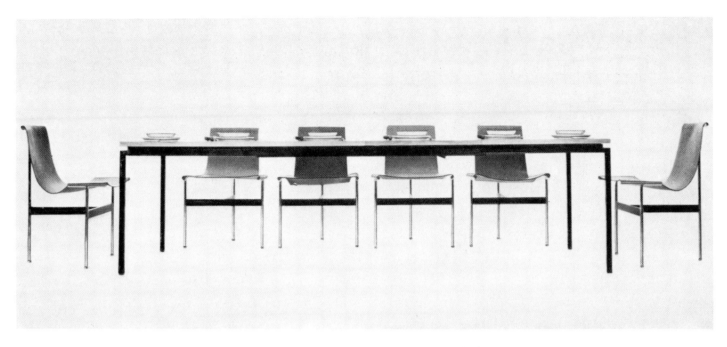

626 + 627 Jørgen Høj 1960/63 Denmark   ▷

Circular table "54" with four legs and cross-bar of mat finished
anodized aluminum, top veneered in oak or rosewood on both
sides. The table can be extended by four ring sections with light
frame constructions, grey plastic laminate and edging of oak or
rosewood
Runder Tisch »54« mit vier Beinen und Kreuzzarge aus mattgeschliffenem, eloxiertem Aluminium; Platte beidseitig mit Eichen-
oder Palisanderfurnier. Der Tisch kann vergrößert werden durch
Anschluß von vier viertelkreisförmigen Erweiterungsringen in leich-
ter Rahmenkonstruktion mit grauer Kunststoffbeschichtung und
Kanten mit Eiche oder Palisander furniert
Niels Vitsøe

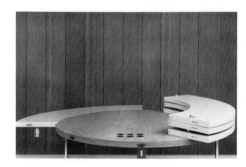

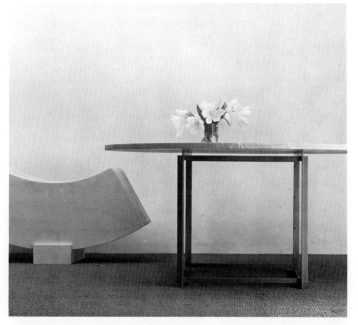

628 + 629 Poul Kjaerholm 1963 Denmark   ▷

Table "54" with base of satin finished chrome-plated steel and
top of marble. Can be extended by attaching six ring sections of
solid maple
Tisch »54« mit Gestell aus matt verchromtem Stahl und Platte aus
Marmor. Kann durch Anfügen von sechs Ringelementen aus massi-
vem Ahorn vergrößert werden
E. Kold Christensen

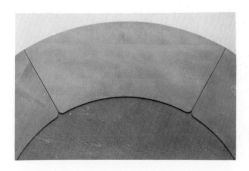

630 + 631 Wolfram Elwert 1976 Germany

Table with base of chrome-plated tubular steel, twin top of black or white oak veneer finish or white formica, height adjustable

Tisch mit Untergestell aus verchromtem Stahlrohr, Doppelplatte aus furnierter Eiche, schwarz oder weiß, oder aus weißem Resopal, höhenverstellbar
Tecta Möbel

632 Joe Colombo 1967 Italy

Game and dining table "Poker" with twin top laminated in plastic, height-adjustable legs of chrome-plated steel. A green cloth can be snapped to underside of upper top when needed. At corners, four small shelves with stainless steel ashtrays can be pulled out

Spiel- und Eßtisch »Poker« mit kunststoffbeschichteter Doppelplatte und höhenverstellbaren Beinen aus verchromtem Stahlrohr. Zum Spielen wird ein grünes Tuch mit Druckknöpfen an der Unterseite der oberen Platte befestigt. An den Ecken lassen sich vier Platten mit Aschenbechern aus rostfreiem Stahl herausdrehen
Zanotta

633 Carlo Viganò 1968 Italy

Low table of lacquered wood with sliding tops, flap doors, drawers, and recesses that can be used for various purposes
Niedriger Tisch aus lackiertem Holz mit Schiebeplatten, Klapptüren, Schubladen und Nischen, die für viele Zwecke eingerichtet werden können
Cesare Augusto Nava

634 Angelo Mangiarotti 1967/68 Italy

Dining table "Idilor" with four attached containers on casters fitting
under the central top when not in use. Made of rosewood with
table top of green marble or white granite
Eßtisch »Idilor« mit vier angehängten Behältern, die auf Rollen
laufen und nach Gebrauch unter die Tischplatte geschoben werden können. Aus Palisander, Tischplatte aus grünem Marmor oder
weißem Granit
Lorenzon

635 Roberto Pamio, Renato Toso, Noti Massari 1967 Italy

Storage furniture "Lara B/G/LS" of wood, partly laminated in white
plastic, with revolving compartments. "Lara" consists of two parts
of which one is fixed and the other is mounted on casters, with
a built-in extensible table top. Various variations for living and dining area
Kastenmöbel »Lara B/G/LS« aus Holz, zum Teil weiß kunststoffbeschichtet, mit ausschwenkbaren Eckschränken. »Lara« besteht aus
einem festen und einem auf Rollen laufenden Kastenelement mit
eingebauter ausziehbarer Tischplatte. In verschiedenen Ausführungen für den Wohn- und Eßbereich
Stilwood

636 **Isamu Noguchi** 1946 USA

Coffee table with demountable wood base in walnut and glass
top
Couchtisch mit Glasplatte und zerlegbarem Gestell in Nußbaum
Herman Miller

637 **Herbert Hirche** 1953 Germany

Coffee table with chrome-plated steel tube base and glass top
Couchtisch mit verchromtem Stahlrohrgestell und Glasplatte
Stuttgarter Akademie-Werkstätten

638 **Jørgen Høj** 1954 Denmark

Table with steel base and glass top
Tisch mit Stahlgestell und Glasplatte
Jørgen Høj

639 **Nicos Zographos** 1960 USA

Table "406" with frame of polished stainless steel and glass top
Tisch »406« mit Gestell aus poliertem, rostfreiem Stahl und Glasplatte
Albano

640 **Nicos Zographos** 1960 USA

Low table "TA 35 G" with frame of polished stainless steel and glass top
Niedriger Tisch »TA 35 G« mit Gestell aus poliertem, rostfreiem Stahl und Glasplatte
Zographos Designs

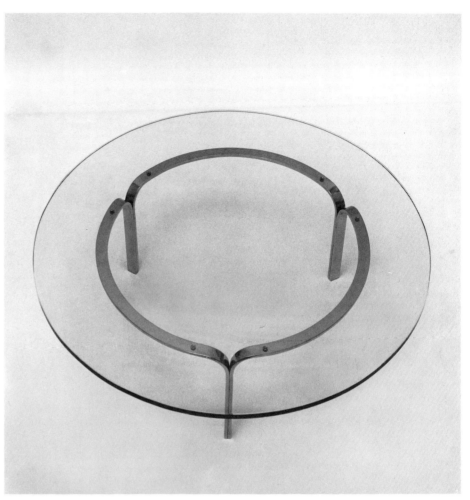

641 **William Armbruster** 1937 USA
  Coffee table with steel frame and glass top
  Couchtisch mit Stahlgestell und Glasplatte
  Edgewood

642 **William Armbruster** 1937 USA
  Small table with steel base and glass top
  Tischchen mit Stahlgestell und Glasplatte
  Edgewood

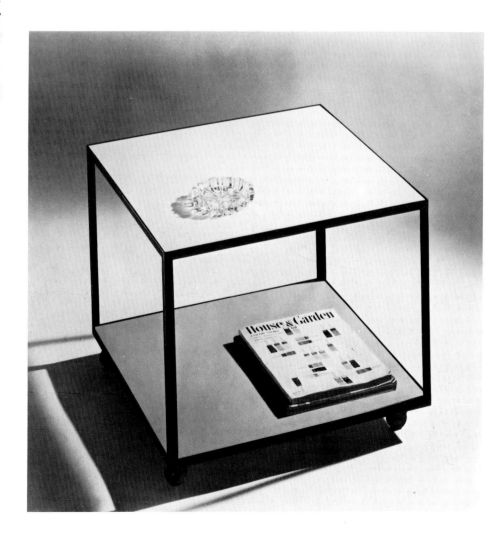

644 **Herbert Hirche** 1959 Germany
  Tea trolley with square tubular steel frame
  and tops in wood or plastic
  Teewagen mit Rahmen aus Vierkantstahlrohr und Platten aus Holz oder Kunststoff
  Christian Holzäpfel

643 **George Nelson** c. 1951 USA
  Tea trolley with angle-iron frame and plas-
  tic tops
  Servierwagen mit Gestell aus Winkeleisen
  und Kunststoffplatten
  Herman Miller

645 **Florence Knoll** 1953 USA

Tables with iron bases and tops of wood
Tische mit Eisengestellen und Holzplatten
Knoll International

646 **George Nelson** c. 1951 USA

Small table with angle-iron frame and plas-
tic top
Tischchen mit Gestell aus Winkeleisen und
Kunststoffplatte
Herman Miller

647 **George Nelson** c. 1951 USA

Coffee table with angle-iron frame and
plastic top
Couchtisch mit Gestell aus Winkeleisen
und Kunststoffplatte
Herman Miller

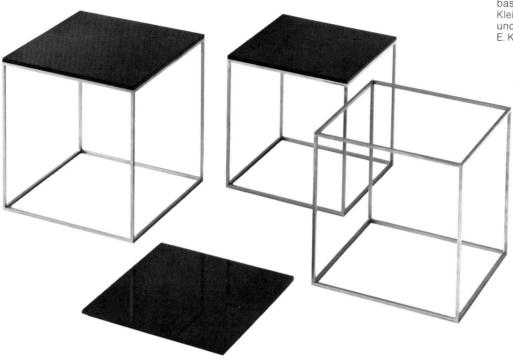

648 Poul Kjaerholm 1957 Denmark

Small stacking tables "71" with metal
bases and plastic tops
Kleine Stapeltische »71« mit Metallgestellen
und Kunststoffplatten
E. Kold Christensen

649 Team Form AG 1963 Switzerland

Nesting tables "K1" with frames of square
tubular steel and inserted tops of crystal
glass or marble
Satztische »K1« mit Gestellen aus Vierkantstahlrohr und eingelegter Kristallglas-
oder Marmorplatte
Ronald Schmitt Tische

650 Works Design 1972 Germany

Nesting tables "121" with frames of
chrome-plated steel tubes and tops of
plastic
Satztische »121« mit Gestellen aus verchromtem Stahlrohr und Platten aus
Kunststoff
Läsko

653 Gae Aulenti 1971 Italy   ▷

Series of dinner and coffee tables "Festo"
with frames of anodized aluminum and
joints of injection-molded aluminum, tops
of crystal glass or plastic laminate
Eß- und Couchtischprogramm »Festo« mit
Gestellen aus eloxiertem Aluminium sowie
Verbindungsstücken aus formgespritztem
Aluminium. Platten aus Kristallglas oder
mit Kunststoffbeschichtung
Zanotta

651 **Poul Kjaerholm** 1956 Denmark

Table "61" with steel base and glass top
Tisch »61« mit Stahlgestell und Glasplatte
E. Kold Christensen

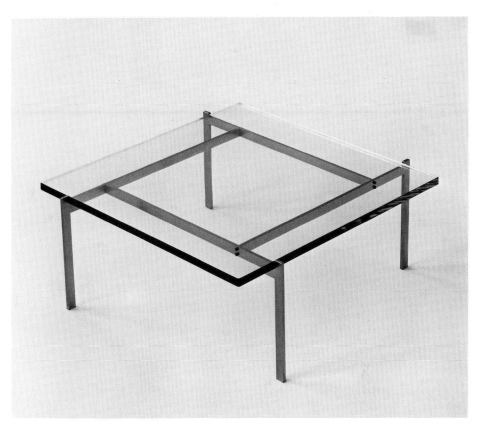

652 **Jørgen Høj** 1959 Denmark

Coffee table "157" with legs of mat finished
anodized aluminum; top of laminated
wood veneered in oak or rosewood on
both sides
Couchtisch »157« mit Beinen aus mattgeschliffenem, eloxiertem Aluminium; Platte
aus Schichtholz, beidseitig mit Eiche oder
Palisander furniert
Niels Vitsøe

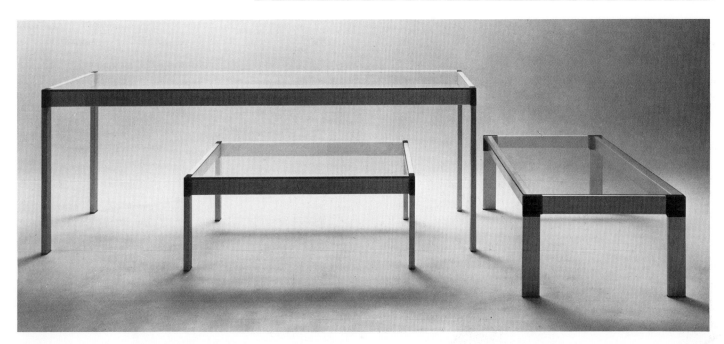

654 **Nardin & Radoczy** c. 1951 USA
Coffee table "TL-1" of solid ash or mahogany with legs of chrome-plated steel tubes
Couchtisch »TL-1« aus Esche oder Mahagoni massiv mit Beinen aus verchromtem Stahlrohr
Habitat

655 **Florence Knoll** 1955 USA
Table with chrome-plated steel base, birch or walnut top
Tisch mit Gestell aus verchromtem Stahlrohr, Platte in Birke oder Nußbaum
Knoll International

656 **Jørgen Høj** 1962 Denmark
Circular coffee table "154" with legs of mat finished anodized aluminum; top of laminated wood veneered in oak or rosewood on both sides
Runder Couchtisch »154« mit Beinen aus mattgeschliffenem, eloxiertem Aluminium; Platte aus Schichtholz, beidseitig mit Eiche oder Palisander furniert
Niels Vitsøe

658 **George Nelson** c. 1953 USA ▷
Coffee table "5452" with base of cast aluminum enamelled in black or white with plastic top and natural birch edgings
Couchtisch »5452« mit Gestell aus weiß oder schwarz emailliertem Aluminiumguß, Platte aus Kunststoff mit Kanten in Birke
Herman Miller

△ 657 **Eero Saarinen** 1957 USA

Table series with single pedestals of aluminum and marble
or plastic tops
Tischprogramm mit Säulenfüßen aus Aluminium und Mar-
mor- oder Kunststoffplatten
Knoll International

▽ 659 **Robert Haussmann, Fred Hochstrasser** 1960 Switzerland

Tables "T 304" with pedestals of anodized aluminum and wooden or mar-
ble tops
Tische »T 304« mit Säulenfuß aus eloxiertem Aluminium und Holz- oder
Marmorplatten
Hans Kaufeld

660 Vico Magistretti 1969 Italy

Demountable table "Stadio" of reinforced resin in various colors and sizes
Zerlegbarer Tisch »Stadio« aus verstärktem Kunstharz in verschiedenen Größen und Farben
Artemide

661 Helmut Bätzner 1969 Germany

Stacking table of fiberglass-reinforced polyester, designed to match "Bofinger" chair (see ill. 386 + 387)
Stapeltisch aus glasfaserverstärktem Polyester, passend zum »Bofinger-Stuhl« entworfen (vgl. Abb. 386 + 387)
Menzolit-Werke

662 Giovanni Offredi 1968 Italy

"Gruppo Carola" including cupboard of molded plywood in lacquer finish, and matching demountable table composed of three identical parts
»Gruppo Carola« aus verformtem, farbig lackiertem Sperrholz mit Geschirrschrank und zerlegbarem, aus drei gleichen Teilen zusammengesetztem Tisch
Alberto Bazzani

663 Vico Magistretti 1967 Italy

Square occasional table "Demetrio 70" of
fiberglass-reinforced polyester
Quadratischer Beistelltisch »Demetrio 70«
aus glasfaserverstärktem Polyester
Artemide

664 + 665 Olaf von Bohr 1971 Italy

Collpasible tables in various sizes and
heights. Frame of four identical parts in
ABS resin, simply put together and
screwed. Top of plastic laminate in various
colors
Zerlegbare Tische in verschiedenen Größen und Höhen. Gestell aus vier gleichen
Teilen aus ABS-Kunstharz, zusammengesteckt und verschraubt. Platte farbig
kunststoffbeschichtet
Kartell

666 John Mascheroni 1968 USA

Stacking tables "422/18" of acrylic pla-
stic
Stapeltische »422/18« aus Acrylglas
John Mascheroni

667 Wolfgang Feierbach 1965 Germany

Side tables "fg 2001" of fiberglass in various sizes, shapes, and colors; some with casters
Beistelltische »fg 2001« aus Fiberglas in verschiedenen Größen, Formen und Farben; teilweise mit Rollen
Wolfgang Feierbach

668 + 669 Rodolfo Bonetto 1969 Italy

Plastic table "700 Quattroquarti" in four units which can be stacked and grouped as desired
Kunststofftisch »700 Quattroquarti« mit vier Elementen, die beliebig gestapelt und gruppiert werden können
Bernini

670 Giotto Stoppino 1969 Italy

Stacking table "Scagno" of injection-molded plastic. Tables may also be arranged horizontally
Stapeltisch »Scagno« aus Kunststoff, im Spritzgußverfahren hergestellt. Die Tische können auch horizontal aufgereiht werden
Fiarm

672 Mario Bellini 1966 Italy

Stacking tables "I quattro gatti" of plastic
Kunststoff-Beistelltische »I quattro gatti«
B & B Italia

671 Kenneth Brozen 1968 USA

"Highlight" magazine table of plexiglass
with joints of chrome-plates steel
Zeitschriftentisch »Highlight« aus Plexiglas mit Verbindungsstücken aus verchromtem Stahl
Robinson, Lewis & Rubin

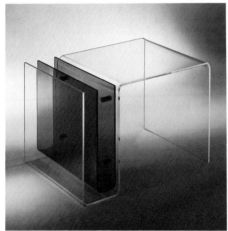

673 Alberto Rosselli 1972 Italy

Open container elements in plastic on casters. Can be put together to various
heights with corner elements of different
lengths and built-in slots
Offene Rollbehälter aus Kunststoff. Durch
verschieden lange Stützen mit Ausparun-
gen zum Einhängen der Fachböden zu beliebiger Höhe zusammenzustecken
Kartell

674 **Verner Panton** 1965 Denmark

"Barboy" of molded wood on casters in lacquer finish
»Barboy« aus Formholz, farbig lackiert, auf Rollen laufend
Bisterfeld & Weiss

674	
675	676
677	678

675 **Emma Schweinberger-Gismondi** 1967 Italy

Small cylindrical table "Giano" and "Giano Vano" (with or without
recess) of fiberglass-reinforced polyester
Kleiner runder Tisch »Giano« und »Giano Vano« (mit oder ohne
Nische) aus glasfaserverstärktem Polyester
Artemide

676 **Chiara Briganti** 1968 Italy

Small cylindrical table on casters with storing space and two drawers; molded plywood lacquered white
Kleiner runder Tisch auf Rollen mit offenem Fach und zwei Schubladen; verformtes, weiß lackiertes Sperrholz
Lorenzon

679+680 Verner Panton 1965 Denmark

"Party Set" of molded wood, to be used
as stools (with loose cushions), occasional
tables, and bar. Being of varying diameter,
tables stack inside each other
»Party Set« aus Formholz, als Hocker (mit
Sitzkissen), Beistelltische oder Bar zu verwenden. Der Satz ist ineinander stapelbar
Bisterfeld & Weiss

681 Anna Castelli Ferrieri 1970 Italy

Range of cylindrical plastic containers
"4953–4956" in two sizes, with or without
sliding doors and casters; can be combined as desired
Runde, beliebig kombinierbare Kunststoff-
behälter »4953–4956« in zwei Größen mit
oder ohne Schiebetüren und Laufrollen
Kartell

682 Eugenio Gerli 1967 Italy

Bar "Jamaica B.106" on casters in veneered wood or lacquer finish
Bar »Jamaica B.106« auf Rollen in furniertem Holz oder lackiert
Tecno

◁ **677+678 Sergio Mazza** 1968 Italy

Bar "Bacco" of fiberglass-reinforced polyester
Bar »Bacco« aus glasfaserverstärktem Polyester
Artemide

683 **Works Design** c. 1952 Switzerland
  Desk with steel tube legs and separate cabinet units on casters
  Schreibtisch mit Stahlrohrbeinen und separatem Kastenelement auf Rollen
  Wohnbedarf Zürich

Most office furniture today is made of metal. This form has a long tradition, as can be seen from the fact that filing cabinets at the turn of the century were usually made of this material. If one views the development in the past thirty years, the most convincing examples are those that operate most clearly within this tradition and whose merit is contained in their robust inconspicuousness. This is especially true of the office furniture of Pohlschröder (ills. 727–731). When one comes across these articles of furniture in places where they are still being used, in the offices of the publisher Hatje, for instance, one feels that the correct form for office furniture has been found. These objects were, of course, never beautiful in the proper meaning of the word, just always sensible and therefore a pleasure to look at. One had the impression that they had been developed by a well trained expert but not especially by a designer. At the time they were planned they could manage without any "styling", which is often somewhat superfluous in objects that have to serve a quite ordinary purpose. Subsequent developments always seemed rather ambitious. They had overtones of elegance that were unsuitable for the way they were to be used.

The system designed by the group of architects B.B.P.R. and produced by Olivetti is an exception (ills. 734–738). The details were styled so precisely that an impression of great functionality was produced. A good deal of thought went into the distinct structure of the furniture. It was easy to see how the individual elements could be put together in different ways. At first sight they appeared old-fashioned but the special intelligence of this Italian system could be seen in the conscious recourse to traditional details (in the formation of the legs, for example).

Just as convincing was George Nelson's idea in 1964 of resurrecting the old standing-desk (ills. 743–745). This object, together with the characteristic detail of the roll-top, served to evoke the atmosphere of a "classic" office. However, it could not quite resolve the problem that the object's styling, although excellent, seemed overdone in relation to the simple purpose it was supposed to serve.

In the category of more straightforward office furniture, the table with its movable box elements that Wohnbedarf in Zürich produced (ill. 683) is still very convincing today. The principle behind it was often used afterwards with variations. One cannot help wondering why it was necessary to modify this uniquely successful design. In comparison with its maturity, all the others appear conspicuously affected. In this design the elements are co-ordinated excellently without any inset or projecting parts; the composition of the materials is extremely sensitive: chrome-plated steel tubes, light wood and black linoleum. A perfect piece of furniture of great precision; an ingenious piece of furniture.

Büromöbel sind heute vorwiegend aus Blech, und in dieser Form haben sie schon eine längere Tradition. So gab es bereits um die Jahrhundertwende vorzügliche Karteischränke aus diesem Material. Sieht man die Entwicklung der letzten dreißig Jahre durch, dann wirken am überzeugendsten jene Beispiele, die sich am deutlichsten in dieser Tradition bewegen und ihren Vorzug mehr in einer soliden Unauffälligkeit besaßen. Das gilt besonders für die Büromöbelserie von Pohlschröder (Abb. 727–731). Begegnet man heute diesen Dingen dort, wo sie noch in Benutzung sind, etwa in den Räumen des Verlegers Hatje, dann hat man das Gefühl, daß hier die richtige Form für Büromöbel überhaupt gefunden worden ist. Diese Gegenstände waren wohl nie im eigentlichen Sinne schön, aber stets sinnvoll und damit auch wohltuend für das Auge. Es waren Möbel, bei denen man den Eindruck hatte, daß sie von einem versierten Praktiker entwickelt worden waren, aber nicht unbedingt von einem Designer. Sie konnten seinerzeit, als sie entworfen wurden, noch ohne jene »Gestaltung« auskommen, die bei Dingen, die recht profanen Zwecken dienen müssen, oft eine störendes Zuviel ist. In ihrer Nachfolge wirkten spätere Entwicklungen immer etwas unglücklich ehrgeizig, sie wiesen eine Halb-Eleganz auf, die für die Art ihrer Benutzung unpassend war.

Eine Ausnahme bildete das System, das die Architektengruppe B.B.P.R. entworfen und das von Olivetti vertrieben worden war (Abb. 734–738). Die Einzelheiten waren hier so prägnant gestaltet, daß der Eindruck einer besonders hohen Funktionalität entstand. Die deutliche Gliederung der Möbel wirkte sehr überlegt, man begriff schnell, wie sie aus Einzelteilen wechselnd zusammengesetzt werden konnten. Ihr Aussehen war im ersten Moment etwas altmodisch, aber gerade in diesem bewußten Rückgriff auf traditionelle Details (zum Beispiel bei der Ausbildung der Füße) zeigten sich die besonderen Vorzüge dieses italienischen Systems.

Ähnlich überzeugend war 1964 der Einfall von George Nelson, das alte Stehpult wieder aufleben zu lassen (Abb. 743–745). Zusammen mit der charakteristischen Einzelheit des Rollverschlusses war dieser Gegenstand geeignet, eine »klassische« Büroatmosphäre zu erwecken. Nicht ganz aufzulösen war dabei jedoch der Umstand, daß dieser Gegenstand eine Gestaltung erfahren hatte, die zwar hervorragend war, aber dennoch überzogen erschien für den einfachen Zweck, dem sie dienen sollte.

In der Kategorie der etwas einfacheren Arbeitsmöbel wirkt heute immer noch sehr überzeugend der Tisch mit den lose untergeschobenen Kastenelementen, den die Firma Wohnbedarf in Zürich herausgebracht hat (Abb. 683). Sein Prinzip ist später oft variiert worden, aber dann stets um Grade weniger gut. Man fragt sich unwillkürlich, wozu es nötig war, diese einmalig gelungene Gestaltung überhaupt noch abzuwandeln. Neben dieser ausgereiften Leistung wirkten alle anderen auffallend geziert. Die Abstimmung der Elemente aufeinander ist hier sehr sinnvoll gehandhabt worden, ohne störende Vor- und Rücksprünge; die Materialzusammensetzung ist äußerst sensibel: verchromtes Stahlrohr, helles Holz und schwarzes Linoleum. Ein fertiges Möbel von großer Bestimmtheit, ein wirklich kluges Möbel.

690 **Alfred Altherr** c. 1954 Switzerland

Desk in white maple, sliding doors and
pulls with dark veneer
Schreibtisch in weißem Ahorn, Schiebetüren und Griffe mit Edelholzfurnier
K.H. Frei

691 + 692 **Alberto Rosselli** c. 1953 Italy

Desk of molded wood with plastic lami-
nate, glass top
Schreibtisch aus verformtem Holz mit
Kunststoffbeschichtung, Glasplatte
RIV

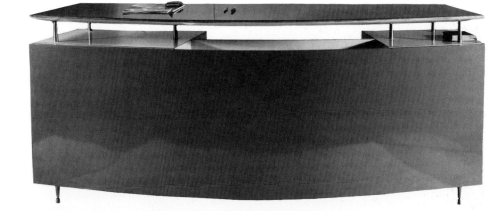

◁ 684 **Franco Albini** c. 1950 Italy

Desk with metal frame and glass top
Schreibtisch mit Metallgestell und Glas-
platte
Knoll International

◁ 685 **Gianemilio, Piero and Anna Monti** 1954
Italy

Desk with metal frame, opaque glass top,
plastic-laminated drawer units
Schreibtisch mit Metallgestell, Opalglas-
platte, kunststoffbeschichteten Unterschränken
Senna

◁ 686 + 687 **Alberto Rosselli** c. 1950 Italy

Desk with steel tube frame, top and drawer
fronts of glass
Schreibtisch mit Stahlrohrgestell, Platte
und Schubladenfronten aus Glas
Vis

◁ 688 + 689 **Jens Risom** c. 1953 USA

Office furniture series "Group Eight" in
birch or walnut with brass handles
Büromöbelprogramm »Group Eight« in
Birke oder Nußbaum mit Beschlägen aus
Messing
Jens Risom

693 + 694 Florence Knoll c. 1950 USA
Desks of wood with square steel tube frames and attached drawers
Schreibtische aus Holz mit Gestellen aus Vierkantstahlrohr und an-
gehängten Schubladenelementen
Knoll International

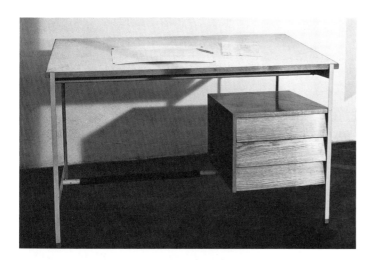

699 + 700 **George Nelson** 1947/1955 USA

"Executive Office Group" of walnut with wooden or plastic tops, chrome-plated legs
Büromöbelprogramm »Executive Office Group« in Nußbaum mit Platten aus Holz oder Kunststoff, verchromte Gestelle
Herman Miller

◁ ◁ 695 **Luisa Castiglioni** c. 1952 Italy

Desk with steel frame, wooden drawer unit and plastic-laminated top
Schreibtisch mit Stahlgestell, Schubladenelement aus Holz und kunststoffbeschichteter Platte
Ettore Canali

◁ 696 **Oliver Lundquist, Julian von der Lancken** 1958 USA

"Architective Furniture" desk with walnut top and drawer fronts, two pedestals of ebonized walnut
Büromöbelprogramm »Architective Furniture«. Schreibtisch mit Platte und Schubladenfronten in Nußbaum, Unterschränke in dunkel gebeiztem Nußbaum
John Stuart

◁ ◁ 697 **Gio Ponti** c. 1952 Italy

Desk with steel frame and plastic-laminated top
Schreibtisch mit Stahlgestell und Kunststoffplatte
Rima

◁ 698 **Robin Day** c. 1954 Great Britain

Desk with metal legs, wooden pedestals and linoleum covered top
Schreibtisch mit Metallbeinen, Unterschränken aus Holz, linoleumbeschichteter Platte
Hille

701 Charles Eames c. 1952 USA

Desk, part of "Eames Storage Units", with top of walnut or birch, frame of chrome-plated steel
Schreibtisch aus dem Programm »Eames Storage Units« mit Platte in Nußbaum oder Birke, Gestell aus verchromtem Stahl
Herman Miller

702 Fred Ruf 1953 Switzerland

Desk with metal frame, wooden top and drawers
Schreibtisch mit Metallgestell, Platte und Schubladen aus Holz
Wohnbedarf Zürich

703 Kurt Thut 1955 Switzerland

Executive desk "KT 124-34" with inter-changeable pedestals in rosewood or wal-nut and frame of chrome-plated profile steel
Chefschreibtisch »KT 124-34« mit aus-wechselbaren Korpuselementen in Pali-sander oder Nußbaum und Gestell aus verchromten Stahlprofilen
Teo Jakob

704+705 Jaap Penraat 1956 Netherlands

Desk and typewriter desk with beech base, colored drawers and linoleum-covered top
Schreib- und Schreibmaschinentisch mit Gestell in Buche, farbigen Schubladen und Linoleumbelag
Pentagonia

702	704
703	705

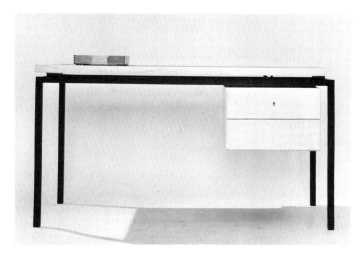

706 **Poul Kjaerholm** 1956 Denmark
Drawing table with flat steel frame, top and drawer of plywood
Zeichentisch mit Gestell aus Flachstahl, Platte und Schublade aus Sperrholz
Rud. Rasmussens Snedkerier

707+708 **Henning Jensen, Torben Valeur** 1961 Denmark
Modular office furniture "M-40"; solid oak, fittings of chrome-plated metal in mat finish
Modulares Büromöbelprogramm »M-40« aus Eiche massiv, Beschläge aus mattiertem, verchromtem Metall
Munch Møbler

709+710 **Herbert Berry, Christopher Cattle** 1962 Great Britain
Series of office furniture in chipboard slab construction with teak or mahogany veneers, fittings and handles of aluminum. Shown here are double pedestal desk "LD 46" and L-shaped work station "LS 52/LTY 36"
Büromöbelprogramm aus Spannplatten mit Teak- oder Mahagonifurnier, Beschläge und Griffe aus Aluminium. Hier gezeigt sind ein Schreibtisch mit zwei Unterschränken »LD 46« und ein L-förmiger Arbeitsplatz »LS 52/LTY 36«
Lucas

707	709
708	710

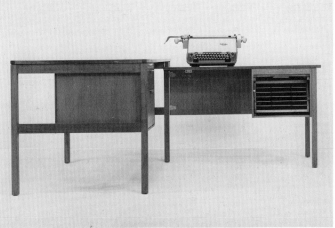

711 Dieter Rams 1957 Germany

Double-top desk "RZ 57" in beech or walnut veneer; detachable legs of anodized aluminum
Schreibtisch »RZ 57« mit Doppelplatte in Buchen- oder Nußbaumfurnier; abschraubbare Beine aus eloxiertem Aluminium
Vitsoe + Zapf

712 Frank Bolliger 1960 Switzerland

Desk with metal frame in black or grey lacquer finish and rosewood pedestal. Reversible table top of rosewood on one side, plastic on the other
Schreibtisch mit schwarz oder grau lackiertem Metallgestell und Korpus in Palisander, Tischplatte umdrehbar, auf einer Seite Palisander, auf der anderen Kunststoff
Globus

713 Werner Blaser 1960 Switzerland

Desk in white plastic with chrome-plated steel frame
Schreibtisch mit weißer Kunststoffbeschichtung und verchromtem Gestell
Ernst Nielsen

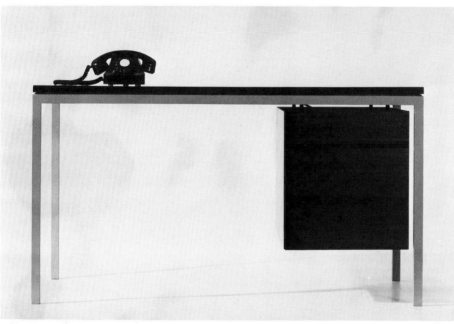

716 Jens Risom 1959 USA ▷

"Group Nine" office furniture series consisting of desk arrangements and cabinets of walnut with aluminum fittings
Büromöbelprogramm »Group Nine« mit Schreibtischkombinationen und Kastenelementen in Nußbaum mit Aluminiumbeschlägen
Risom Design

717 Herbert Hirche 1957 Germany ▷▷

Desk and sideboard in teak, interiors of white maple, bases of square steel tubes
Schreibtisch und Kastenelement in Teak, innen Ahorn weiß, Gestelle aus Vierkantstahlrohr
Christian Holzäpfel

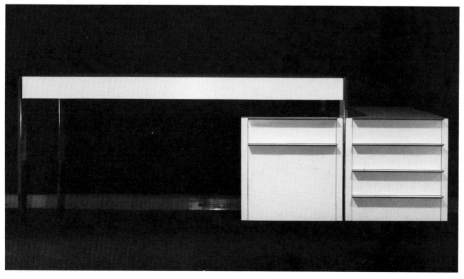

718 Robin Day 1958/59 Great Britain ▷

"Status Group" office furniture of walnut, mahogany, or teak, with square steel frames and wooden or plastic tops
Büromöbelprogramm »Status Group« in Nußbaum, Mahagoni oder Teak mit Untergestellen aus Vierkantstahl, Platten aus Holz oder Kunststoff
Hille

719 Alain Richard 1960 France ▷▷

"Direction" office furniture series consisting of desk arrangements, filing cabinets, and telephone table in rosewood and plastic, all interiors of oak, frames of black lacquered or chrome-plated steel
Büromöbelprogramm »Direction« aus Schreibtischkombinationen, Kastenmöbeln und Telefontischchen in Palisander und Kunststoff, alle Innenteile in Eiche, schwarz lackierte oder verchromte Stahlgestelle
Meubles T.V.

714+715 **Hugh Acton** 1962 USA
Executive desk "ET3377" with frame of chrome-plated steel and
various storage elements
Chefschreibtisch »ET3377« mit Gestell aus verchromtem Stahl und
verschiedenen Kastenelementen
Hugh Acton

720 + 721 **Friso Kramer** 1956 Netherlands

"Revolt" desks of pressed sheet steel, frames of square steel tubes, interchangeable drawer units
Schreibtischprogramm »Revolt« aus gepreßtem Stahlblech, Gestelle aus Vierkantstahlrohr, auswechselbare Schubladeneinheiten
Oda Staalwerk

722 **Works Design** 1958 USA

"Steelcase 1300 Line" desk with lacquered metal frame, colored pedestal and back panel, plastic laminated top
Schreibtisch »Steelcase 1300 Line« mit Fußgestell aus lackiertem Metall, Unterschränke und Verkleidung der Rückwand farbig, Arbeitsplatte mit Kunststoffolie beschichtet
Steelcase

723 **Skidmore, Owings & Merrill** 1957 USA

"Inland Steel Furnishings" desk with black steel frame, baked-enamel steel pedestals, white plastic top
Schreibtisch aus dem Programm »Inland Steel Furnishings« mit schwarzem Stahluntergestell, einbrennlackierten Unterschränken und weißer Kunststoffplatte
Steelcase + Allsteel

724–726 **Arne Jacobsen, Niels Jørgen Haugesen** 1969/70 Denmark

Office furniture series "Djob". Frames of desks and typing tables of aluminum with rounded foot pieces and angular joints of steel. Typing table changeable into a suspension filing cabinet. Table tops, drawers, and cabinet units in wood with dark blue or ochre plastic laminate
Büromöbelprogramm »Djob«. Gestelle der Schreib- und Schreibmaschinentische aus Aluminiumprofilen und abgerundeten Füßen sowie verschieden großen Eckstücken aus Stahl zusammengesteckt. Der Schreibmaschinentisch kann in eine Hängeregistratur umgewandelt werden. Tischplatten, Unterschränke und Kastenmöbel aus dunkelblau oder ocker beschichtetem Holz
Scandinavian Office Organisation

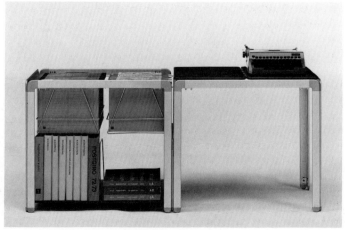

727+728 **Georg Leowald** c. 1953 Germany

Desks with frames of chrome-plated steel
tubes, interchangeable drawer units of
sheet steel, and plastic-laminated
tops
Schreibtische mit Gestellen aus verchromtem Stahlrohr, auswechselbaren Schubladeneinheiten aus Stahlblech und kunststoffbeschichteten Platten
Pohlschröder

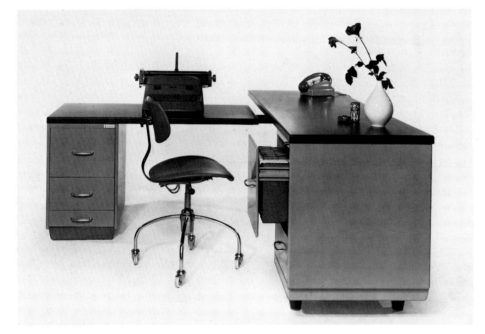

729+730 **Georg Leowald** c. 1957 Germany

Desks "3800" with metal legs or bases, lacquered steel pedestals in varying drawer
arrangements, plastic tops
Schreibtischprogramm »3800« mit Metallbeinen oder -sockeln, lackierten Stahlun-
terschränken mit verschiedener Schubla-
denaufteilung, Arbeitsplatten mit Kunststoffbeschichtung
Pohlschröder

731 Works Design 1960 Germany

Office furniture "WF-System" with metal
bases, lacquered steel pedestals in varying
drawer arrangements, plastic tops
Büromöbelprogramm »WF-System« mit
Metallsockeln, lackierten Stahlunter-
schränken mit verschiedener Schubladen-
aufteilung, Arbeitsplatten mit Kunststoffbeschichtung
Pohlschröder

732 + 733 Works Design 1963 Germany

Modular series of office furniture "3900".
Table tops in various sizes and pedestals
of different depths, with interchangeable
drawer units and variable interior equipment, ensure a wide range of combinations. Legs of square profile metal in dark
grey lacquer finish; pedestals lacquer-finished in two different states of grey; tops
plastic-laminated
Modulares Büromöbelprogramm »3900«.
Durch verschieden große Tischplatten und
unterschiedlich tiefe Unterschränke mit variabler Schubladeneinteilung und -Einrich-
tung ist das Programm vielseitig zu variie-
ren. Gestelle aus anthrazitfarbenen Vier-
kantprofilen; Untersätze lichtgrau oder
platingrau; Tischplatten mit Kunststoffbeschichtung
Pohlschröder

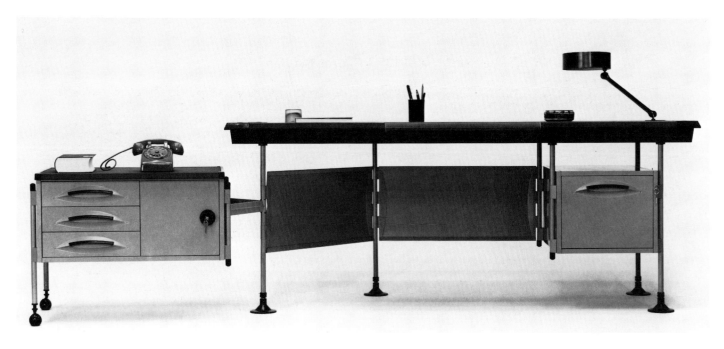

734–738 **Studio B.B.P.R.** 1959 Italy
"Spazio" office furniture series composed of interchangeable units.
All elements in metal, table tops plastic-laminated
Büromöbelprogramm »Spazio« aus auswechselbaren Elementen.
Alle Teile aus Metall, Tischplatten mit Kunststoffbeschichtung
Olivetti

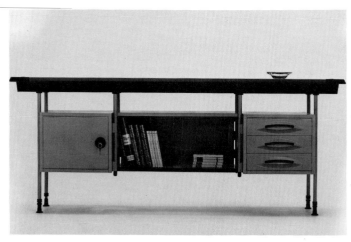

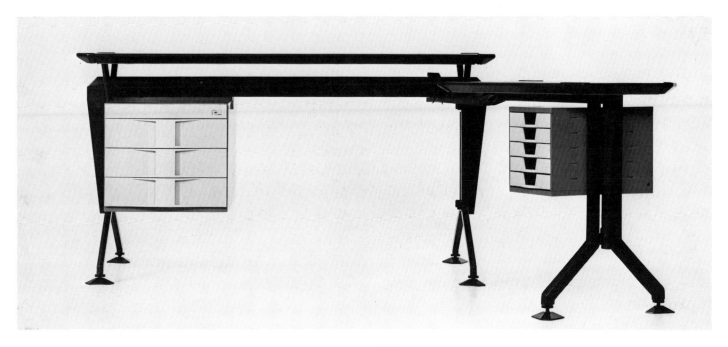

739 **Studio B.B.P.R.** 1963 Italy

Office furniture "Arco" with supporting frames in three sizes and drawers of stove-enamelled steel, tops plastic-laminated or covered with imitation leather or cloth
Büromöbelprogramm »Arco« mit Rahmenkonstruktion in drei Größen und Schubladen aus einbrennlackiertem Stahl, Tischplatten kunststoffbeschichtet oder mit Kunstleder oder Stoff bespannt
Olivetti

740–742 **Alberto Rosselli** 1960 Italy

Office furniture series composed of interchangeable units with wooden tops and frames of chrome-plated or black lacquered steel
Büromöbelprogramm aus auswechselbaren Elementen mit Holzplatten und verchromten oder schwarz lackierten Stahlgestellen
Arflex

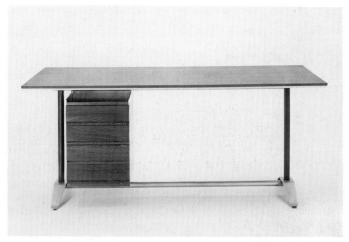

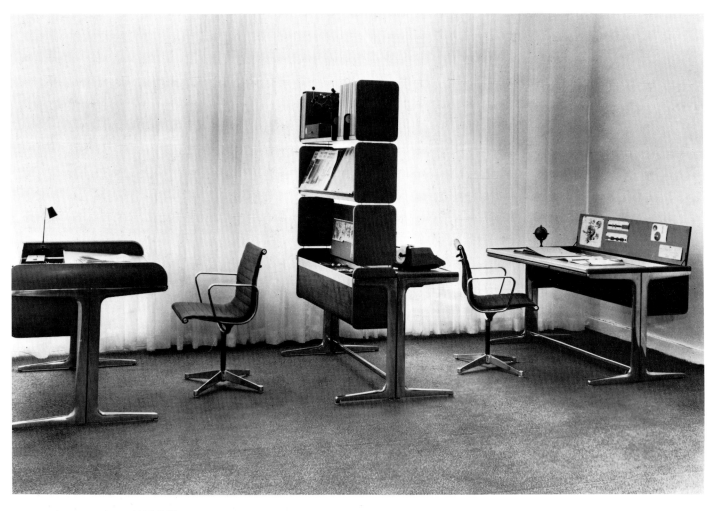

743–745 **George Nelson** 1964 USA

"Action Office" furniture system. Two types of desks with cast aluminum legs and chrome
foot rail, molded plastic end panels, filing bins with roll or flipper tops of ash or walnut,
writing surfaces of plastic laminate. Matching height-adjustable swivel perch and cabinet
unit which can be combined with desks or be hung on a wall
Büromöbelprogramm »Action Office«. Zwei Schreibtischtypen mit Füßen aus Aluminiumguß
und Querstange aus Chromstahl, Seitenwangen aus Kunststoff, Aktentrögen mit Klappdek-
keln oder Rolljalousien aus Esche oder Nußbaum, Schreibflächen kunststoffbeschichtet. Passender, höhenverstellbarer Drehhocker und Kasten- bzw. Regalelemente, die mit den Schreibtischen kombiniert oder an der Wand befestigt werden können
Herman Miller

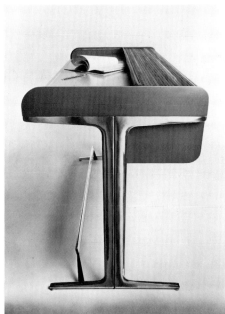

746 Robert Probst 1970 USA

"Action Office 2", a wall panel system based on the former "Action Office" with shelves, storage elements and writing tops
»Action Office 2«, ein Trennwandsystem, das auf dem früheren »Action Office« basiert und Regale, Kastenelemente sowie Schreibplatten umfaßt
Herman Miller

747 Studio Igl 1970 Germany

All-plastic desk "IGL-Tisch" of cast-molded polyurethane-Duromer foam in various colors, drawer fronts and top in imitation leather or plastic combined with wood. Communication panel can be equipped as desired
Vollkunststoff-Schreibtisch »IGL-Tisch« aus Polyurethan-Duromer, im Reaktions-gießverfahren hergestellt. Schubladenfronten und Schreibfläche auch in Kunstleder oder in Kunststoff mit Edelholz kombiniert. Das Funktionsfeld kann nach Wahl ausgestattet werden
Wilhelm Werndl

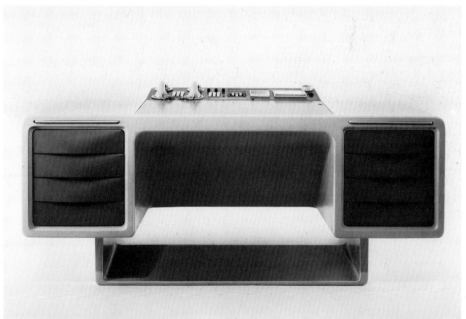

748 + 749 Works Design 1971 Germany

Modular office furniture series "exklusiv" with various red colored cabinet elements and grey table tops of polyurethane, supports of grey lacquer-finished cast aluminum. All these components can be assembled in various combinations to form desks, shelves and cabinet units
Modulares Büromöbelprogramm »exklusiv« mit verschiedenen roten Kastenelementen und grauen Schreibtischplatten aus Polyurethan sowie Gestellen aus grau lackiertem Aluminiumguß. In beliebiger Kombination können Schreibtische, Kastenmöbel und Regale zusammengesetzt werden
Viessmann

750–754 **Peter Raake** 1958/59 Germany

Office furniture series "ZG-System" composed of interchangeable units; desks, tables, and cabinets of wood, colored steel or plastic, frames of square tubular steel
Büromöbelprogramm »ZG-System« aus auswechselbaren Elementen; Schreibtische, Tische und Schränke aus Holz, Stahl oder Kunststoff in verschiedenen Farben, Gestelle aus Vierkant-Stahlrohr
Voko Büromöbelfabriken

755 Fritz Haller 1964/70 Switzerland

Series of storage furniture for offices with modular frames of
chrome-plated steel tubes screwed with spheric joints. Shelves and
side panels of lacquer-finished sheet metal or of plastic-laminated
wood. Matching table with frame of chrome-plated steel and plastic
top
Modulares Kastenmöbelsystem für Büros mit Rahmen aus verchromten Stahlrohren, die über Kugelverbindungsstücke miteinander verschraubt werden. Fachböden und Seitenwände aus farbig
lackiertem Metall oder aus kunststoffbeschichtetem Holz. Passender Tisch mit Gestell aus verchromtem Stahlrohr und Kunststoffplatte
Schärer

756 Osvaldo Borsani, Eugenio Gerli 1968 Italy

Modular office furniture system "Graphis" with three basic elements
of sheet steel in white or grey enamel finish: two types of container
units, one L-shaped supporting element, and various panels in
plastic laminate. The system allows a wide variety of combinations
and is particularly suited for open-plan offices
Modulares Büromöbelsystem »Graphis« mit drei Grundelementen
aus grau oder weiß emailliertem Stahlblech: zwei Kastenelementen
und einem L-förmigen Stützelement, sowie kunststoffbeschichteten
Platten in verschiedenen Größen. Das System zeichnet sich durch
vielseitige Kombinationsmöglichkeiten aus und eignet sich daher
besonders für Großraumbüros
Tecno

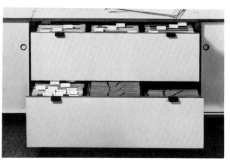

757+758 Hans Gugelot 1961 Switzerland

Series of desks "M 125 S" with adjustable
interior equipment, designed on the same
module as the demountable furniture
group "M 125" (see ill. 779). All surfaces
covered in dull white plastic, edges in
afrormosia. Matching filing cabinets
Schreibtischprogramm »M 125 S« mit variabler Inneneinteilung, abgestimmt auf die
Maßeinheiten des zerlegbaren Möbelsy-
stems »M 125« (siehe Abb. 779). Alle Ober-
flächen matt weiß kunststoffbeschichtet,
Kanten in Afrormosia. Passende Registra-
turschränke
Habit

759 Walter Wirz 1960 Switzerland

Desk "WR 403" of walnut with a variety of
pedestal elements, metal frame in grey lacquer or chrome finish
Schreibtisch »WR 403« in Nußbaum mit
Unterschränken und Seitenkästen in verschiedenen Ausführungen; Gestell aus anthrazit lackiertem oder verchromtem
Metall
Wilhelm Renz

760+761 Works Design 1962 USA

Office furniture series "Formal Line" with
chrome-plated or painted steel frames.
Table tops may be selected from a wide
range of natural wood finishes or plastic
laminates. Cabinets with various drawers
and drop-door storage
Büromöbelprogramm »Formal Line« mit
verchromten oder lackierten Stahlgestellen. Tischplatten in verschiedenen Furnie-
ren oder mit Kunststoffbeschichtung.
Kastenelemente mit unterschiedlich einge-
teilten Schubfächern und Klapptüren
Peerless Steel Equipment

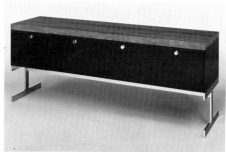

762 **Marco Zanuso** 1970 Italy

Desk series "Cartesio" of plywood with
noise-absorbing white resin laminate; connection of single elements with plastic ten-
ons
Schreibtischprogramm »Cartesio« aus
Sperrholzplatten mit weißer, schalldämp-
fender Kunstharzbeschichtung; Verbindung der Platten durch Kunststoffzapfen
fen
mim mobili

763 **Karl-Heinz Teufel** 1974 Germany

Office furniture series "Interfunction",
desks in plastic laminate, frames of mat
aluminum, tops with resin laminate. Desks
and cabinet units are supplied as kits of
individual components easily ready for use
through a combination of mating joints
and threaded fasteners
Schreibtisch aus dem Büromöbelprogramm »Interfunction« mit Kunststoffbeschichtung, Gestell und Profile aus mattem
Aluminium, Platten mit Melaminharzbe-
schichtung. Tische und Schränke werden
zerlegt geliefert, ein kombiniertes Steck/
Schraubsystem erlaubt mühelosen Aufbau
Interfunction

764 + 765 **Pierre Guariche** 1963 France

Desks and drawing tables of chrome-
plated square tubular steel and tops of dull
white plastic laminate. Shelves and pedestals of plastic imitation walnut. Cabinet unit
in front of window with eight drop-doors
Schreib- und Zeichentische mit Gestellen
aus verchromtem Vierkantstahlrohr und
Tischplatten aus mattweißem Kunststoff.
Regale und Kastenelemente aus Kunststoff
mit Nußbaumtextur. An der Fensterwand
langes Kastenelement mit acht Klapptüren

766–768 Works Design/Karl Dittert 1972 Germany

Office furniture series "Modulares Element-Programm" with all components for the techno-
logically equipped office. Desk frames of steel in various widths and depths, tops in wood
with plastic laminate. Each desk has raceways for electric equipment covered with a metal
lid with molded trays of plastic. Larger desks with built-in filing bins. Several desks can
be linked by curved elements in different angles or by square elements
»Modulares Element-Programm« zur Einrichtung von voll technisierten Büros. Schreibtisch-
gestelle in verschiedenen Breiten und Tiefen aus Stahl, Arbeitsplatten aus kunststoffbeschichtetem Holz. Jeder Schreibtisch enthält einen Kabelkanal für die notwendigen elektrischen
Anschlüsse, abgedeckt durch eine Metallplatte mit eingesetzten Ablageschalen aus Kunststoff. Größere Schreibtische haben eingebaute Registraturkästen. Mehrere Arbeitsplätze werden durch quadratische oder in verschiedenem Winkel gebogene Verbindungselemente kombiniert
Voko Bürmöbelfabriken

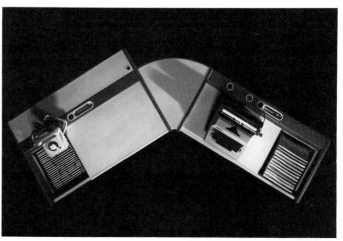

769–772 **Hartmut Esslinger** 1976 Germany

Modular office furniture series "RCO". Frames of tubular steel; tops with rounded corners,
cabinet units and shelves of resin laminate in various colors. Tubular supports for telephone
or file bins (770), power supply through tubular table legs (771), infinitely variable mechanism
for adjusting the height of writing and typing desks (772). The range comprises also such
other office furniture items as cabinets, drawers, trolley-type containers on castors, or room
dividers
Modulares Büromöbelprogramm »RCO«. Untergestelle aus Stahlrohr; Tischplatten mit abgerundeten Ecken, Kastenelemente und Regale aus Melaminharz in verschiedenen Farben.
Aufsatzrohre für Telefon oder Ablagetableaus (770), Stromkabel können durch die Rohrfüße
zur Tischplatte durchgezogen werden (771), stufenlose Höhenverstellung der Schreib- und
Maschinentische (772). Das Programm kann darüber hinaus mit verschiedenen Ausführungen von Schränken, Schüben, Rollwagen, Trennwänden vervollständigt werden
Christian Holzäpfel

770

771

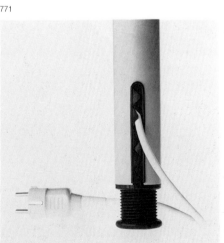

772

773–775 **Works Design** 1970 Germany

"Raum-in-Raum-System" of office furniture. Wall partitions in two heights of sound-absorbing panels covered with fabric. Connection of panels by posts of anodized aluminum with height-adjustable foot plates. The posts also serve to hang various pieces of office furniture as desk tops, shelves and storage elements
»Raum-in-Raum-System« zur Möblierung von Großraumbüros mit Wandelementen in zwei Höhen aus stoffbespannten, schallschluckenden Lochblenden. Verbindung durch Pfosten aus eloxiertem Aluminium mit höhenregulierbaren Fußtellern. Schreibtische, Fachböden und Kastenelemente werden in Schienen der Pfosten eingehängt
Pohlschröder

776–778 Ettore Sottsass jr. 1970/71 Italy

Office furniture series "Synthesis 45" consisting of two chair models
(see ill. 277), desks with legs and stiffeners of light grey enameled
sheet metal and tops of plastic laminate which can be combined
in numerous ways, drawer pedestals and free standing cabinets
of dark or light blue lacquer-finished sheet metal with ABS handles,
also on casters, various shelving and storage units. Room dividers
are assembled of free standing bookshelves and acoustic screens
in brown with hinges and adjusting screws of ABS. All elements
can be combined in many ways

Büromöbelprogramm »Synthesis 45« mit zwei Stuhlmodellen (siehe
Abb. 277), Schreibtischen mit Beinen und Querträgern aus hellgrau
lackiertem Stahlblech und kunststoffbeschichteten Platten, Unterschränken und frei stehenden Kastenelementen aus dunkel- oder
hellblau lackiertem Stahlblech mit Griffen aus ABS, auch auf Rollen,
verschiedenen Regal- und Karteischränken. Als Raumteiler frei ste-
hende Bücherregale und schalldämmende Stellwände in Braun mit
Scharnieren und Stellschrauben in ABS. Alle Elemente sind vielfältig
kombinierbar
Olivetti

779 **Hans Gugelot** 1953 Switzerland

Modular group "M 125" consisting of metal rods and panels covered with light grey plastic, afrormosia edging. Components can be assembled as desired
Möbelsystem »M 125« aus Metallstäben und Brettern mit hellgrauer Kunststoffbeschichtung und Kanten in Afrormosia. Die Elemente können beliebig kombiniert werden
Habit

It is probably very difficult for us to realize, thirty years later, what kind of innovation Nisse Strinning's shelving system was when it first appeared. "String" became the guiding object for a design freed from unnecessary bulk (ills. 849, 850). The light grille structure was extremely spartan in its use of materials and the pieces that slot into it, most of them simple in design, strengthened the impression that here was a very uncluttered piece of furniture. In addition, "String" hung on the wall and did not touch the floor; it hovered. The whole system may seem rather too fragile and delicate for today's tastes but when it was created (1950) it was revolutionary. "String" broke the predominance of free-standing storage furniture and heavy shelving, it lifted the structure off the floor and introduced cheerfulness into a matter that had previously been dealt with much too solemnly. The ladder system may have tempted people to let stuffed animals and wooden monkeys clamber over it but even that was better than the bronze figures and porcelain knick-knacks that used to serve as ornamentation. That sort of thing did not match "String". Liberation really entered people's houses with this system, one could breathe freely, and suddenly had an amazing amount of space. And that was also necessary because the cramped living conditions after the war and the spare dimensions of new flats did not leave much space for larger pieces of furniture. Nevertheless, "String" was more than just a practical and timely solution to the problem of storing books, magazines, glasses, plates and cutlery. It represented in fact an idea, and it possessed a convincing affinity to the ideas that were influencing architecture at that time. The material economy that the war had previously enforced was transposed here into a statement advocating conscious renunciation. The recent increased demand for "String" proves that the basic thought behind it is still operative.

It should not come as much of a surprise that none of the subsequent systems was equally satisfactory. Modifications, often involving replacing the ladders with vertical rods jammed between ceiling and floor, appeared heavier and therefore more complicated than the original. In this, they violated the principles behind the whole concept.

The simple fact that a room seems much smaller when a piece of furniture stands higher than table-top height explains why the low sideboard was so popular in the modest flats of the postwar era. Just as "String" replaced the terrible old bookcase, the sideboard did the same for the "buffet" which used to dominate the dining-room. At the very beginning of this development there was an almost classic model by Florence Knoll, where bast fabric replaced the usual showy veneer (ill. 791). A large amount of Japanese influence was evident in this piece of furniture, which also had sliding doors.

Among the compact systems, Hans Gugelot's was both one of the first and has remained one of the best (ill. 779). Newer developments dispensed with the combination of individual side, top and connecting elements, which often only appeared to be cheap. They functioned according to the principle of units that could be arranged in any order. Old ship's dressers served as a model for them (ill. 873). In another case of constructive reminiscence, the former wardrobe-trunk celebrated a fine comeback (ills. 937–940).

Es ist heute, dreißig Jahre danach, wahrscheinlich nur noch schwer nachzuvollziehen, welche Neuerung seinerzeit das Regalsystem von Nisse Strinning in die Welt gesetzt hat. »String« wurde zum Leitgegenstand für eine von unnötigem Möbelballast befreite Wohnform (Abb. 849 + 850). Das leichte Gitterwerk war vom materiellen Aufwand her äußerst sparsam, und die zumeist einfach gehaltenen Einsatzteile bestärkten den Eindruck, es mit einer sehr unaufwendigen Einrichtung zu tun zu haben. Hinzu kam noch, daß »String« an der Wand hing und den Boden nicht berührte, also gleichsam schwebte. Mag sein, daß für unser heutiges Empfinden das ganze System etwas zu fragil und zart erscheint, zur Zeit seiner Entstehung (um 1950) war es revolutionär. »String« löste die alleinige Vorherrschaft der stehenden Kastenmöbel und schwerfälligen Regale auf, es hob die Einrichtung vom Boden ab und brachte Heiterkeit in eine Sache, die bisher mit zuviel Ernst behandelt worden war. Zwar verlockte das Leitersystem dazu, Stofftiere und hölzerne Affen daran herumklettern zu lassen, aber auch das war besser als die Bronzefiguren und der Porzellan-Nippes, der früher als Möbelzierrat gedient hatte. Mit »String« vertrug sich dergleichen nun nicht mehr. Mit diesem System kam wirklich Befreiung in die Wohnungen, man konnte aufatmen und hatte auf einmal überraschend viel Platz. Das war allerdings auch notwendig, denn die beengten Wohnverhältnisse nach dem Kriege und die sparsamen Dimensionen von Neubauwohnungen ließen nur wenig Raum für größere Möbelstücke. Trotzdem war »String« mehr als nur eine praktische und zeitgerechte Lösung des Problems, Bücher, Zeitschriften, Gläser, Teller und Besteckteile unterzubringen. Es stellte tatsächlich eine Idee dar, und es besaß eine überzeugende Affinität zu den Vorstellungen, die damals die Architektur bewegten. Die Ökonomie im Materiellen, zu der vorher der Krieg gezwungen hatte, wurde hier transportiert zu einem Bekenntnis, das für einen bewußten Verzicht eintrat. Die in letzter Zeit wieder angestiegene Nachfrage beweist, daß der Gedanke, der »String« zugrundeliegt, noch wirksam ist.

Nicht verwundern durfte es, daß keines der Systeme, die in der Nachfolge entstanden, in gleicher Weise überzeugen konnte. Die Abwandlungen, die oft die Leitern ersetzten durch senkrechte Stäbe, die zwischen Fußboden und Decke eingespannt wurden, wirkten immer gewichtiger und damit anspruchsvoller als das Urbild. Sie verletzten damit die Grundidee der ganzen Erfindung.

Die einfache Erfahrung, daß ein Raum wesentlich kleiner wirkt, wenn ein Möbelstück über Tischhöhe hinausragt, kann man in den bescheidenen Verhältnissen der Nachkriegszeit begründen, warum das niedere Sideboard damals so beliebt war. Ähnlich wie »String« den schrecklichen alten Bücherschrank ersetzte, so tat es das Sideboard mit dem »Buffet«, das früher in Speisezimmern dominiert hatte. Ein geradezu klassisches Modell stand auch hier gleich am Anfang der Entwicklung, nämlich das von Florence Knoll, bei dem der übliche Furnierprunk an den Türen einer Bastbespannung gewichen war (Abb. 791). Ein gutes Stück Japan steckte in diesem Möbel, dessen Türen deshalb auch zum Schieben waren.

Unter den geschlossenen Systemen ist das von Hans Gugelot auch eines der zugleich ersten und besten geblieben (Abb. 779). Neuere Entwicklungen verzichten auf die – oft nur scheinbar billige – Kombination einzelner Wand-, Decken- und Verbindungselemente und funktionieren nach dem Prinzip der beliebig aneinanderzureihenden Bausteine. Das Modell alter Schiffskommoden hat hierbei als Anregung gedient (Abb. 873). In einem anderen Fall der konstruktiven Erinnerung hat der Schrankkoffer von einst eine schöne Widerkehr gefunden (Abb. 937–940).

785 **Taichiro Nakai** c. 1954 Japan

Demountable wardrobe and sideboard of molded plywood
Auseinandernehmbarer Schrank und Anrichte aus geformtem
Sperrholz
Yamada Kogyo Co.

786 + 787 **Robin Day, Clive Latimer** c. 1950 Great Britain

Cabinets of molded plywood with legs of metal
Kommoden aus verformtem Sperrholz mit Metallbeinen

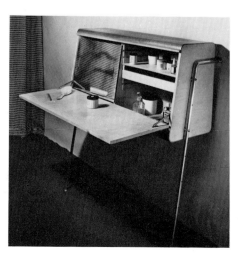

780	781	
782	783	784
785		
786	787	

◁ 780 **A. Patijn** c. 1951 Netherlands

Sideboard of wood with folding doors
Anrichte aus Holz mit Falttüren
Ums-Pastoe

◁ 781–784 **Cees Braakman** c. 1951 Netherlands

Cabinet series of wood comprising sideboards, bookshelves with writing desks,
cupboards, and chests; legs of molded
wood
Kastenmöbelprogramm aus Holz, das Anrichten, Bücherregale, Schreibschränke,
Wäscheschränke und Kommoden umfaßt;
Füße aus verformtem Holz
Ums-Pastoe

788 + 789 **Hans J. Wegner** c. 1952
Denmark

Chest in oak with doors in teak, also with
additional bookshelves for use as writing
desk
Kommode in Eiche mit Türen in Teak, auch
mit Regalaufsatz als Schreibschrank
Ry Møbler

790 **Franz Füeg** 1950 Switzerland

Series of storage furniture of wood, comprising sideboard, chest of drawers, and
wardrobe of wood
Kastenmöbelprogramm aus Holz mit Anrichte, Kommode mit Schubladen und
Schrank
Franz Füeg

791 **Florence Knoll** 1950 USA

Sideboard with bast-covered sliding
doors
Anrichte mit bastbespannten Schiebetüren
Knoll International

792 **Nardin & Radoczy** c. 1951 USA

Wall cabinet of wood with lacquered drawers and door, sliding doors of glass, adjustable shelves
Anrichte mit Wandbefestigung aus Holz,
Schubladen und Tür farbig lackiert, Schiebetüren aus Glas, verstellbare Fachböden
Habitat

793 **Robin Day** c. 1953 Great Britain

Sideboard of wood with lacquered sliding
doors and legs of metal
Anrichte aus Holz mit lackierten Schiebetüren und Metallfüßen
Hille

794 **Charles Eames** c. 1950 USA

Storage units with steel construction and plastic-laminated plywood
shelves and drawers
Kastenmöbel mit Stahlgestell sowie Fachböden und Schubladen
aus kunststoffbeschichtetem Sperrholz
Herman Miller

795 **Alfred Altherr** c. 1953 Switzerland

Sideboard composed of chest and storage units with bench base
and metal legs
Anrichte aus Anbauelementen mit Bank-Untergestell und Metallfüßen
K.H. Frei

796 George Nelson c. 1950 USA
Sideboard with sliding doors and legs of
chrome-plated tubular steel
Anrichte mit Schiebetüren und Füßen aus
verchromtem Stahlrohr
Herman Miller

797 George Nelson c. 1952 USA
Chest of drawers in oak, legs and pulls
of lacquered steel tubes
Kommode in Eiche, Füße und Griffe aus
lackiertem Stahlrohr
Herman Miller

798 George Nelson 1952 USA
Chest of drawers in rosewood and natural
cane bench
Kommode in Palisander und Bank mit
Rohrgeflecht
Herman Miller

801 Charles Eames c. 1950 USA ▷
Chest of drawers "ESU 275", part of
"Eames Storage Units" series, with frames
of chrome-plated steel, drawer fronts in
birch, tops in walnut or birch; side panels
in various colors
Kommode »ESU 275« aus dem Programm
»Eames Storage Units«, mit Rahmen aus
verchromtem Stahl, Schubladen in Birke,
Abdeckplatten in Birke oder Nußbaum; Sei-
tenwände in verschiedenen Farben
Herman Miller

802 George Nelson c. 1953 USA ▷▷
"Steelframe Series" of storage units with
frames of black or white painted steel,
drawers and shelves in various colors and
tops of glass or black or white plastic
»Steelframe series«, Kommodenprogramm
mit Rahmen aus schwarz oder weiß lak-
kiertem Stahl, Schubladen und Fachböden
in verschiedenen Farben und Abdeckplatten aus Glas oder schwarzem oder weißem
Kunststoff
Herman Miller

799 + 800 **George Nelson** c. 1951 USA
Sideboard and miniature chest in teak with pulls of white porcelain and legs of turned brass
Anrichte und Aufsatzschränkchen in Teak mit Griffen aus weißem Porzellan und Füßen aus Messing
Herman Miller

803 **Florence Knoll** c. 1953 USA

Chests of drawers "135/136/137" with white or black fronts and metal legs
Kommoden »135/136/137« mit weißen oder schwarzen Fronten und Metallfüßen
Knoll International

804 **Jens Risom** c. 1953 USA

Chest of drawers composed of wooden units
Anbaukommode aus Holz
Jens Risom Design

805 **Paul McCobb** 1954 USA

Drawer chest with rectangular brass legs
Kommode mit Füßen und Kanten aus winkelförmigem Messing
Sacks & Sons

806 **William Pahlmann** c. 1952 USA
Series of chests of drawers in wood
Kommodenprogramm in Holz
Grand Rapids Bookcase & Chair Co.

807 **Edward J. Wormley** c. 1950 USA
Series of chests of drawers with legs of
molded wood
Kommodenprogramm mit Füßen aus ver-
formtem Holz
Dunbar

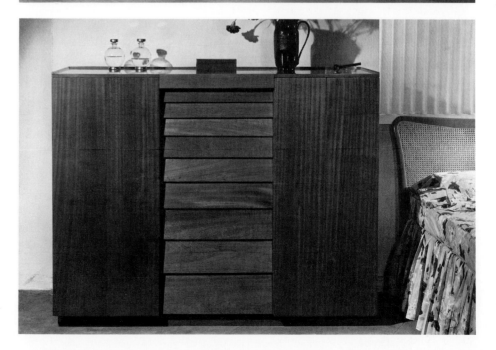

808 **Edward J. Wormley** c. 1950 USA
Wardrobe cabinet with hinged doors and
drawers of different heights
Kleiderschrank mit Seitentüren und Schub-
laden unterschiedlicher Höhe
Dunbar

809 + 810 **Hans J. Wegner** c. 1957 Denmark

Teak cabinets with wood or tubular steel legs
Kastenmöbel in Teak mit Füßen aus Holz oder Stahlrohr
Ry Møbler

▽ 811–813 **Cees Braakman** c. 1957 Netherlands

Modular teak or walnut group with detachable legs of square tubular steel and black plastic pulls. Top cabinets with white flap doors are removable
Zerlegbares Kastenmöbelsystem in Teak oder Nußbaum mit verstellbaren Füßen aus Vierkantstahlrohr, Griffe aus schwarzem Kunststoff. Die Aufsetzkästen mit weißen Klapptüren sind abnehmbar
Ums-Pastoe

816 **Alain Richard** 1957 France ▷▽

Dining room furniture group, all parts collapsible. Exteriors in wood or plastic laminate, interiors in mahogany, underframes of chrome-plated steel
Eßzimmermöbelserie, alle Teile zerlegbar. Wände außen Holz oder Kunststoff, innen Mahagoni, Untergestelle verchromtes Stahlrohr
Meubles T.V.

814 Herbert Hirche 1959 Germany

"LIF" modular group of collapsible elements in walnut, white maple interior, fixtures and underframe of chrome-plated square tubular steel
Zerlegbares Möbelsystem »LIF« in Nußbaum, Innenausführung weiß Ahorn, Beschläge und Untergestelle aus verchromtem Vierkant-Stahlrohr
Christian Holzäpfel

815 Herbert Hirche 1957 Germany

Rosewood sideboard of the "DHS-40" furniture series. White maple interior, underframe of lacquered square tubular steel
Vierteilige Anrichte in Palisander aus dem Programm »DHS-40«. Innenausführung weiß Ahorn, Untergestell aus lackiertem Vierkantstahlrohr
Christian Holzäpfel

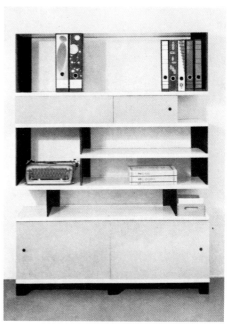

817+818 Reni Trüdinger c. 1957 Switzerland
Modular bookshelves consisting of lacquered wooden shelves with grooves for sliding doors, black brackets and base parts
Beliebig kombinierbares Bücherregal aus lackiertem Holz, bestehend aus Fachböden mit Rillen für Schiebetüren, schwarzen Winkelstützen und Sockelteilen
Werkgenossenschaft Wohnhilfe

819–821 Works Design 1955 USA
Chests with metal drawer slides, fronts of natural or white lacquered wood, tops of wood or in white plastic laminate, backs white plastic laminate
Kommoden mit Schubladen mit Metallgleitschienen, Fronten Holz natur oder weiß lackiert, Deckplatten aus Holz oder mit weißer Kunststoffbeschichtung, Rückseiten weiß kunststoffbeschichtet
Knoll International

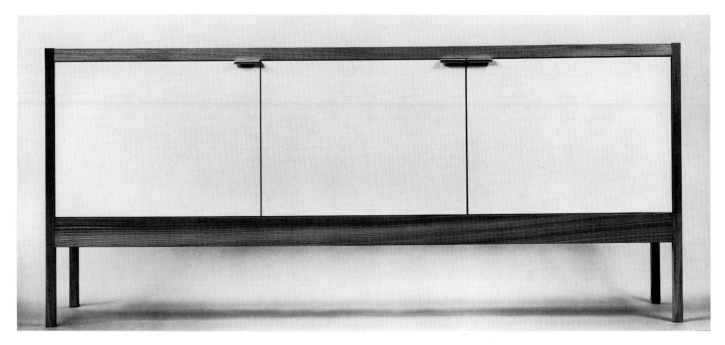

822 + 823 Dieter Waeckerlin 1963 Switzerland

Storage units "Serie III (H 110)" with frames of Japanese elm or Brazilian rosewood and white plastic surfaces. Three basic units of different lengths with doors or drawers and with a wide variety of interior equipment may be combined to meet individual needs. Also with doors on both sides for use as room-divider
Wohn- und Speisezimmerprogramm »Serie III (H 110)« mit Rahmen in japanischer Ulme oder Rio-Palisander und weiß kunststoffbeschichteten Flächen. Die drei verschieden breiten Grundelemente mit Türen oder Schubladen und vielseitiger Innenausstattung können nach Wunsch kombiniert werden. Auch mit Türen auf beiden Seiten als Raumteiler
Idealheim/Karl Haiges

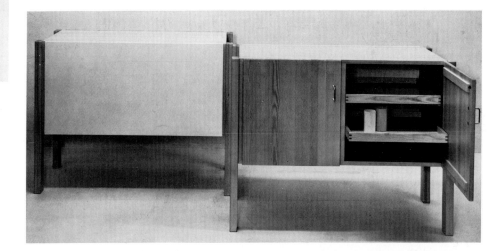

824 Pirkko Stenros 1959 Finland

Cabinet units of pine, partly laminated in white plastic
Kastenelemente in Kiefer, teilweise weiß kunststoffbeschichtet
Artek

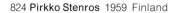

825 Arne Karlsen 1960 Denmark

Sideboard "ak-26" consisting of two units in oak
Anrichte »ak-26« aus zwei Elementen in Eiche
Interna

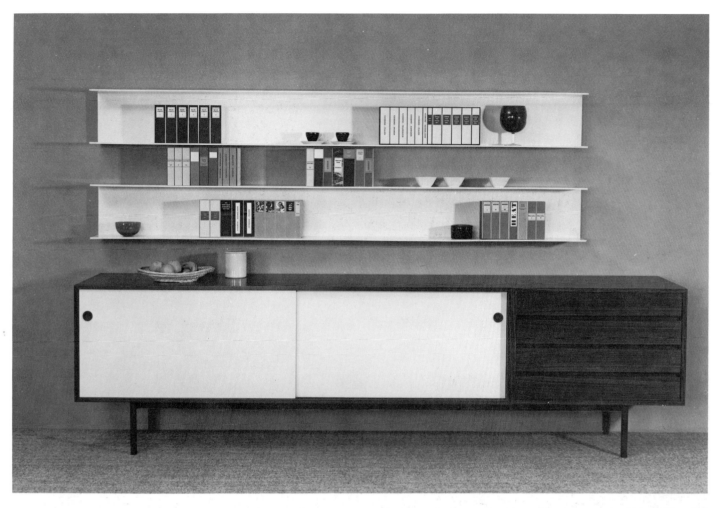

◁ 826 **Gianfranco Frattini** 1960 Italy

Sideboards "502" and "503" with drawers and tambour doors of jacaranda or teak. Units are supported by benchlike frames and may be stacked
Anrichte »502« und »503« mit Schubfächern und Rolläden. Die Kastenelemente aus Jacaranda oder Teak stehen auf bankähnlichen Untergestellen und sind stapelbar
Bernini

◁ 827 **Walter Wirz** 1960 Switzerland

Sideboard in rosewood or teak, underframe of lacquered metal
Anrichte in Palisander oder Teak, Untergestell aus lackiertem Metall
Wilhelm Renz

◁ 828 **Dieter Waeckerlin** 1959 Switzerland

Sideboard "B 40", part of the extensive furniture series "behr waeckerlin-massmöbel", in teak with black lacquered metal underframe
Anrichte »B 40« aus dem Programm »behr waeckerlin-mass-möbel« in Teak mit schwarz lackiertem Metall-Untergestell
Behr

829 **Walter Wirz** 1960 Switzerland

White lacquered bookshelves "190" and "191" and sideboard "192" in rosewood or wengé with white lacquered sliding doors and metal under-frame
Weiß lackiertes Bücherregal »190« bzw. »191« sowie Anrichte »192« in Palisander oder Wengé mit weiß lackierten Schiebetüren und Untergestell aus Metall
Wilhelm Renz

830 **Hugh Acton** 1960 USA

Modular group in wood with adjustable metal frames. Components are adaptable for living room, bedroom, and studio use, and can be assembled in various combinations as chests, cabinets, sideboards, shelves, and room dividers
Regalsystem in Holz mit verstellbaren Metallgestellen, geeignet für Wohn-, Schlaf- und Arbeitszimmer. Beliebig zu Kastenmö-beln, Beistelltischen, Regalen, Schränken und Raumteilern kombinierbar
Hugh Acton

831+832 **Florence Knoll** 1961 USA

Sideboard "119H" with four doors of natural-finished walnut with maple interiors, or with doors covered in white plastic laminate. Underframe of solid walnut or of chrome-plated steel
Anrichte »119H« mit vier Türen; Korpus außen Nußbaum natur, innen Ahorn, oder Türen weiß kunststoffbeschichtet. Untergestell in Nußbaum oder aus verchromtem Stahlrohr
Knoll International

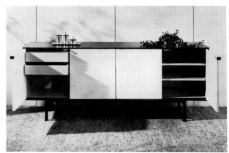

833 **Helmut Fuchs** 1961 Germany

Sideboard "A240/4-105" of rosewood with white plastic fronts and macoré interior; nickel-plated legs
Anrichte »A240/4-105« aus Rio-Palisander, Türfronten mit weißer Kunststoffbeschichtung, Innenausführung Macoré; vernickelte Fußbügel
Dux

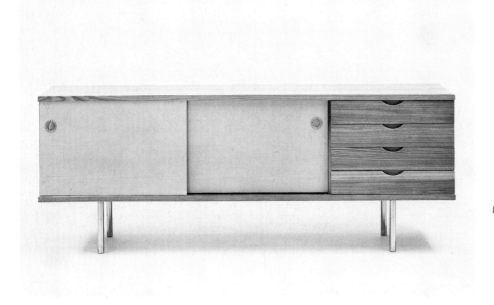

834 **Frank Bolliger** 1960/61 Switzerland

Sideboard in larch, plastic-faced sliding doors, legs of chrome-plated tubular steel
Anrichte in Lärche, Schiebetüren mit Kunststoffbeschichtung, Füße aus verchromtem Stahlrohr
Globus

835 Helmut Magg 1964 Germany

Sideboard of Brazilian rosewood with plastic edges and wooden or marble top
Anrichte aus Rio-Palisander mit Zargen in
weißem Kunststoff und Holz- oder Marmorplatte
Karl Haiges

836 Etienne Fermigier 1961 France

Sideboard "D. 183" of rosewood with three
doors and one drop-flap, top in white marble or travertine, anodized aluminum base.
Matching low collapsible table with flat
profile aluminum legs and rosewood top
Anrichte »D. 183« in Palisander mit drei Türen und einem Klappfach, Abdeckplatte
weißer Marmor oder Travertin, Gestell aus
eloxiertem Aluminium. Passender, zerlegbarer niedriger Tisch mit Füßen aus flachen Aluminiumprofilen und Palisanderplatte
Meubles et Fonction

837 Ib Kofod-Larsen 1962 Denmark

Sideboards "K 6024" and "K 6025" of rosewood or teak with mat finished chrome-
plated steel frames and fittings; maple interiors
Anrichten »K 6024« und »K 6025« in Palisander oder Teak mit matt verchromten
Stahlgestellen und Beschlägen; Innenausführung Ahorn
Laauser

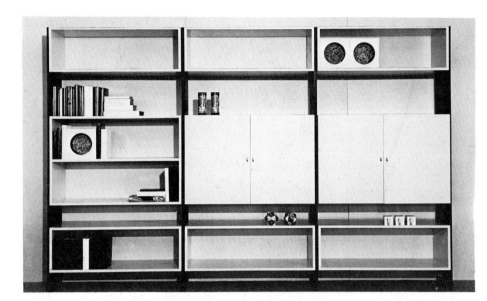

838 + 839 **Works Design** 1969 Netherlands
Modular wall unit "AK" with supporting
side panels of two heights in natural wood
or white lacquer finish; cabinet elements
and shelves finished in white lacquer
Anbauwand »AK« mit Seitenwangen in
zwei Höhen aus Naturholz, auch weiß lakkiert. Kastenelemente und Fachböden
weiß lackiert
Ums-Pastoe

840 **Mogens Koch** 1932/1948 Denmark
Modular storage and bookshelving
unit
Modulares Schrank- und Bücherwand-
system
Rud. Rasmussens Snedkerier

841+842 **Hans J. Wegner** c. 1952 Denmark

Series of chests, cabinets and shelves in oak and teak which can
be assembled to larger storage units
Kastenmöbelprogramm mit Kommoden- und Regalelementen, die
zu größeren Anbauwänden zusammengestellt werden können
Ry Møbler

843 + 844 **Hans Bellmann** c. 1950 Switzerland

Adjustable bookshelves of wood
Verstellbares Bücherregal aus Holz
Wohnbedarf Zürich

845	846
847	848

845 **Hendrik van Keppel, Taylor Green** c. 1954 USA ▷

Bookshelves with folding metal frame and marble shelves
Bücherregal mit zusammenklappbarem Metallgestell und Fachböden aus Marmor
Van Keppel-Green

846 **Bruno Mathsson** c. 1950 Sweden ▷

Bookshelves with L-shaped shelves of molded plywood
Bücherregal mit Fachböden aus L-förmig gebogenem Sperrholz
Karl Mathsson

847 **Olof Pira** 1956 Sweden ▷

Shelving system with pressure-fitted frame of perforated square steel tubing, spring steel brackets and adjustable shelves of wood
Regalsystem mit verspannten Stützen aus gelochtem Vierkantstahlrohr, Federstahlkonsolen und verstellbaren Fachböden aus Holz
Olof Pira

848 **Terence Conran** 1962 Great Britain ▷

"Summa" storage unit of pine, ash, or teak to be put against wall or used as a room divider
Regalwand »Summa« aus Kiefer, Esche oder Teak, auch als Raumteiler verwendbar
Conran

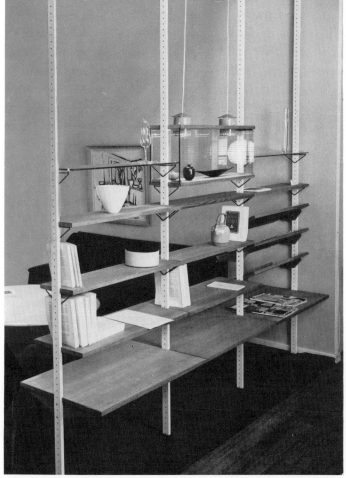

849 + 850 **Karin and Nisse Strinning** c. 1950
Sweden

Bookshelves with plastic-covered iron rod
construction, adjustable shelves and writ-
ing desk
Bücherregal mit kunststoffüberzogenen
Metalleitern, verstellbaren Fachböden und
Schreibfach
String Design

851 **Egon Eiermann** c. 1950 Germany

Bookshelves of wood with supports of per-
forated tubular steel
Bücherregal mit Fachböden aus Holz und
Trägern aus gelochtem Stahlrohr
Wilde & Spieth

852 **Angelo Mangiarotti** c. 1950 Italy

Adjustable bookshelves of molded plywood,
mounted on black-lacquered steel tubes
Verstellbares Bücherregal mit Fachböden
aus verformtem Sperrholz, befestigt an
schwarz lackierten Stahlrohrträgern

854 **Luisa Castiglioni, Margherita Mori** c. 1951 ▷
Italy

Bookshelving system for free standing use
with frame of wood and adjustable shelves
and cabinets
Frei stehendes Bücherregal mit Rahmen
aus Holz sowie verstellbaren Fachböden
und Schrankelementen
Ettore Canali

855 **Jaap Penraat** c. 1951 Netherlands ▷▷

Adjustable bookshelves with lacquered
shelves and cabinets, frame of metal
Verstellbares Bücherregal mit lackierten
Fachböden und Schrankelementen, Rahmen aus Metall

853 Herbert Hirche 1955 Germany
Bookshelving system with chests in teak, maple interiors, black lacquered back panels for stiffening purposes. White lacquered steel tube ladders

Regalsystem mit Fachböden und Schrankelementen in Teak, innen Ahorn, und schwarz lackierten Rückwänden zur Versteifung. Weiß lackierte Stahlrohrleitern
Christian Holzäpfel

856–864 George Nelson 1958 USA

Flexible, assembled "Comprehensive Storage System" which may
be used against a wall or as floor-to-ceiling room divider. Numerous
basic components including shelves, drop-front desks, cabinets
with sliding doors or drawers. Units are suspended on brackets
at any desired height between adjustable aluminum poles pressure-
fitted between floor and ceiling
Vielseitig kombinierbares, demontables Regal- und Raumteilungs-
system »Comprehensive Storage System« mit zahlreichen einsetz-
baren Elementen wie Fachböden, Schreibplatten, Schränken mit
Schiebetüren und Schubladen. Tragkonstruktion aus zwischen Boden und Decke verspannten, höhenverstellbaren Aluminiumprofil-
stangen; Befestigung der Regalbretter und Kastenelemente auf verstellbaren Konsolen
Herman Miller

865 Alfred Altherr c. 1957 Switzerland

"Team" bookshelves combined with cabinet and drawer units, supported by pressure-fitted metal poles
Bücherregal »Team« mit Kasten- und Schubladenelementen, Spannstützen aus Metall
K.H. Frei

866 Pierre Guariche 1958 France

Shelving system with ladder frames of chrome-plated steel tubing; cabinet units of elm, fronts of units for stereo equipment in white plastic laminate
Regalwand mit Leitergestell aus verchromtem Vierkantstahlrohr; Fachböden und Schränke in Rüster, Fronten der Radio- und Musikschränke mit weißem Kunststoff beschichtet
Dassas

867 Ico Parisi 1958 Italy

"Urio" wall unit with interchangeable shelves and cabinets, open and closed compartments, supported by metal poles and brackets
Regalwand »Urio« mit verstellbaren Fachböden und Kastenelementen, offenen und geschlossenen Fächern, die von Metallstangen und Drahtbügeln getragen werden
M.I.M. Mobili Italiani Moderni

868 Dieter Rams 1960 Germany

Wall unit "RZ 60"; shelves and cabinets in
beech or walnut veneer or with light grey
plastic laminate. Framework of anodized
profile aluminum
Wandregal »RZ 60« mit Fachböden und
Kastenelementen in Nußbaum oder Buche,
auch mit lichtgrauem Kunststoff beschichtet. Seitenteile und Wandleisten aus matt
eloxierten Aluminiumprofilen
Vitsoe + Zapf

869 Jürg Bally 1961 Switzerland

Wall unit "WK 299" with shelves and cabinets of natural-finished walnut or white
plastic laminate, suspended between aluminum poles which are pressure-fitted between floor and ceiling. Units may also be
fixed to wall by means of wall panels
Regalsystem »WK 299« mit Fachborden
und Kastenelementen aus Nußbaum natur
oder weißer Kunststoffbeschichtung. Stützen aus Aluminium, zwischen Fußboden
und Decke zu verspannen. Die Elemente
können auch mit Vertäfelungsplatten an
der Wand befestigt werden
WK-Möbel

870 Rudolf Lübben 1963 Germany

Wall storage units "WA" of rosewood or
oak with aluminum ladders
Anbauwand »WA« in Eiche oder Palisander mit Aluminiumleitern
Wilhelm Albrecht

871+872 **Hans Gugelot** c. 1953 Switzerland

Modular storage and shelving system in maple with lacquered sliding doors and tubular steel supports
Regal- und Kastenmöbelsystem in Ahorn mit lackierten Schiebetüren und Stahlrohrträgern
Wohnbedarf Zürich

873 **Peter Biedermann** 1972 Germany

Range of containers "addition", fitted with doors, drawers, flaps, of black-stained ash with red-brown mahagony frames. The underside of each unit is fitted with adhesive discs; twenty different units may be assembled to a variety of combinations
Kastenmöbelserie »addition«, mit Türen, Schubfächern oder Klappen, aus schwarz gebeiztem Eschenholz mit Rahmen aus rotbraunem Mahagoni. Auf der Unterseite jedes Elements sind Haftscheiben angebracht; zwanzig verschiedene Einheiten lassen sich vielseitig kombinieren
Mobilia Collection

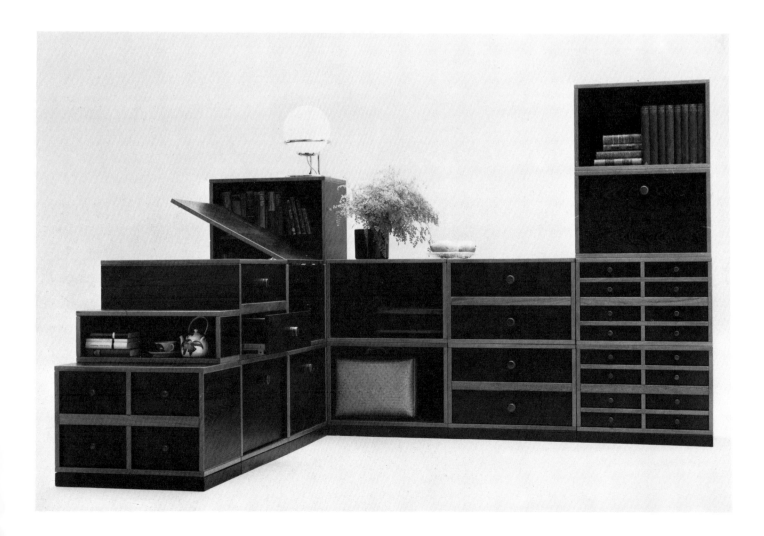

874 Joe Colombo 1968 Italy

Range of containers "Square Plastic System" comprising six units and a number of plastic parts; units may be mounted on wall, stacked, linked, or placed back-to-back to form a variety of combinations such as wall units, partitions, or separate pieces of furniture; available also with casters and in three different colors
Kastenmöbelserie »Square Plastic System« aus Kunststoff. Die sechs Grundeinheiten lassen sich mit den ebenfalls aus Kunststoff bestehenden Verbindungselementen zu Anbauwänden, Raumteilern oder frei stehenden Kastenmöbeln jeder Art und Größe beliebig kombinieren. Auch mit Rollen und in drei verschiedenen Farben lieferbar
Elco

875 Horst Brüning 1969 Germany

Modular range of furniture that can be mounted on a wall or stand free; may be combined individually as desired. Cabinet or shelf units are suspended between side panels. Doors and drawer fronts in natural or white lacquered wood or in anodized aluminum
Modulares Möbelprogramm, das frei aufgestellt oder an der Wand montiert werden kann. Kästen und Fachböden werden zwischen den Seitenwangen eingehängt; die Fronten der Kästen und Schubladen sind aus Naturholz, auch weiß lackiert oder in eloxiertem Aluminium
Hipp-Möbel

876 Dieter Rams 1957 Germany

Wall unit "RZ 57" with cabinet doors and back panels in light grey plastic laminate, shelves and side panels with beech veneer. Supporting construction of anodized aluminum
Anbauwand »RZ 57«; Türen der Kastenelemente und Rückwände mit lichtgrauem Kunststoff beschichtet, Seitenwände und Fachböden mit Buchenfurnier. Tragekonstruktion aus matt eloxiertem Aluminium
Vitsoe + Zapf

877 Helmut Magg 1964 Germany

Storage units "DeWe 500" with matching table and chairs. All frames and edges of solid oak, drawer and door fronts and back panels white plastic. Seat and back of chairs covered with black leather, table top of plywood with grey plastic laminate
Möbelprogramm »DeWe 500« mit passendem Tisch und Stühlen. Stollen und alle Kanten Eiche massiv, alle Flächen einschließlich der Rückwände mit weißem Kunststoff beschichtet. Sitz und Rückenlehne der Stühle mit schwarzem Leder bezogen; Tischplatte aus Sperrholz mit grauer Kunststoffbeschichtung
Deutsche Werkstätten

880 + 881 Enrico Somaini 1968 Switzerland ▷

Furniture group "Squadra" consisting of five basic elements (open-frame base, two cabinet units, U-shaped combination pieces of book height, and shelf) of white laminated plastic; can be combined horizontally and vertically as desired. Smaller arrangements may be mounted on casters
Möbelsystem »Squadra« mit fünf weiß kunststoffbeschichteten Grundelementen (offener Sockelrahmen, zwei Kastenelemente, U-förmige Zwischenstücke in Buchhöhe, Zwischen- oder Abschlußplatte), die sich horizontal und vertikal zu beliebigen, auch auf Rollen beweglichen Kombinationen zusammenstellen lassen
Victoria-Werke

878 Jürgen Lange 1970/71 Germany

"behr 1600 paneel" series consisting of
wall panels of various heights and widths
with aluminum edges, fixed on rails of anodized aluminum; joints between panels are
covered with plastic extrusions, hiding the
wall fastening. Shelves, storage elements,
mirrors, lighting fixtures, hooks and tables
can be hung into the joints at any desired
position
Programm »behr 1600 paneel« aus verschieden breiten und hohen, weiß lackierten Wandtafeln mit Aluminiumkanten, an
Schienen aus eloxiertem Aluminium montiert. Die Fugen sind mit Kunststofflamellen
verblendet, um die Wandbefestigung zu
verdecken. Regalböden, Kastenelemente,
Spiegel, Lampen, Garderobehaken und
Tische werden an beliebiger Stelle in die
Fugen eingehängt
Behr

879 Team Form AG 1969 Switzerland

Living room and bedroom complex "Umgebung 121" with a wide range of modular
elements finished in grey white lacquer
creating individual environments. Complex
includes beds of various sizes, seats,
shelves, chests of drawers, cupboards, numerous table combinations, and a variety
of interior storage facilities
Möbelprogramm »Umgebung 121« mit vielen Kombinationsmöglichkeiten zur Gestaltung eines individuellen Wohn- und
Schlafbereichs. Das weißgrau lackierte
Programm umfaßt unter anderem Betten
in verschiedenen Breiten, Kastenborde,
Kommoden, Schränke, zahlreiche Tisch-
kombinationen; die Inneneinteilung ist vielseitig und variabel
Interlübke

882 **Eduard Ludwig** c. 1950 Germany

Demountable sideboard of wood with colored sliding doors
Auseinandernehmbare Anrichte mit farbigen Schiebetüren
Domus

883 **Fred Hochstrasser** 1956 Germany

Bookshelves in birch or teak with black lacquered supports of various heights
Bücherregal mit Fachböden in Birke oder Teak und verschieden hohen, schwarz lackierten Winkelträgern
Bofinger

884–886 **Jaap Penraat** 1956 Netherlands

Bookshelves consisting of interlocking plywood panels which can be assembled as desired
Bücherregalsystem aus Sperrholzplatten, die beliebig zusammengesteckt werden können
Pentagonia

887–889 **Angelo Mangiarotti, Bruno Morassutti** 1955 Italy ▷

Bookshelves composed of wood elements stacked on each other
Bücherregal, aus einzelnen Holzelementen zusammengesteckt
Fratelli Frigerio

890–892 **Angelo Mangiarotti, Bruno Morassutti** 1957 Italy ▷

"Multi-Use" collapsible bookshelves of wood or plastic. Two vertical boards support a series of horizontal and vertical partitions joined by fillets, without screws or any other metal components. The fillets also provide grooves for sliding doors
»Multi-Use«, zerlegbares Regalsystem in Holz oder Kunststoff. Zwei vertikale Elemente tragen eine Reihe von horizontalen und vertikalen Trennplatten, die von profilierten Leisten ohne Schrauben oder andere Metallteile zusammengehalten werden. Die Leistenprofile dienen auch als Gleitrillen für die Schiebetüren
Fratelli Frigerio

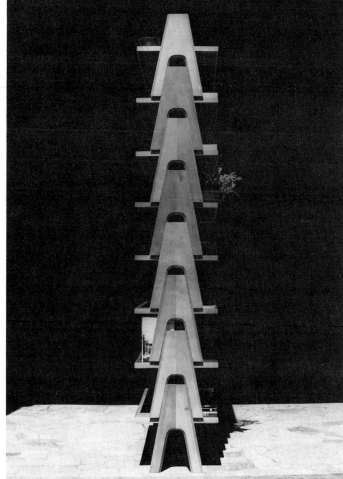

887	889
888	
890	891
	892

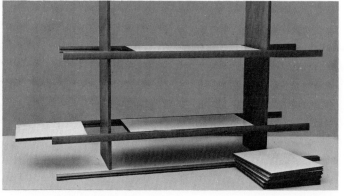

893 Ueli Berger 1961 Switzerland

Multi-purpose units "UBE 61" of fir or beech in natural or lacquer finish. Single elements are joined by means of nylon linking devices. Units may be combined with drawers of plastic, glass tops, seat cushions and filing equipment
Mehrzweck-Kastenelemente »UBE 61« aus Tanne oder Buche natur oder lackiert. Montage mit Nylonverbindern. Als Ergänzung Kunststoffschubladen, Glastablare, Sitzkissen oder Hängeregistratureinsätze
Wohngestaltung Heydebrand

894 Emanuele Ponzio 1960 Italy

Bookshelves "LB-4" of walnut or rosewood; shelves are inserted into notches in side panels. Cabinet units can be added at various heights
Bücherregal »LB-4« aus Nußbaum oder Palisander; senkrechte Seitenwangen und Fachböden sind ineinander verzahnt. In bestimmten Höhen lassen sich Kastenelemente einstecken
Cantieri Carugati

895–897 Gianfranco Frattini 1960 Italy

Bookshelves "540" of jacaranda or teak. Side panels equipped with guide-rails, into the grooves of which shelves are inserted
Anbau-Bücherregal »540« aus Jacaranda oder Teak. Die Seitenwangen sind mit Führungsleisten versehen, in deren Einschnitte die Fachböden eingeschoben werden
Bernini

898 + 899 Mario Ravegnani Morosini 1954 Italy   ▷

Modular bookshelves of wood with fronts in plywood and metal fittings
Bücherregalsystem aus Holz mit Außenseiten aus Sperrholz und Metallbeschlägen
Plotini

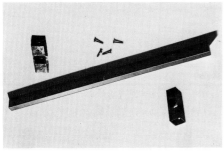

900 Hans Ebbe Nielsen 1975 Denmark

Modular bookshelf system "Cubex" of light pinewood with acid-fast varnish or white lacquer finish; bases and panels in different lengths can be assembled by connectors of black plastic without tools. Units may be supplemented with sliding doors, table tops, or back panels
Bücherregalsystem »Cubex« aus hellem Kiefernholz mit säurefestem farblosem oder weißem Lack; Sockel und Bretter in verschiedenen Längen werden mit einer Steckverbindung aus schwarzem Kunststoff ohne Werkzeug zusammengefügt. Die Elemente können mit Schiebetüren, Tischplatten oder Rückwänden ergänzt werden
Royal System – Cado

901 + 902 Heinz Witthoeft 1964 Germany

Furniture system "Tail 12", assembled from modular basic elements of beech, punctured at regular intervals; steel fittings. Accessoires are chipboard panels finished in plastic laminate and seat slings of leather or canvas
Möbelsystem »Tail 12« aus gelochten Stäben in Rotbuche, Stahlbeschläge. Als Fachböden werden kunststoffbeschichtete Spanplatten verwendet; Sitze und Bespannungen aus Leder oder Segeltuch
Witthoeft

905 Hans Staeger, Manfred Malzacher 1964 ▷
Germany

Room divider and shelving complex "raum
technik system rts" can be set up in many
combinations including separate pieces of
furniture. Panels of glass or white laminated plastic, also veneered panels, are
assembled by grey or clear plastic or
chromed corner caps. Accessoires include
panels with built-in lighting fixtures, slide-
projector boxes, mirrors, drawers, hinged
or sliding doors
Vielseitig kombinierbares Regalsystem
»raum technik system rts«, das auch zu
frei stehenden Einzelmöbeln zusammengesetzt werden kann. Platten aus Glas, mit
weißer Kunststoffbeschichtung oder mit
Furnier werden mit Eckstücken aus
grauem Kunststoff, auch glasklar oder verchromt, zusammengesteckt. Das Zubehör
umfaßt auf Platten montierte Leuchten,
Diakästen, Spiegel, Schubladen, Dreh-
oder Schiebetüren
Staeger

903 Christoph-Albrecht Kühn zu Reineck 1968 Germany

Shelf complex "C3" of chipboard may be used for circular shelving. Shelf units are assembled
from four paired, interlocking boards that are connected with each other by turning them
at a 90 degree angle
Regalsystem »C3« aus Spanplatten mit vielen Kombinationsmöglichkeiten, auch für runde
Regalwände. Die Kastenelemente werden aus vier paarweise gleichen Platten zusammengesteckt und dann jeweils um 90 Grad verdreht ineinandergeschoben
Poul Kold Møbler

904 Enzo Mari 1969 Italy

Shelf complex with side panels of corrugated cardboard and shelves of transparent plastic
Regalsystem mit Seitenteilen aus Wellpappe und Fachböden aus transparentem
Kunststoff
Danese

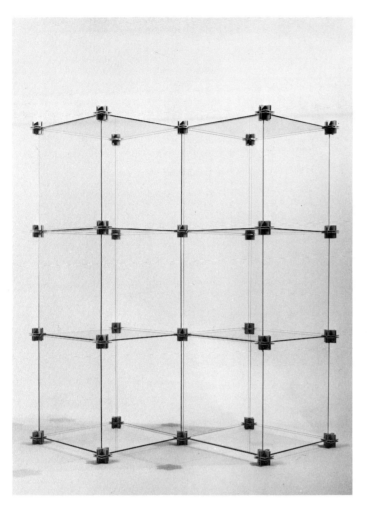

906 **Dieter Schempp** 1967 Germany

Shelving system "easy" of colored or white plastic panels, assembled by connectors of black plastic
Regalsystem »easy« aus farbigen oder weißen Kunststoffplatten, die in schwarze Eckstücke aus Kunststoff eingesteckt werden
Pes Schwenk

907 **OMK Design Ltd**. 1971 Great Britain

"T" shelving system in two heights, assembled of chrome-plated steel tubes and knuckle joints. Shelves of glass
»T«-Regalsystem in zwei Höhen, zusammengesteckt aus verchromten Stahlrohren und Verbindungsstücken. Fachböden aus Glas
OMK Furniture

908 **Corrado Cocconi, Fabio Lenci** 1970 Italy

Shelf system of cubes in clear or smoked Plexiglas. Fittings and linking devices of chrome-plated metal, bases of polished aluminum and black Plexiglas
Regalsystem mit Würfeln aus klarem oder rauchfarbenem Plexiglas. Beschläge und Verbindungsstücke aus verchromtem Metall, Sockel aus poliertem Aluminium und schwarzem Plexiglas
Ilform

911+912 **Jonathan De Pas, Donato D'Urbino, Paolo Lomazzi** 1971
Italy

Shelf system "Jeep" of injection-molded ABS. End panels with slide
connections and bolted with plastic stoppers. Shelves with wide
edges for stiffening purposes fixed to the end panels
Regalsystem »Jeep« aus ABS, im Spritzgußverfahren hergestellt.
Die Seitenteile werden ineinandergeschoben und mit Kunststoffbol-
zen verriegelt. Fachböden mit breiten Kanten zur konstruktiven Aus-
steifung auf die Seitenwangen aufgesteckt
BBB Bonacina

▷ 913 **Ernesto Gismondi** 1971 Italy

Shelf system "Dodona 300" of ABS resin.
Hidden connection of side panels and
shelves with angular linking devices,
pushed from above into the slots of side
panels and fitting into the ends of the
shelves
Regalsystem »Dodona 300« aus ABS-
Kunstharz. Unsichtbare Verbindung von
Seitenteilen und Fachböden durch Metall-
winkel, die von oben in die Rillen der Seitenteile eingeschoben werden und in die
hohlen Fachböden eingreifen
Artemide

◁ ◁ 909 **Rolf Heide** 1969 Germany

"Montageregal", shelf system of lacquer-
finished sheet steel in three heights and
two depths. Shelves, punched frame posts
and stiffening elements screwed. Writing
top can be mounted in horizontal or slant-
ing position. Base edges protected with
black rubber blocks
»Montageregal« aus farbig lackiertem
Stahlblech in drei Höhen und zwei Tiefen;
Fachböden, gelochte Winkelpfosten und
Versteifungsbleche verschraubt. Die
Schreibtischplatte kann waagrecht oder
schräg montiert werden. Fuß aus schwarzem Gummi
Wohnbedarf Hamburg

◁ 910 **Sergio Mazza** 1969 Italy

Book shelf "Sergesto" of ABS resin. Side
panels assembled of single elements to desired height. Shelves pushed into built-in
tracks of side panels
Bücherregal »Sergesto« aus ABS-Kunstharz. Seitenteile aus Einzelelementen zu
beliebiger Höhe zusammenzustecken.
Fachböden in Schienen der Seitenteile eingeschoben
Artemide

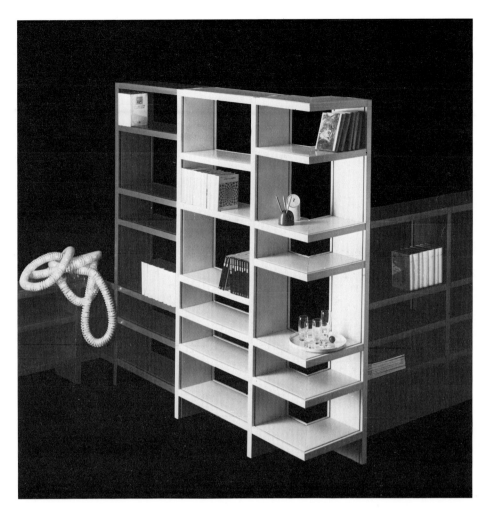

914 **H. Maier-Aichen** 1968 Germany

Open cubes of molded wood finished in
lacquer; elements in three sizes may be
combined to shelving units
Offene Formholzwürfel, farbig lackiert, in
drei Größen lieferbar. Sie können einzeln
oder als Regaleinheiten verwendet werden
Holzmanufaktur Oberaichen

915 **Olaf von Bohr** 1969 Italy

Shelf complex of injection-molded plastic; four vertical and three horizontal units may be
interlocked as desired. Maximum stability and load-bearing capacity is achieved without
any fittings
Regalsystem aus Kunststoff, im Spritzgußverfahren hergestellt; vier vertikale und drei horizon-
tale Elemente lassen sich nach Belieben zusammenstecken. Die Regale sind ohne jede Verbindungselemente äußerst stabil und belastbar
Kartell

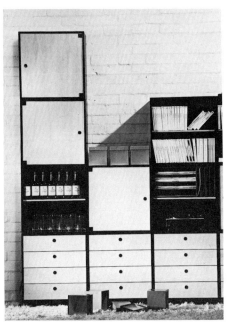

916 **Works Design** c. 1958 Netherlands

"Stabilux" sheet steel wall unit for residental and office interiors, with detachable shelves, drawer inserts, open and closed compartments, sliding writing top, and back panels
Anbauregal »Stabilux« für Wohnung und Büro aus Stahlblech mit verstellbaren Fachböden, Schubladeneinsätzen, offenen und geschlossenen Fächern, ausziehbarer Schreibplatte und Rückwänden
De Cirkel

917 **The Conran Design Group** 1967 Great Britain

Storage system "Stowaway", built up from five units. Boxes are stained dark brown, with backs, shelves, doors and drawers in natural beech. Units are located on pins
Schrankwandsystem »Stowaway« aus fünf Grundelementen, die durch Dübel miteinander verbunden werden. Die Kastenelemente sind dunkelbraun gebeizt; Rückwände, Türen, Fachböden und Schubladen aus Buche natur
Conran

918 **Gino Marotta** 1967/68 Italy

Furniture system "Koan Bonde" of lacquer finished wood. All elements including matching beds are demountable and can be combined as desired
Möbelsystem »Koan Bonde« aus farbig lackiertem Holz. Alle Elemente, darunter ein passendes Bett, sind zerlegbar und können nach Belieben montiert werden
Lorenzon

919 + 920 **Joe Colombo** 1967 Italy

"Triangular System" with units which can be combined as desired. Basic elements in three heights, of white plastic-laminated panels with black edges, are mounted on casters; interior storage facilities include various kinds of shelves and drawers
»Triangular System«, Kastenmöbelprogramm mit beliebig kombinierbaren Elementen aus weiß kunststoffbeschichteten Platten mit schwarzen Kanten in drei Höhen, auf Rollen befestigt; Inneneinteilungen mit Fachböden und Schubladen in verschiedenen Formen
Elco

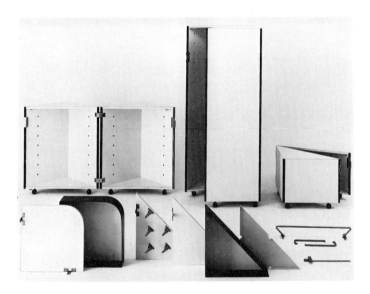

921 + 922 **Jonathan De Pas, Donato D'Urbino, Paolo Lomazzi** 1970 Italy

Furniture system "Dado & Vite" with panels in different sizes of natural or white lacquer-finished plywood which can be joined by bolts and nuts of plastic to individual pieces of furniture in a great variety. Several additions like drawers, round table tops and cushions
Möbelsystem »Dado & Vite« mit verschieden großen Platten aus Sperrholz, natur oder weiß lackiert, die durch Schrauben und Würfelmuttern aus ABS zu beliebigen Möbelstücken verbunden werden können. Verschiedene Ergänzungen wie Schubladen, runde Tischplatten und Polster
BBB Bonacina

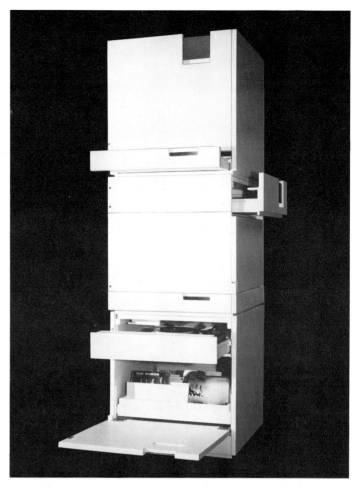

923 Claudio Salocchi 1967 Italy

Free-standing revolving bookcase "Centro HiFi"; the lower element can be equipped with a complete hi-fi-set. Wooden parts of rosewood or in lacquer finish, plastic-laminated door fronts, central support of stove-enameled metal
Frei stehendes, drehbares Bücherregal »Centro HiFi«, dessen unterer Teil mit einer kompletten Stereoanlage ausgestattet werden kann. Holzteile in Palisander oder lakkiert, Türen kunststoffbeschichtet, Mittelstütze aus einbrennlackiertem Metall
Sormani

924 Carlo Viganò 1968 Italy

Modular container series "Euro 2" of wood in lacquer finish. Units with a great variety of interior equipment are composed of six elements which can be combined horizontally and vertically as desired
Modulares Kastenmöbelsystem »Euro 2« aus lackiertem Holz. Die einzelnen Behälter können aus sechs Grundelementen beliebig zusammengesetzt, horizontal und vertikal kombiniert sowie mit verschiedener Inneneinteilung je nach Wunsch ausgestattet werden
Cesare Augusto Nava

925 Gerhard Schneider 1970 Germany

Open cubes "WR 390/391" with or without casters; may be used individually as side table or tea trolley, or, combined horizontally or vertically, as storage units; wood, lacquer finished
Offene Würfelelemente »WR 390/391« aus farbig lackiertem Holz, mit oder ohne Rollen, die einzeln als Teewagen oder Beistelltisch, horizontal und vertikal kombiniert als frei stehendes Regal verwendet werden können
Wilhelm Renz

923	924
925	926

927 Joe Colombo 1969 Italy

Range of containers "Square Plastic System", comprising six units and a number of plastic connecting parts. Units may be mounted on a wall, stacked, linked, or placed back-to-back to form a variety of combinations such as wall units, partitions, or separate pieces of furniture
Kastenmöbelsystem »Square Plastic System« aus Kunststoff. Die sechs Grundeinheiten lassen sich mit Verbindungselementen ebenfalls aus Kunststoff zu Anbauwänden, Raumteilern oder frei stehenden Kastenmöbeln jeder Art und Größe kombinieren
Elco

928 Works Design 1971 Italy

Stackable shelf cubes "Questo" of plastic-laminated chipboard panels, open or with drawers
Stapelbare Regalwürfel »Questo« aus kunststoffbeschichteten Spanplatten, offen oder mit Schubladen
Essex

929 Ristomatti Ratia 1970 Finland

"Palaset", range of cubic elements with various interior compartments manufactured in one piece of injection-molded polystyrol, lacquer finished. Can be assembled as desired for various purposes. Additional drawers, doors and base frames can be added
»Palaset«, Würfelelemente mit verschiedenen Inneneinteilungen in einem Stück aus Polystyrol im Spritzgußverfahren hergestellt und farbig lackiert. Beliebig zu größeren Einheiten kombinierbar und durch Schubladen, Türen sowie Bodenrahmen zu ergänzen
Treston Oy

◁ **926 Cini Boeri** 1968 Italy

Chest of drawers, movable on casters, made of wood and finished in plastic laminate
Auf Rollen bewegliches Kastenmöbel mit Schubladen, Holz mit Kunststoffbeschichtung
Arflex

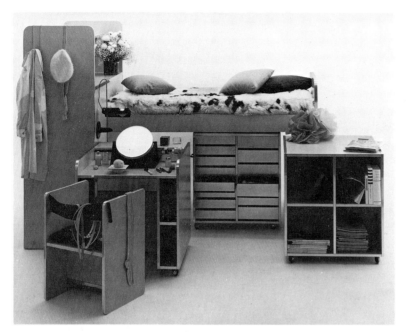

930–932 Joe Colombo 1967/68 Italy

"Box 1", a monoblock comprising all furniture one person needs for sleeping, dressing, reading, playing and so on: bed, bedside, table, closet, drawers, bookcase, desk/dressing table, and a chair that can be used as steps, all fitting together to form a space-saving block. Units are made of wood panels with plastic laminate, and trimmed in metallized plastics

Möbelblock »Box 1«, der alles umfaßt, was eine Person zum Schlafen, Ankleiden, Lesen, Spielen usw. braucht: Bett, Nachttisch, Schrank, Schubfächer, Bücherregal, Schreib- und Toilettentisch sowie einen Stuhl, der umgedreht als Trittstufe dient. Die Einzelelemente bestehen aus kunststoffbeschichteten Holzplatten mit Umleimern aus metallisch wirkendem Kunststoff und können zu einem raumsparenden Block zusammengeschoben werden
La Linea

933 Jonathan De Pas, Donato D'Urbino, Paolo Lomazzi 1970 Italy

Furniture system "Dado & Vite" with panels in different sizes of natural or white lacquer-finished plywood which can be joined by bolts and nuts to individual pieces of furniture in a great variety. Several additions like drawers, round table tops and cushions available

Möbelsystem »Dado & Vite« mit verschieden großen Platten aus Sperrholz natur oder weiß lackiert, die durch Schrauben und Würfelmuttern aus farbigem ABS zu beliebigen Möbelstücken verbunden werden können. Verschiedene Ergänzungen wie Schubladen, runde Tischplatten und Polster
BBB Bonacina

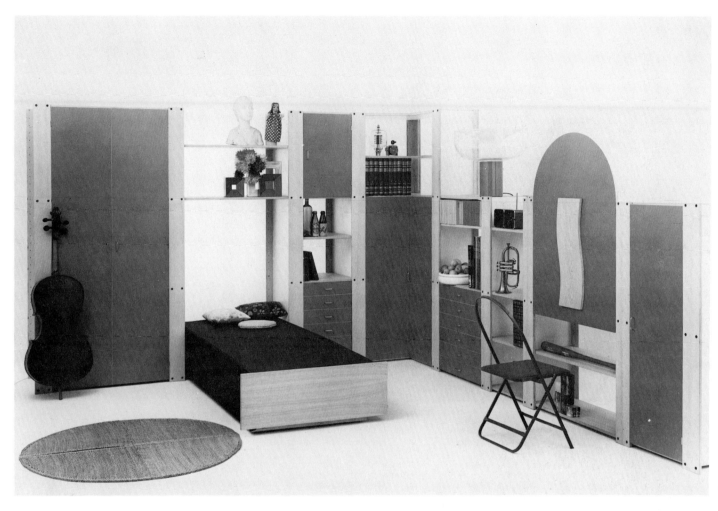

934–936 Roberto Pamio, Renato Toso, Noti Massari 1969 Italy

Modular wall unit "Carioca" with elements (plywood supports, ply-wood frames veneered in ash, side and back panels of plywood covered in plastic) which are set up by a special pressure-fitting method and can be combined vertically and horizontally as desired. Equipment for the storage units includes shelves, hinged doors laminated in plastic, translucent, screened glass doors, drawers of beech with laminated plastic fronts, and also a folding table and a bed. Nickel-plated metal fittings

Anbaumöbelserie »Carioca« für Wohnräume und Küchen. Die Elemente (Sperrholzständer, mit Esche furnierte Sperrholzrahmen sowie Seiten- und Rückwände aus Sperrholz mit Kunststoffbeschichtung) werden mit einer speziellen Einspannmethode horizontal und vertikal nach Belieben kombiniert. Der so entstehende Stauraum kann mit Fachböden, Türflügeln in farbiger Kunststoffbeschichtung, Türen aus transparentem Drahtglas, Schubladen aus Buche mit kunststoffbeschichteten Fronten ausgestattet werden; zum Zubehör gehören außerdem Bett und Klapptisch. Vernickelte Beschläge Stilwood

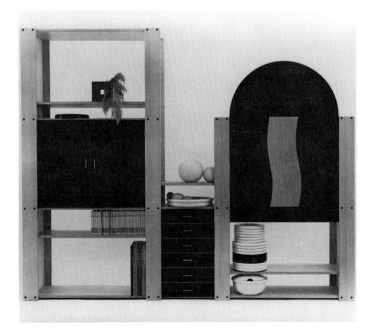

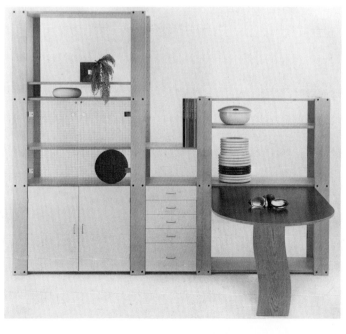

937–940 Joe Colombo 1964/65 Italy

Series of foldable containers, equipped for a variety of purposes. Shown here are: Closed and locked container in walnut, with metal fittings (938), container for men (937), container for ladies (939), container for living room (940)
Aufklappbare Container mit vielseitiger Inneneinteilung. Hier abgebildet sind ein raumsparend zusammengeklappter Behälter aus Nußbaum mit Metallbeschlägen (938), ein Behälter für Herren (937) und Damen (939) sowie ein für den Wohnraum ausgestatteter Behälter (940)
Arflex

937	938
939	940

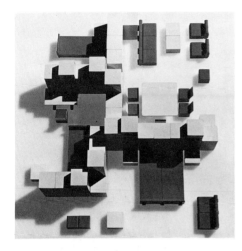

941 + 942 Joe Colombo 1966/67 Italy

Flexible furniture program, designed for
production on an industrial scale and for
distribution by department stores. The system comprises seating and lighting elements, beds, and a variety of cabinet units,
all of which can be arranged and rear-
ranged according to individual needs.
Cabinet units, which are joined magneti-
cally, are finished in plastic laminate;
upholstered seating elements and beds
are supported by L-shaped metal
parts
Vielseitig kombinierbares Möbelsystem,
das speziell für industrielle Serienproduk-
tion und zum Vertrieb durch Kaufhäuser
entworfen wurde. Das System umfaßt Sitzmöbel, Leuchten, Betten und zahlreiche
Kastenelemente, die beliebig kombiniert
und umgruppiert werden können. Die
kunststoffbeschichteten Kastenelemente
sind mit Magneten untereinander verbunden; Polstersitze und Betten haben L-förmige Metallgestelle
La Rinascente

943 + 944 Rolf Heide 1971 Germany

Container units "Rollschränke" with side and back panels of sheet steel; doors, shelves,
foot and head parts of wood, stained or lacquered. The units are mounted on casters
and can be linked with metal coupling devices
»Rollschränke« mit Seiten- und Rückwänden aus Stahlblech sowie Türen, Fachböden, Ab-
deck- und Bodenplatten aus farbig lackiertem oder gebeiztem Holz. Die Schränke sind auf
Rollen montiert und können durch Kupplungslaschen aus Metall miteinander verbunden
werden
Wohnbedarf Hamburg

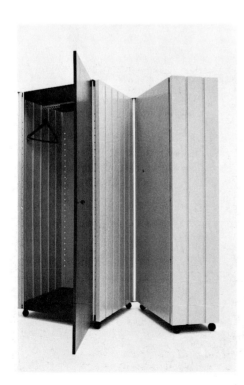

945 **Willy Guhl** c. 1950 Switzerland

Demountable wardrobe cabinet
Auseinandernehmbarer Kleiderschrank
Wohnbedarf Zürich

946 **Works Design** c. 1958 Germany

Beech wardrobe "2702" with square tubular steel legs, plastic-laminated doors, adjustable shelves and drawers
Kleider- und Wäscheschrank »2702« in
Buche mit Füßen aus Vierkantstahlrohr,
kunststoffbeschichteten Türen sowie verstellbaren Fachböden und Schubladen
Knoll International

947 + 948 **Angelo Mangiarotti** c. 1950 Italy   ▷

Wall storage unit, composed of four basic
elements. Frame of wood, front and side
panels lacquered white, fittings of chrome-
plated steel
Anbauwand, aus vier Grundelementen zusammengesetzt. Rahmen aus Holz, Fronten weiß lackiert, Beschläge aus verchromtem Stahl

949 + 950 **Viljo Rewell, Antti Nurmesniemi**   ▷
c. 1954 Finland

Collapsible wardrobe with front and side
panels in white and frame of wood
Zerlegbarer Kleiderschrank mit Front und
Seitenwänden in Weiß und Rahmen aus
Holz
Askon Tehtaat Oy

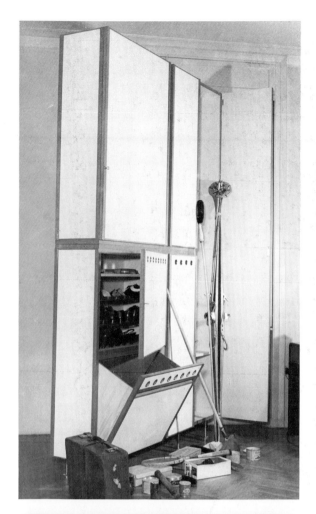

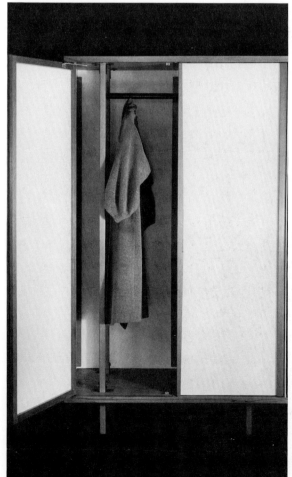
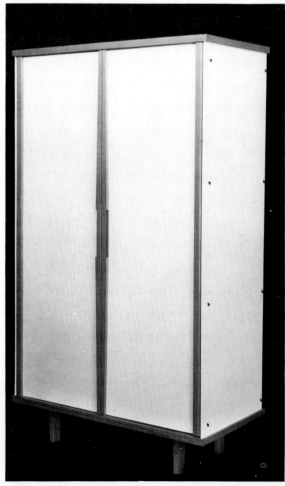

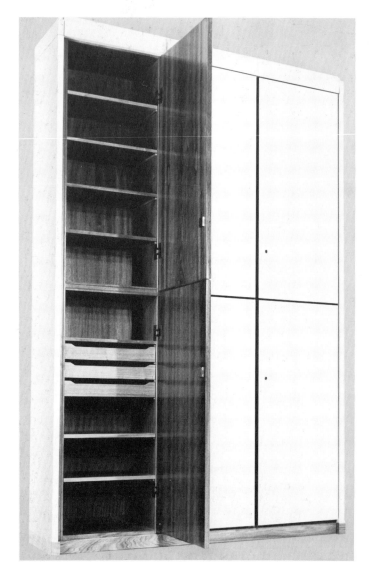

951 **Osvaldo Borsani** 1957 Italy

Collapsible wardrobe "A 57" consisting of interchangeable closed compartments, drawers, and shelves. Mahogany interior, lacquered doors and side panels
Zerlegbarer Kleiderschrank »A 57« aus kombinierbaren Kästen, Schubladen und Fachböden. Innenausführung in Mahagoni, Türen und Seitenwände farbig lackiert
Tecno

952 + 953 **Silvio Coppola** 1970 Italy

Wardrobe of polyurethane, assembled of U-formed wall elements, similar foot and head pieces; doors with built-in partitions
Schrank aus Polyurethan, zusammengesetzt aus U-förmigen Wandelementen sowie gleichen Fuß- und Abschlußstücken; Türen mit Facheinteilung
Bernini

954–956 **Pierluigi Molinari** 1970 Italy

"Box-System", storage units with tambour doors of plastic in various colors and two heights which can be assembled to large combinations. Many varieties for interior partitions: drawers, wardrobe installations and folding tables etc. possible. Table tops can be hung between the storage units with metal supports

»Box-System«, Schränkchen mit Rolljalousien in zwei Höhen aus verschieden gefärbtem Kunststoff, die beliebig verbunden werden können. Inneneinteilung variabel, neben Fachböden, Schubladen und Kleiderstangen ist auch ein Klapptisch-Einsatz erhältlich. Mit Metallbügeln lassen sich außerdem Tischplatten zwischen den Kästen einhängen
Asnaghi Rinaldo & Figli

958+959 **Cees Braakman** 1961 Netherlands

Modular range of wardrobes of Oregon pine, fronts of sliding doors in white lacquer finish with recessed wooden handles; drawers of molded mahogany. Interior equipment can be arranged as desired

Anbauschränke aus Oregon Pine, Fronten der Schiebetüren weiß lackiert, eingelassene Holzgriffe. Inneneinrichtung variabel, darunter Schubfächer aus formgepreßtem Mahagoni
Ums-Pastoe

◁ 957 **Grethe Meyer, Børge Mogensen** 1957
Denmark

"Boligens Byggeskabe" versatile storage units which can be arranged to accommodate all space and storage requirements. Fiberboard sides, bottoms, and backs; Oregon pine front frames with visible brass screws; teak veneered doors. Lacquered interiors; drawers in three sizes have grooves for loose partitions. Hinged and sliding doors of top cabinets lacquered. Brass hardware
Anbauwand »Boligens Byggeskabe« aus variablen Kastenelementen, deren Maße den verschiedensten Wohnbedürfnissen angepaßt werden können. Seitenwände, Böden und Rückwände aus Holzfaserplatten; Vorderrahmen aus Oregon-Kiefer mit sichtbaren Messingschrauben; teakfurnierte Türen. Innenwände der Schränke lackiert; Schubladen in drei Größen mit Rillen zum Einstecken von Trennungen. Hänge- und Schiebetüren der Oberschränke lackiert. Messingbeschläge
Boligens Byggeskabe

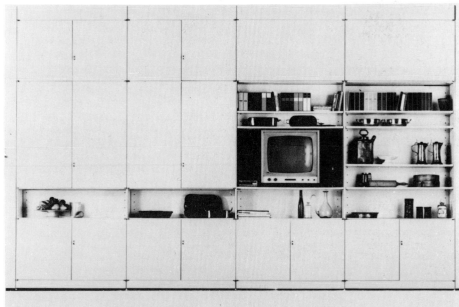

960–962 **Atelier Herbert Hirche** 1959–62
Germany

Demountable wall unit and room dividing system "INwand" of combinable, prefabricated elements. For room dividing, units are available with built-in doors and windows and with cabinets accessible from one or both sides; elements may also be assembled to form built-in cabinets attached to solid walls. Elements are constructed on a module of 12.5 cm in length and 7.5 cm in height
Demontables Schrankwand- und Trennwandsystem »INwand« aus beliebig kombinierbaren, vorfabrizierten Bauteilen zur Aufteilung von Räumen mit ein- und zweiseitig benutzbaren Schränken, auch mit Durchgangstür und Fenster; ferner zur Verwendung als normaler Einbauschrank vor fester Wand. Modul der Elemente: 12,5 cm Breite, 7,5 cm Höhe
Christian Holzäpfel

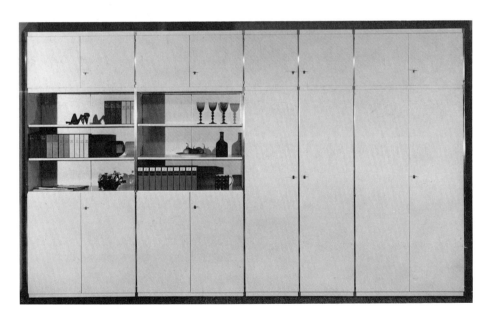

965 + 966 **Arno Votteler** 1964 Germany

Modular wall storage system in knock-down construction with a wide variety of combinations. Supports of U-shaped profile aluminum poles which are connected at both ends by wooden rails. Side and back panels in light grey plastic laminate, visible wooden parts of teak, ash, walnut, rosewood, or with plastic laminate. Adjustable interior equipment may be installed to meet any individual needs

Zerlegbare modulare Schrankwand mit zahlreichen Variationsmöglichkeiten. Tragende U-Profilstollen aus Aluminium, die oben und unten durch Holzzargen eingerahmt werden. Seiten- und Rückwände beidseitig mit Kunststoff beschichtet; Ausführung der sichtbaren Holzteile in Teak, Esche, Nußbaum, Palisander oder in Kunststoff. Variable Inneneinteilung Hans Mäder

◁ 963+964 **Charles Eames** 1961 USA

"Eames Contract Storage", a flexible system of storage, study, and sleeping units with minimum space requirements, including two different hanging units, one dressing unit, one folding bed unit, and a study unit with desk and bookshelves, all mounted free from floor and ceiling and hung from standard unstrut section secured to wall. Fronts of birch plywood, side and back panels of plywood with black resin coating

»Eames Contract Storage«, ein zerlegbares, raumsparendes Schrankwandsystem für Studentenheime aus drei verschiedenen Schranktypen, einem Klappbett und einem Studierelement mit Arbeitstisch und Bücherborden, frei vom Boden und der Decke an Standardschienen an der Wand aufgehängt. Fronten in Birkensperrholz, Seiten- und Rückwände aus Sperrholz mit schwarzem Kunstharzüberzug
Herman Miller

967+968 **Hans Gugelot** 1964 Switzerland

Modular wardrobe units with space-saving folding doors, which may be pressure-fitted between floor and ceiling or used free-standing. Any number of units with a variety of adjustable interior equipment may be joined

Schrankwand mit raumsparenden Falttüren, deren Grundeinheit (mit verstellbarer und variabler Inneneinteilung) beliebig aneinandergereiht werden kann. Die Schrankwand wird zwischen Boden und Decke verspannt oder frei stehend aufgestellt
Bofinger

969+970 **Works Design** 1963 Germany

Modular wall storage system; basic elements can be assembled to any desired length. Great variety of interior equipment. Door fronts of walnut or larch, also in lacquer finish

Schrankwand, aus türbreiten Elementen beliebig lang zusammensetzbar. Zahlreiche Variationsmöglichkeiten der Inneneinteilung. Türfronten aus Nußbaum oder Lärche, auch farbig lackiert
Interlübke

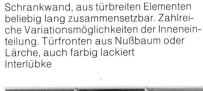

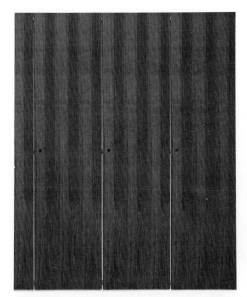

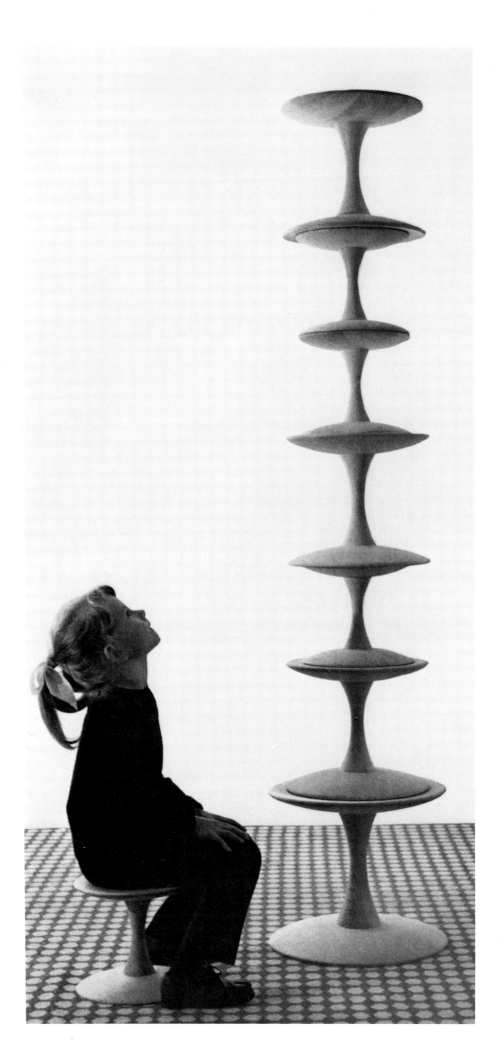

971 **Nanna Ditzel** 1962 Denmark
Stools and tables of different heights and diameters in Oregon pine
Hocker und Tische in verschiedenen Höhen und Durchmessern aus Oregon Pine
Kolds Savværk

Of necessity, children's furniture looks the way adults think children imagine it should look. The consumers' judgement is irrelevant because it is partly influenced by that of others. The fact is that children do not possess the necessary experience really to be able to know what they like. So they have to put up with what others have chosen for them with a greater or lesser amount of care and understanding.

It is generally believed that children prefer simple things which allow their fantasy plenty of scope. This means things that do not proclaim loudly what they are for, but whose possibilities can be gradually discovered. In this respect, the round stools by Nanna Ditzel (ill. 971) are very successful examples because their form is beautiful, clear and stimulating. They can be used to sit on or as tables, and if they are put on their side, they can be rolled. Children can use them to discover what an axle and two wheels is, and—as the picture shows—how to make a tower. In addition, the stools are sturdy, robust and not dangerous.

The wooden boxes that Hans Gugelot designed as play furniture (ills. 977, 978) are similarly sensible. It appears that their educational value was so great that they later moved into adults' rooms in a modified form. The simple idea of stacking up cube-shaped containers and filling them as required is really so obvious one wonders why it is not more common. The traditional attitude was that a piece of furniture must always be a complete object which, although it may be taken apart, cannot be assembled in various ways. This was so widespread that it appeared that a different concept had hardly any chance of gaining acceptance. It took children's furniture to teach us the error of our ways.

And so the position is now exactly the opposite of what it used to be. Whereas children's furniture was often a smaller-scale version of things adults used, the furniture we adults have now seems to be a continuation of what we grew up with. Children's furniture tended to act as preparation for adulthood and contained in its supposed childishness a clearly domesticating style. Today one could often think that furniture allows adults to carry on their childhood games. This is true above all for "do-it-yourself" furniture in kit form. It is based on the experience gathered with children's furniture. This observation reminds us of the influence a toy—Fröbel's building set—had on modern architecture (the American architect Frank Lloyd Wright freely admitted the important stimuli he obtained from this quarter). At the root of it all lies the rediscovery of primary needs and the attempt to face up to them instead of artificially suppressing them.

So the nursery has been regarded for some time as a place for experimenting and making observations. Accordingly, education is seen these days as training in essential experiences, and not so much as the anticipation of adulthood.

Kindermöbel sehen notgedrungen so aus, wie Erwachsene meinen, daß Kinder sie sich vorstellen. Das Urteil der Konsumenten ist insofern irrelevant, weil es ihnen zum Teil suggeriert wird. Kindern fehlt nun einmal die nötige Erfahrung, um wirklich wissen zu können, was sie möchten. Also müssen sie mit dem vorlieb nehmen, was man mehr oder minder einsichtig und verständnisvoll für sie aussucht.

Im allgemeinen wird die Ansicht vertreten, Kinder hätten am liebsten einfache Dinge, die ihrer Phantasie genügend Spielraum lassen. Gemeint sind Sachen, die ihren Sinn und Zweck nicht vorlaut verkünden, sondern die in ihren Möglichkeiten erst allmählich entdeckt werden können. In dieser Hinsicht sind die runden Hocker von Nanna Ditzel (Abb. 971) sehr gelungene Beispiele, weil ihre Form sowohl schön, einleuchtend und anregend ist. Sie können in gleicher Weise zum Sitzen wie auch als Tisch benutzt werden, und wenn man sie umlegt, lassen sie sich rollen. Das Erlebnis, was eine Achse mit zwei Rädern ist, läßt sich an ihnen machen und dann auch – wie das Bild es zeigt – das des Turmbaues. Außerdem sind die Hocker stabil, ungefährlich und robust.

In ähnlicher Weise sinnvoll sind die Holzkästen, die Hans Gugelot als Spielmöbel entwickelt hat (Abb. 977 + 978). Ihr pädagogischer Wert war offensichtlich so groß, daß sie später in abgewandelter Form auch Einzug gehalten haben in den Zimmern der Erwachsenen. Das simple Prinzip, würfelförmige Behälter aufzuschichten und sie je nach Anspruch zu füllen, ist eigentlich so naheliegend, daß man fragen muß, warum es nicht viel gebräuchlicher ist. Die Vorstellung, daß ein Möbel immer ein fertiger Gegenstand sein muß, den man zwar zerlegen kann, der aber in seiner Zusammenstellung nicht variabel ist, war so verbreitet, daß etwas anderes daneben offenbar kaum eine Aussicht hatte, sich durchzusetzen. Erst über den Umweg Kindermöbel wurde uns diese Lehre zuteil.

Der Weg läuft damit gerade umgekehrt wie früher. Waren Kindermöbel in der Vergangenheit oft die Verkleinerungen von Dingen, die Erwachsene benutzten, so scheinen heute die Möbel, mit denen man lebt, die Fortsetzung von denen zu sein, mit denen man groß geworden ist. Kindermöbel dienten gern zur Vorbereitung auf das Erwachsensein und besaßen gerade in ihrer vermeintlichen Kindlichkeit eine deutlich domestizierende Note. Heute könnte man nun meinen, daß Möbel oft den Erwachsenen erlauben, die Spiele ihrer Kindheit fortsetzen zu können. Vor allem für die aus Einzelteilen zusammenfügbaren »Bastelmöbel« gilt das. Sie bauen ganz offensichtlich auf Erfahrungen auf, die man zuerst an Kindermöbeln gemacht hat. Diese Beobachtung vermag daran zu erinnern, welchen Einfluß einmal ein Spielzeug – der Fröbelsche Steckbaukasten – auf die moderne Architektur gehabt hat (der amerikanische Architekt Frank Lloyd Wright bekannte gern, welche wichtigen Anregungen er von dort bezogen hatte). Dahinter steht die Wiederentdeckung primärer Bedürfnisse und der Versuch, sich ihnen zu stellen, statt sie künstlich zu überdecken.

Das Kinderzimmer ist also schon seit geraumer Zeit als Experimentier- und Beobachtungsfeld im Blick, und Erziehung wird dementsprechend heute angesehen als Einübung in lebenswichtige Erfahrungen und nicht so sehr als Vorwegnahme des Erwachsenenseins.

972 **Marcel Breuer** c. 1950 USA
Nursery furniture
Kinderzimmermöbel

973 **Jaap Penraat** c. 1952 Netherlands
Nursery furniture
Kinderzimmermöbel

974 **Eduard Ludwig** c. 1950 Germany
Nursery, table and stools with demountable legs
Kinderzimmer, Tisch und Hocker mit abschraubbaren Beinen
Domus

975 **Herbert Hirche** 1954 Germany ▷
Shelf for toys with steel tube frame and detachable wooden cases
Spielzeugregal mit Stahlrohrgestell und herausnehmbaren Kästen
Christian Holzäpfel

976 **Nisse Strinning** 1955 Sweden ▷▷
Nursery furniture
Kinderzimmermöbel
String Design

977 + 978 **Hans Gugelot** 1953/1964 Germany ▷
Nursery and play furniture of four basic units: long bridge, short bridge, lacquered panel (to be used as blackboard), open box. All elements of pine with hardboard edging, panels with red, yellow, green, and blue lacquer finish. Unites may be used for various purposes and combined in any desired way
Kinderzimmer- und Spielmöbel aus Kiefernholz mit Hartholzkanten und lackierten Farbflächen, deren vier Grundelemente (große Brücke, kleine Brücke, Tafelbrett mit Tafellack, Kubus) zu den verschiedensten Zwecken verwendet werden können und sich beliebig kombinieren lassen
Albin Grünzig

979 + 980 **Nanna Ditzel** 1963 Denmark ▷
Range of nursery furniture, comprising a variety of single units: wardrobes, open and closed cabinets of different sizes with drawers and shelves, tables for play and hoolwork. Wooden parts of Oregon pine, back panels in colored plastic laminate. Units may be used for adults
Kinderzimmermöbel mit einer Vielzahl kombinierbarer Einzelelemente: Schränke, offene und geschlossene Kastenelemente verschiedener Größe mit Schubladen und Fachböden, Spiel- und Arbeitstische. Holzteile aus Oregon Pine, Rückwände der Regaleinheiten mit farbigem Kunststoff beschichtet. Umgruppierung der verschiedenen Elemente ist jederzeit möglich. Das Programm kann auch für Erwachsene verwendet werden
Kolds Savværk

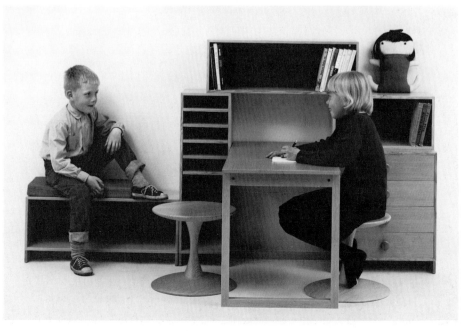

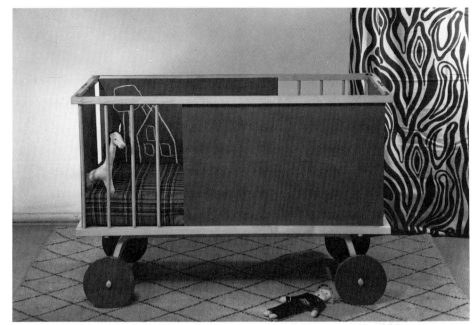

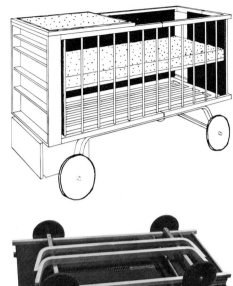

△ 981–983 **Franz Füeg** c. 1953 Switzerland

Demountable cot
Demontierbares und zusammenlegbares
Kinderbett
Franz Füeg

◁ 984 **Vera Catz** c. 1952 Netherlands

Cot
Kinderbett

▽ 985–987 **Emil Guhl** c. 1956 Switzerland

Adjustable cot with removable wood pen
and chest
Verstellbares Kinderbett mit abnehmbarem
Holzgitterställchen und einem Aufsatz-
schränkchen
Emil Guhl

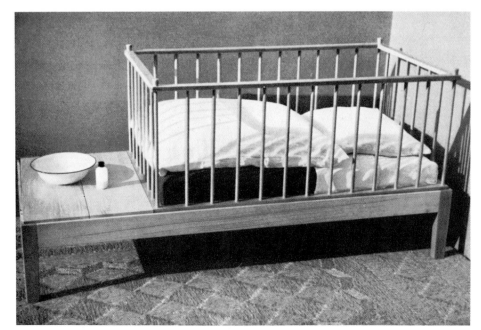

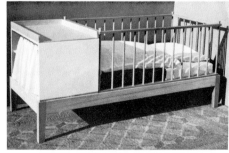

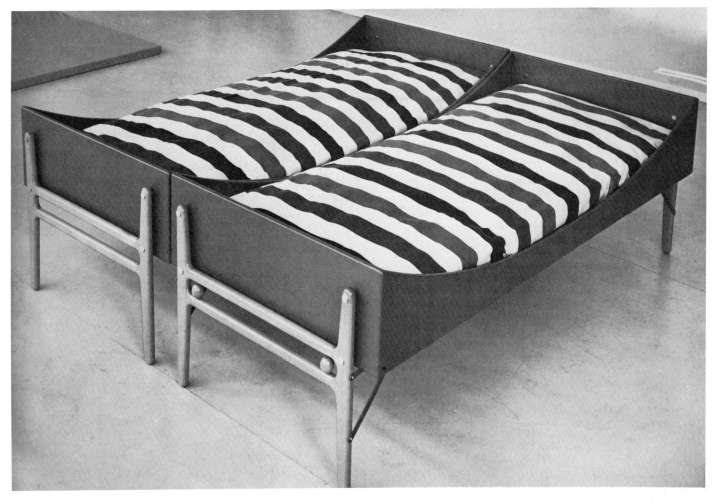

△ 988+989 **Thea Leonhard** c. 1950 Sweden

Cots with polished wooden frame and lacquered wooden beds; can be pushed one under the other
Kinderbetten aus poliertem Holzgestell mit gestrichenen Bettladen, übereinanderstellbar
Boklund & Davidson

▽ 990–992 **Nanna Ditzel** 1964 Denmark

Demountable children's bed of Oregon pine with adjustable railing; without rails to be used as sofa
Zerlegbares Kinderbett aus Oregon Pine mit verstellbarem Gitter; ohne Gitter als Sofa verwendar
Kolds Savværk

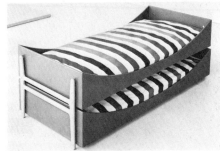

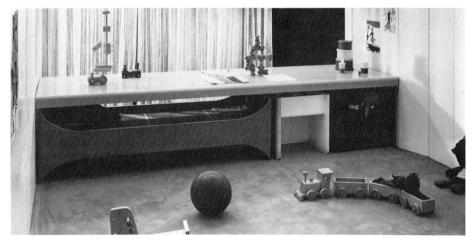

993 **Eva and Nils Koppel** 1952 Denmark

Children's beds to be placed one upon the other
Übereinanderstellbare Kinderbetten
Bech Jensen

994 **René Jean Caillette** 1964 France

Nursery furniture of Formica; bed and cab-
inet unit in front of window red, play box
black, stool white
Kinderzimmermöbel aus Formica; Bett und
Schrankelement vor dem Fenster in Rot,
Spielzeugkiste in Schwarz, Hocker in
Weiß
Charron

995 **Gigi Sabadin** 1971 Italy

Bunk bed "Bibo" of natural ash. Beds can
be hung at any height, joints with metal
pegs which fit into borings of the posts.
Pedestal drawers on casters in two
widths
Doppelstockbett »Bibo« aus Esche natur.
Betten in beliebiger Höhe einzuhängen;
Verbindungsstücke mit Metallstiften, die in
die Bohrungen der Pfosten eingreifen.
Passende Rollschubladen in zwei Breiten
zum Unterschieben
Gigi Sabadin

998 **Roberto Pamio, Renato Toso, Noti
Massari** 1969 Italy   ▷

Children's desk "Grillo" with wooden top
and folding frame in blue, red or white
Kinderschreibtisch »Grillo« mit Holzplatte
auf blauem, rotem oder weißem Klappgestell
Stilwood

999 **Giancarlo Piretti** 1972 Italy   ▷ ▷

Folding table "Platone" with frame of
chrome-plated steel tube and plastic top
in various colors with molded tray
Klapptisch »Platone« mit Gestell aus verchromtem Stahlrohr, Platte aus Kunststoff
in verschiedenen Farben mit Ablagevertie-
fungen
Anonima Castelli

996+997 Marc Berthier 1972 France

Children's furniture range "Twentytube" of lacquer-finished steel
tube in yellow, red or green. Canvas slings, shelves and table tops
with white plastic laminate. The range consists of single and double
beds, wardrobes and shelves, tables and desks with matching
chairs
Kinderzimmerprogramm »Twentytube« aus gelb, rot oder grün lak-
kiertem Stahlrohr mit Segeltuchbespannungen sowie Tisch- und
Regalplatten mit weißer Kunststoffbeschichtung. Das Programm
umfaßt Einzel- und Doppelbetten, Schrank- und Regaleinheiten,
Tische und Schreibtische mit passenden Stühlen
Roche-Bobois

1000 + 1001 **Angelo Mangiarotti, Bruno Morassutti** 1955 Italy
Collapsible nursery school tables composed of beech elements
Zerlegbare Kindergartentische aus Buchenholzelementen
Fratelli Frigerio

1002 **Wilhelm Kienzle** c. 1952 Switzerland
Kindergarten tables in manifold combinations
Kindergartentische in verschiedenen Kombinationen
Horgen-Glarus

1005–1007 **Kristian Vedel** 1956/57 ▷
Denmark
Children's furniture with molded plywood backs, adjustable seats and boards. Various possibilities of use as chair, playtable and swing
Kindermöbel mit gewölbtem Rückenteil aus geformtem Sperrholz und verstellbarem Sitz- und Tischbrett. Verschiedene Verwendungsmöglichkeiten als Stühlchen, Spieltisch, Schaukel
Torben Ørskov

1003 **Alain Richard** c. 1953 France

Toy cases
Spielzeugkisten
Charron

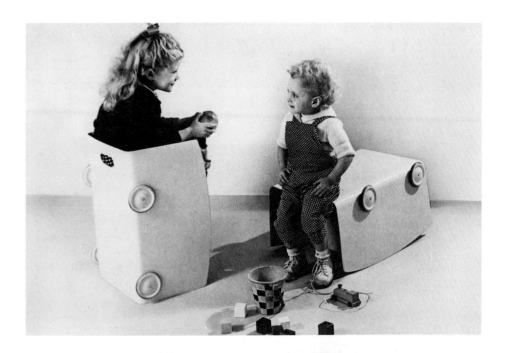

1004 **Kristian Vedel** 1956/57 Denmark   ▷

Play-table composed of one table and
four chairs
Spieltisch, zusammengefügt aus einer
Platte und vier Stühlchen
Torben Ørskov

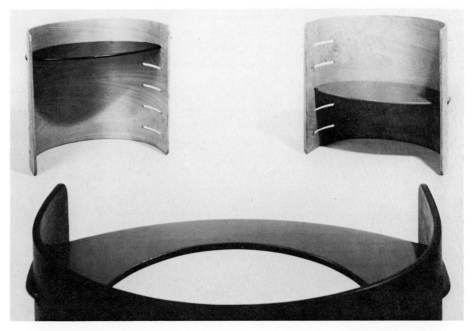

1008–1012 **Works Design** 1969 Germany
"Die Baukiste", a range of children's play
furniture, consisting of ten items of strong
corrugated board in three shapes (trian-
gle, square, circle); may be combined to
form a variety of furniture and playthings;
units are laminated in plastic in various
colors on one side, the other side is left
untreated to be painted or decorated by
the children; parts are combined by
means of easy-to-handle big, plastic
screws with rounded corners
»Die Baukiste«, Baukastensystem für Kin-
derspielmöbel aus starker Wellpappe. Die
zehn Einzelteile einer Serie werden in drei
Grundformen (Dreieck, Quadrat, Kreis)
geliefert und können vielfältig kombiniert
werden. Die Teile sind auf einer Seite mit
farbigem Kunststofflack beschichtet; die
andere Seite blieb unbeschichtet, damit
die Kinder sie nach Belieben bemalen
oder bekleben können. Große, leicht zu
handhabende Kunststoffschrauben mit
gerundeten Ecken verbinden die einzelnen Teile
3h Design Hübner + Huster

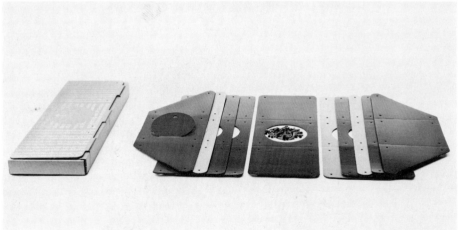

1013 + 1014 Jonathan De Pas, Donato D'Urbino, Paolo Lomazzi 1973 Italy

Children's chair "Chica" of injection die-casted ABS resin in yellow or red, consisting of four parts which can be put together as desired
Kinderstuhl »Chica«, aus blau, gelb oder rot gefärbtem ABS im Spritzgußverfahren hergestellt. Seine vier Einzelteile können beliebig zusammengesteckt werden
BBB Bonacina

1015 + 1016 Marco Zanuso, Richard Sapper 1964 Italy/Germany

Children's chair "K 1340" of injection molded low density polyethylene, available in white, yellow, blue, or red, consisting of three elements which are joined under pressure (seat, legs, gliders). Developed for nursery and small school children, chairs may be used as building units
Kinderstuhl »K 1340« aus Niederdruck-Polyäthylen, im Spritzgußverfahren hergestellt und in den Farben weiß, gelb, blau und rot lieferbar. Der Stuhl besteht aus drei Elementen (Sitz, Beine, Gleiter), die durch Druck zusammengefügt werden. Der Stuhl wurde für Kindergärten und erste Grundschulklassen entwickelt und läßt sich auch zum Bauen verwenden
Kartell

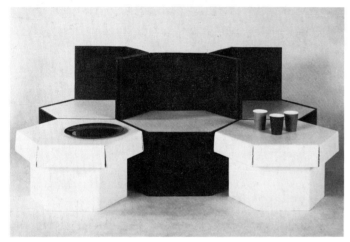

1017–1019 **Peter Raake** 1968 Germany

Folding furniture of specially stabilized, corrugated cardboard with
kraftliner covering, unfinished or with plastic laminate
Faltmöbel aus besonders stabiler Spezialwellpappe mit schwerem
Deckpapier, unbeschichtet oder mit Kunststoffbeschichtung
Papp-Faltmöbel Ellen Raake

1020 **Works Design** 1973 Germany

Multi-purpose cube "Papperlapapp" of strong cardboard with
plastic laminate in various colors. Available in three sizes
Sitz- und Spielwürfel »Papperlapapp« aus Hartpappe mit bunter
PVC-Beschichtung. Lieferbar in drei verschiedenen Größen
3h design Hübner + Huster

1021–1024 **Richard Thern** 1969/1974 Germany

Playing units of hard surfaced, foamed polyurethane, white or
colored; can be used in a multiplicity of ways
Spielelemente aus weißem oder farbigem geschäumtem Polyurethan-Duromer, das auf vielfältige Weise als Spielzeug oder Möbel
verwendet werden kann

1025–1030 **Works Design** 1971–74 Germany

"Mobilix" children's playing and constructing system. Solid colored plastic panels with notches may be combined with cross slats of extruded plastic to form a variety of playthings and furniture. Supplement elements are panels with round cutout, table tops, drawers, casters, bed mattresses, wheels and chrome-plated steel axles

»Mobilix«-Bauspielsystem. Farbige Stabilplatten aus Kunststoff mit umlaufender Nut können belastungssicher durch Kreuzschienen aus extrudiertem Kunststoff verbunden und vielfältig zu Spielgegenständen oder Möbeln kombiniert werden. Als Ergänzungselemente gibt es Platten mit rundem Ausschnitt, Tischplatten, einschiebbare Boxen, Doppellaufrollen, Bettpolster, Räder und verchromte Stahlachsen

Top System Burkhard Lübke

1031 + 1032 Stanley Selengut 1970 USA

Children's environmental system. Grill
structure consisting of solid maple or
birch dowels with threaded ends and
cubic wooden joints. Can be extended
with bed boards, side and end panels,
ladders, swings and other play equipment. Basic system can also be combined
to form tables and shelves
Einrichtungssystem für Kinderzimmer.
Gitterstruktur aus Stäben mit Schraubge-
winde und würfelförmigen Verbindungsstücken aus Birke oder Ahorn, in die Betten, Platten aus Holz oder Kunststoff,
Hängeleitern und Turngeräte eingebaut
werden. Konstruktion von Einzelmöbeln
wie Regalen oder Tischen ebenfalls möglich
Children's Motivational Environments Inc.

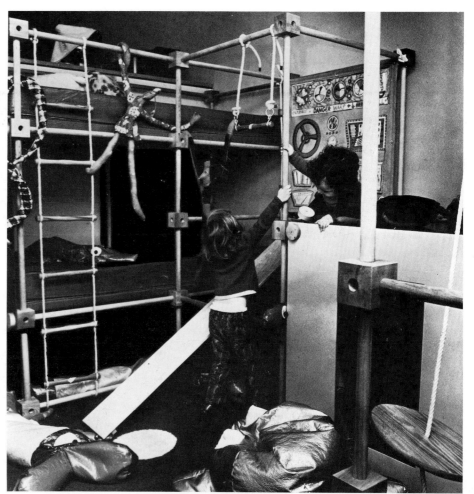

1033 Günter Renkel 1976 Germany

"Robinson" children's environmental system of solid pine. The basic element is
the wide ladders, on the range of which
beds, bookshelves, desks, and drawers
are suspended
»Robinson«-Einrichtungssystem für Kinderzimmer. Grundelement sind Sprossen-
leitern, in die Betten, Bücherborde,
Schreibplatten oder Schubladen eingebaut werden können
ZE Möbel

Manufacturers · Hersteller

Designers · Entwerfer

Photographers · Photographen